Sports Travel Security

Sports Travel Security

Peter E. Tarlow

President and founder, Tourism & More

Butterworth-Heinemann
An imprint of Elsevier
elsevier.com

Butterworth-Heinemann is an imprint of Elsevier
The Boulevard, Langford Lane, Kidlington, Oxford OX5 1GB, United Kingdom
50 Hampshire Street, 5th Floor, Cambridge, MA 02139, United States

Notices
Knowledge and best practice in this field are constantly changing. As new research and experience
broaden our understanding, changes in research methods, professional practices, or medical treatment
may become necessary.

Practitioners and researchers must always rely on their own experience and knowledge in evaluating and
using any information, methods, compounds, or experiments described herein. In using such information
or methods they should be mindful of their own safety and the safety of others, including parties for
whom they have a professional responsibility.

To the fullest extent of the law, neither the Publisher nor the authors, contributors, or editors,
assume any liability for any injury and/or damage to persons or property as a matter of products liability,
negligence or otherwise, or from any use or operation of any methods, products, instructions, or ideas
contained in the material herein.

British Library Cataloguing-in-Publication Data
A catalogue record for this book is available from the British Library

Library of Congress Cataloging-in-Publication Data
A catalog record for this book is available from the Library of Congress

ISBN: 978-0-12-805099-6

For Information on all Butterworth-Heinemann publications
visit our website at https://www.elsevier.com

Working together
to grow libraries in
developing countries

www.elsevier.com • www.bookaid.org

Publisher: Candice Janco
Acquisition Editor: Sara Scott
Editorial Project Manager: Hilary Carr
Production Project Manager: Priya Kumaraguruparan
Designer: Mark Rogers

Typeset by MPS Limited, Chennai, India

They will soar on wings like eagles; they will run and not grow weary, they will walk and not be faint. (Isaiah 40:31)

This book is dedicated to my grandchildren and to athletes of good will around the world. May today's athletes teach the next generation how to be strong not only in body, but also in their convictions so as to make the world a better place.

Contents

Acknowledgments

Every book represents not only the author but also those who helped and encouraged the author during the many long hours of writing and rewriting. This book is of course no exception. I want to thank both Tom Stover and Hilary Carr of Elsevier for their guidance and insistence that I write this book, even when I had my own doubts.

I also want to thank the following people, listed in alphabetical order, for allowing me to interview them: Hector Enrique Amador Ruíz, Jovana Dimovic, Erin Lechler, Salomón Libman Pastor, Cory Maltz, T. J. Marcum, Seth McKinney, Anthony (Tony) Paige, Dinis Resende, Jake Rother, and Timothy Speakman. I also wish to thank Ann Kellett who tirelessly read every word.

Additionally I want to thank my stepson, Josh Frager, my son-in-law, Menelaos, and my children, Nathaniel and Lysandra for all of their love. Finally, I want to thank my wife, Sara for having put up with me during the writing of this book and for all of her support.

To each of you, I send my love and give special thanks.

Peter E. Tarlow
College Station, TX, United States
September 2016

CHAPTER 1

Understanding the Issues

Sports and athletics play a major role in tourism. They also play a major social role in the life of many nations. In much of the United States, football—especially collegiate football—is almost a religion. The same can be said of the world of soccer (known as football in much of the world) in Latin America and most of Europe. Soccer is so popular that the World Cup is the world's largest event.

We see the importance of sports simply by browsing through the world's newspapers and magazines. Much of the world's media devote more space to sports news than to domestic or foreign news, politics, or economics. Major sporting events, such as World Cup Soccer, the Olympic Games, the World Series, and the Super Bowl, have become more than mere national pastimes. Often, these events are also real or quasi-real national holidays. We not only pay attention to the games, but also to the people who play the games and the spectators who observe the games. In fact, spectators are both passive observers and active participants in athletic events. The event, then, is more than a game, but a sociological, political, and economic phenomenon that envelops a wide variety of primary and secondary events.

For example, fans both young and old might idolize sports figures, and often see them as role models. This pattern of idealization is so strong that when a sports figure ends up on the wrong side of the law, or in a moral crisis, that situation also becomes major news. Media pundits turn sports figures into symbols of analysis, objectifying them, and transforming their humanity into symbolism.

From a sociological and tourism perspective, we use the term *sports* to mean two different commodities: the quasi-passive commodity called *spectator sports*, and the active commodity called *participatory sports*. Spectator sports are a part of the entertainment industry. In fact, some call the university sports system in the United States "edutainment," as college student-athletes are as much entertainers as students.

1

Sports Travel Security. DOI: http://dx.doi.org/10.1016/B978-0-12-805099-6.00001-4

As Goldblatt notes in his book *Special Events: Creating and Sustaining a New World for Celebration*:

> Before, during, or following the big game, events are used to attract, capture, and motivate spectators regardless of the game's outcome to keep supporting their favorite team. In fact, the line has been blurred between sport and entertainment largely due to the proliferation of events such as pre-game giveaways, post-game fireworks and musical shows, and even promotions such as trivia contests during the games.[1]

An industry as large as athletics is by nature varied and complex. It should not surprise us that athletic games serve multiple needs and goals. They function as emotional releases and, despite the emotions that sports generate, provide people with "safe" and "non-controversial" subjects for conversation. Sports and sporting events are economic generators, and they permit safe forms of controlled physical expenditures of energy and force.

Participatory sports, such as skiing, swimming, or jogging, may or may not have a competitive side, but in all cases, they force the participant to increase his/her skill and physical stamina. In this latter category, success does not depend on the other, but rather on the skill and luck of the doer, or what is known in sociological theory as "the actor." Both spectator and participator sports can play a major role in a community's tourism industry and overall quality of life.

As in much of tourism, sports are a means of escape. The tourism scholar Chris Rojek captures this concept when he paraphrases the early 20th-century sociologist Max Weber: "We stare out from the bars of our iron cage at a world teeming with possibility, but which is always just out of reach."[2]

Although Rojek wrote about tourism in general, his words speak directly to spectator sports. Here, in the world's stadiums, men and women are able to see themselves with physical powers well beyond their everyday capabilities or beyond the capabilities of others. Sports allow people to dream, to create emotionally safe physical experiences in which the athlete proves to the world that he or she can conquer physical danger.

Sports are a major tourism generator. Thousands of people attend major sporting events, such as World Cup events, Super Bowls, or Olympics games, and their attendance generates a great deal of revenue, not only for the teams, but also for the tourism industries that serve these athletic spectacles. Since

---

[1] Goldblatt, J. Special events: Creating and sustaining a new world for celebration. Hoboken: John Wiley & Sons; 1997; 9–10.

[2] Rojek, C. Ways of escape: Modern transformation in leisure and travel. New York: MacMillan Press; 1993, p. 9.

major sporting events bring a locale both prestige and economic development, there is often fierce competition between cities or nations as to which location will host the event. Hotels, restaurants, nightspots, and transportation facilities are only a few of the tourism-related industries that benefit from such sporting events.

Civic leaders also use sports tourism to give their community a new image or reinforce a desired image. Athletics provides a community a sense of "sizzle" and a dynamic image. Sports tourism is also a way to develop a "halo affect" (the effect of this positive image on other parts of the community) that spills over into every aspect of a community's self-image.

Communities use athletics to teach people new skills and, in so doing, attract new visitors. Since many people love to combine travel with skill enhancement, some communities have developed lists of current and former professional athletes or educational centers that might be willing to accept tourists for the purpose of teaching them to learn, improve upon, or perfect an athletic skill. In this way, sports become not only an emotional outlet, but also a health motivator. In a world plagued by the scourge of obesity, sports may motivate people to go from being sedentary to active, and thus, healthier.

Learning a new athletic skill may not be beneficial only for a person's stress levels, but also can teach teamwork and offer participants a new outlook on life. Numerous "sports schools" around the United States and the world accept both groups and individuals. These "sports" schools permit novices to learn a new athletic skill and often bring participants new friendships or even business networking, based on similar interests. These skill enhancement centers are not only good for the individual, but might also be a method to increase a community's tourism business potential.

Not unlike professional sports, sports connected to education, such as programs at universities in the United States, bring thousands of loyal fans to the host community, and pregame, game and after-game activities produce a great deal of economic revenue. Since sports is an important part of many cities' economies, tourism experts work hard to answer such questions as:

- What facilities does my community have?
- Does my community offer visitors the best facilities and equipment possible, or are major improvements needed?
- Should a community build its sports program around participatory activities or spectator activities?
- Does a community's environment and ambience align with the type of sports activities it offers guests and citizens?
- How does a community encourage people to stay in town after the athletic event has ended?

Although a great deal has been written about the athletic event, far less is known about the well-being of both the athlete and the other participants in the sporting event. This is not the first, nor is it the only, book about violence against athletes. Rather, this book seeks to broaden the scope of the intellectual conversation and to view the athlete's challenges both from the perspective of the event and from the perspective of the issues posed by traveling to and from the event, and being at the event.

Many books have been written about violence and sports. For some authors, spectators, and participants, there is a deep connection between sports and violence. Some scholars of sports have even argued that sport is a form of disciplined, or controlled, violence. For example, Jay J. Coakley argues in his book, *Sports in Society*,[3] that there are different forms of physical acts, ranging from nonconformist acts of violence to acts that manifest aggressive behavior. Coakley argues that sports-aggressive behavior has many formats. Among these forms of inappropriate or violent behavior are the following:

- Crimes committed against fans.
- Crimes committed against players.
- Crimes committed against the venue.

Within these three broad categories, however, lie many subcategories, many of which are not "aggressive behavior." This interplay of risks, violence, health, and mental well-being means that there is a need for an overarching, new paradigm when we speak of athletic security and safety.

To complicate the pattern even more, sporting events can be classified as professional, semiprofessional (such as university football games in the United States, which, although technically amateur athletics, are treated as if they were professional), and true amateur events. Sporting matches may also take place between teams or between individuals.

DIFFERENT TYPES OF ATHLETES AND SPORTING EVENTS

The world of athletic events is wide-ranging. Often, we tend to forget that athletes, like all human beings, come in a wide variety of shapes, colors, nationalities, and ethnic backgrounds. Although many people tend to think of athletes only in terms of their physical powers or skills, the truth is that they are human beings who have emotional needs and crises, health needs, family needs, and economic needs. A subtext of this book, therefore, is the fact that

---

[3] Coakley, J. Sports in Society: Issues and Controversies. 11th ed. New York: McGraw Hill; 2014.

too many people tend to forget the athlete's vulnerable side and that physical strength does not necessarily translate into emotional strength.

The athlete might be focused while practicing his or her sport, but once off the field of play (and in the case of health, perhaps on the field) she or he returns to being a human being with all of the needs, wants, and problems that all human beings have.

Boris Godzinevsk, writing in *Bleacher Report*, an online newsletter dedicated to sports, notes:

> An athlete, believe it or not, is a working man like the rest of us. He has responsibilities, and he is expected to perform his job like anyone else. When he is finished for the day, he may go out for some coffee, or he may go for drinks with friends. He may go to the park, go to the movies, or go to a sports game—perhaps a sport he does not play. Yet we, the audience, follow him. For some odd reason when a player leaves his job, his job does not leave him, it is associated with who he is.[4]

To add additional complications to the health and well-being of the athlete, many in the public and the media tend to see athletes not only as heroes, but also as "role models." This prescribed status exists even against a particular athlete's will. This status, especially for those who do not wish to be role models, often puts a great deal of pressure on the athlete. The public, and what the British call the chattering class, tend to forget that although athletes are people blessed with physical talent, this prowess does not mean that they have superior moral or ethical values, nor does it mean that they do not suffer from the same physical, emotional, or social ills the rest of the society. The sports role model paradigm may even lead to subtle forms of racism, under the belief that a person from one racial group has a proclivity to be stronger or faster than a person from another group.

Athletes not only suffer from many of the travails of travel, but they are also often victims of economics. *USA Today's* April 22, 2012 edition noted the problem of the rich-poor athlete:

> The factors contributing to financial ruin are numerous. Most people receiving a sudden windfall would be tempted to spend a good chunk of it quickly. This tendency might be pronounced when there's a sense of entitlement—these are star athletes who have heard how great they are all their lives, after all.
>
> "When a 21-year-old kid gets such big numbers, they go out and buy the big house and the fancy car," said Robert Luna of SureVest Capital Management

---

[4] Bleacher Report. Athletes are entertainers, leave the personal problems out of the headlines, http://bleacherreport.com/articles/379123-the-entertainers-their-job-is-to-entertain/; 2010 [accessed 15.04.10].

in Phoenix and the financial adviser to Arizona Cardinals offensive lineman Levi Brown. "Before they know it, they're out of the league and their income drops significantly." Then there are the legions of hangers-on who flock to the rich and famous.

"All sorts of people and advisers started calling," said Brown, recalling what happened to him after being selected as the fifth overall pick in the 2007 NFL draft. "In any business where you make a lot of money, there are people trying to get their hands on it."[5]

In this way, many athletes not only are objectified, but they also appear more often in the media. This means that their private lives are often not their own, and their notoriety exposes them to unscrupulous people. To protect athletes, the media is supposed to follow very specific guidelines, as ESPN's Jim Caple notes, below. Nevertheless, there is often a wide distance between what the media are supposed to do and what the media actually do.

The media must follow stringent guidelines when covering the personal lives of athletes. Here are the unwritten rules:

1. The media doesn't report an athlete's marital transgressions, because that's his personal life. The athlete in question may be on pace to break Wilt Chamberlain's career scoring record, but as long as it doesn't affect his performance on the field, his personal life is none of our damn business. What happens in private stays in private. Unless, of course, someone in the media breaks rule No. 1 and reports it first (or the athlete drives into a tree)—in which case the rest of us are free to pile on, because now it's *not* his personal life. Now it's *news*, just like Brangelina or the Gosselins.

2. At this point, the media not only must report the transgressions, but must act shocked—shocked!—to learn an athlete cheated on his wife, even though we have covered sports for years and seen many athletes routinely cheat on their spouses/significant others. (The media shall be especially appalled if the other women turn out to be not really all that beautiful.)

3. The media shall feel betrayed, because now all those stories we reported about him being such a good family man have turned out to be inaccurate. The media reported those stories in good faith, since we really had absolutely no idea what type of a family man he really was, other than the fact that he chose a profession that takes him away from his family for long stretches of the year.

---

[5] USA Today. Pro athletes often fumble the financial ball, http://usatoday30.usatoday.com/sports/story/2012-04-22/Pro-athletes-and-financial-trouble/54465664/1/; 2012 [accessed 22.04.12].

4. Meanwhile, the media will continue to write "He's a good family man" stories about other athletes we cover, even though we have no firsthand knowledge of their family lives, either.

5. The media shall impatiently demand an explanation and question the athlete's wisdom when he doesn't come clean right away to the people who matter most in such a personal affair—us, the media—by admitting embarrassing, intimate behavior in front of the entire world.

6. The media shall express its profound sadness and sympathy for the wife and children. We will do so by dispatching armies of cameramen and reporters to camp outside their house to document their pain and humiliation resulting from the transgressions of an immature, thoughtless husband who is making them go through this painful ordeal in public, rather than allowing them to deal with it privately.

7. The media shall fight like Green Berets to get the exclusive first interview with the troubled athlete, providing him with a sympathetic camera/microphone/notepad to give his side of the story (and then when we lose out to Oprah, the rest of us shall call it nothing but a puff piece).

8. The media shall keep dragging the affair out for cheap punch lines and trite morality lessons until the athlete makes proper amends to his wife and the public by buying her a $4 million diamond ring and winning a championship.

9. Finally, the media will not acknowledge whether we ourselves have ever occasionally strayed in our marriages, because that is none of your damn business.[6]

THE SPORTING EVENT

Just as athletes have different needs, so, too, do sporting events differ from their fans. Sporting events range from elite jacket-and tie-events, such as the Kentucky Derby, to local games where blue jeans or T-shirts and shorts are the normal dress. Spectators may view these sporting events from luxurious "boxes" to mere hard, wooden benches. Each of these events attracts a different type of spectator crowd, and these differences in both the size and makeup of the crowd, its demographic traits, and the interaction between those attending the event itself mean that there is no one size that fits all when it comes to the security of the players, spectators, or venue.

---

[6] ESPN. How to cover athletes' personal lives, http://sports.espn.go.com/espn/page2/story?page=caple/091211; 2015 [accessed 04.09.15].

THE ATHLETIC EVENT AS A SPECTACLE

Sporting events are what John Urry and Jonas Larsen in their book *The Tourist Gaze* call places to see and to be seen. Urry and Larsen argue that we attend major events or go to places of interest not only to view the event, but because our presence at the event also signifies a social statement about who we are and what we want others to think of us. From their perspective, sporting events are not only the event themselves, but also the ambience and environment in which the event takes place. For example, in writing about the 1992 Barcelona Olympic Games, Urry and Larsen include this quote from M. Degen:

> Although there were many heroic performances, it was unanimously agreed that a major winner of the Olympics was the city of Barcelona itself, the Game not only beamed its metamorphosed urban landscape (which often featured as a background to sporting events) into the world's gaze, but also reasserted its Catalan pride and identity. The 1992 Olympic games catapulted Barcelona onto the world stage and into the heart of the world's tourism networks. In less than 5 years the city had been transformed from a run-down industrial metropolis into one of Europe's most desired tourist venues.[7]

Sports are part of this tourism spectacle. As in the case of actors or circus members who travel from one locale to another, athletes, to be part of the spectacle, must also travel. Just as in the word of entertainment, sporting events are not just about the actors (players). Rather, a sporting event is a major production that involves numerous people traveling from one locale to another. These people might be traveling as spectators or as athletes, as part of the spectacle's staff, or as devoted fans. Sporting events are places where the physical activities of the athlete meet the emotions of the fan and become a spectacle in which the fans' gaze merges personal differentiations into a unified sense of team or spectator cohesion.

It is in the world of sport in which we observe the merging of the roles of spectators and athletes. Fan reactions to athletes' successes or failures create a cybernetic loop, an intermingling in which fans and athletes merge. The fan's reaction might impact an individual athlete's performance or might act as a motivation that determines the game's (or performance's) outcome.

This intermingling creates great many challenges for tourism sports security managers. Modern stadiums holding thousands of spectators create security risks that impact not only those in the stands, but also those playing on the field or court.

---

[7] Urry, J., Larsen, J. The tourist gaze. 3rd ed. Thousand Oaks, CA: SAGE Publications; 2011.

In the modern world of spectator sports, it is impossible to divorce travel from the sporting event. For many, the trip is part of the event; for others, it is nothing more than a hassle one must endure to see the event. In all cases, both spectators and athletic teams form traveling units that must be fed, housed, cared for, and protected. This book is about the events that surround the game and thus does not focus on the spectacle of the game or match, but rather about the safety and security of those people, be they the athletes, the behind-the-scenes staff who create the spectacle's emotional magic, or even the fans. In reality, players, staff members, and at times fans, spend much more time going to and from a sporting event then participating in the event, and while the potential for being injured during an event is ubiquitous, in reality, the real dangers lie as much, or to a greater extent, outside the event venue.

Travel safety/Security areas

1. While being transported
2. At places of lodging
3. At places of dining
4. At sports venues (fields, courses, courts)
5. In locker rooms

Travel safety/Security physical concerns

1. Travel-related illnesses
2. Food-borne illnesses
3. Lack of rest
4. Jet lag issues
5. Water issues
6. Climate and geological issues
7. Ecological issues, such as poor air quality

SPORTS AND VIOLENCE

Unfortunately, where there is power, prestige, and money, there also exist security risks. Although most people would like to think of sporting events as "good, clean fun," the reality of sports is quite different. Sports often have been intertwined with issues of politics, intrigue, and crime. These negatives occur in a wide variety of formats: from crimes committed against players, to crimes committed by players, and from acts of violence meant to damage the venue, to acts of violence meant (either intentionally or as a form of collateral damage) against the host community. Germany's experiences with the Olympic Games during both the earlier and latter parts of 20th century demonstrate that governments have used sports as a form of political propaganda and terrorists have used sports as a way to hurt the host community or another country's athletes.

A good case study of how sports and politics intermingle is Germany. In 1936, Germany hosted what has now come to be known as the Nazi Olympics. These Olympic Games were on the surface to be like all other Olympic Games, but in reality, they were less about sport and more about politics. The games were staged to camouflage Hitler's racist policies and to promote the idea that Aryans were part of a superior race. The 1936 Olympics have become a symbol of what sporting events should not be. Viewing the games from the perspective of history, historians now debate if the Western democracies made a major blunder by having participated in these events.

The relationship between Germany and sports is varied and filled with highs and lows. The 1936 Olympic Games were not, however, to be the last time that politics overcame sports on German soil. Almost 40 years later, Germany again hosted the Olympic Games, this time, in the city of Munich. These games were to demonstrate to the world a new, post-Nazi, democratic, and tolerant Germany.

Unfortunately, these games, too, ended in tragedy. This time, the tragic event was not due to intentional planning on the part of the German government, but rather due in part to a lack of planning. The attack on Israeli athletes, terminating in their murder, has become a symbol of poor athletic sports risk management and the interrelationship between sporting events and issues of security. The Munich Olympic Games massacre not only besmirched Germany's attempt to put the 1936 Olympic Games behind it, but also became known as one of the greatest failures of sports security. Furthermore, these security failures not only changed the way that the world media and professionals viewed sports security, but in the case of the Munich Olympic Games, also spurred a number of questions about how far Germany had come (or not come) since the prejudiced days of the Nazi Olympics Games.

The tragedies of 1936 and 1973 were not laid to rest until 2015, when the Jewish Olympic events, known as the *Maccabia* (or Maccabi Games) were held in Berlin. Ironically, these games took place in the very Olympic stadium that Hitler built. Under the watchful and ubiquitous eyes of German security, Germany welcomed Jewish athletes from 36 countries and sent a message of tolerance and openness at Europe's biggest Jewish athletic event. It should also be noted that at the 2016 Olympic Games some 40 years later, the International Olympic Committee finally is coming to terms with the murders of Munich.

Although it is beyond the scope of this book to analyze the interweaving of politics and sports during both 20th century German Olympic Games, the

Germany of 2015 well understood that in a hyper-politicized world, it is almost impossible to divorce sports from political realities, and politics from security.

Germany is not the only country in which terrorism has struck sports. For example, in 1996, Atlanta, Georgia (US), suffered a terrorist attack outside of the Olympic stadium. In 2002, a bomb blasted outside the hotel of the New Zealand cricket team in Karachi, Pakistan. Although no members of the team were hurt, the bomb killed the team's physiotherapists, along with some 11 French Navy experts, and 2 Pakistanis. The year 2002 also saw a major bomb blast just outside Madrid's main soccer stadium, for which Basque separatists took "credit." Other major acts of violence against athletes include the act of a suicide bomber in 2008 against a Sri Lanka New Year marathon and the bombing of the Boston Marathon on April 15, 2013.

The above-mentioned events are examples of why holding a major sporting event is no easy matter. Not only must locations deal with the event itself, but there are also logistics, marketing, and public relations that go hand in hand with major events and the security that surrounds them. Major events are, and will continue to be, targets for terrorism. They also might incite local protests that have nothing to do with terrorism. These acts of violence not only affect the athlete, but also the spectators and host community. The sports security professional well understands that these demonstrations are by-products of the event and may occur before or during the event. Demonstrators use the event to vent frustrations or to piggyback on the event as a way of gaining added leverage or publicity. In all cases, not only is the event potentially harmed, but the community and its tourism component's reputation may also suffer. Sporting events might also induce problems off the field. These sports-related, but not athlete-related, problems range from fans fighting with each other, acts of vandalism and hooliganism, prejudicial or racist acts against people of a particular nationality or religion, and community rampages in which businesses and private property are damaged or destroyed.

ISSUES OF SAFETY, SECURITY, AND SURETY

Many tourism professionals are afraid to speak about sports tourism security and tourism safety. Often, there is a common feeling among professionals that these terms will frighten customers. Their position is often summarized by the dictum that the less said, the better. Ironically, these same people are not afraid of on-field violence and often see this form of violence as part of the spectacle. Sports fans act like other travelers, tourists, or visitors and, for the most part, seek out places where there is a sense of security and safety. In the world of spectator sports and where the potential for a physical mishap is ever-present, this need for security is especially true. It is also true for activities that promote physical contact that might escalate to acts of aggression. In a like manner, athletes need to know that they can work (play) without additional fear of a physical mishap.

From this book's perspective, the terms *security* and *safety* often will be used interchangeably or be combined and called "surety." Surety, a term borrowed from the insurance industry, is the point where safety, security, economics, and reputation meet. When a major distinction between safety and security is needed, then a specific term with a precise definition will be used. The reasons for using the term *surety* are many. From the perspective of the athlete, a physical aliment and a hostile act both may result in a loss, be it athletic or physical. Furthermore, athletes are travelers, and as such, are both observers of the spectacle of tourism and part of the spectacle. Thus, a lack of safety and security impacts athletes both from the active side, being part of the spectacle, and from the passive side, watching the spectacle unfold.

Although there is a small minority of travelers—spectators—who sometimes seek out the dangerous, most people want to know that they can attend the sporting event in safety. In reality, there is no such thing as total security or safety. No one can guarantee one hundred percent an experience that will be incident-free. Instead, security specialists work at lessening the odds that something negative will occur. They realize that the target will always exist, but that they can work to make the target as small as possible. It is for this reason that the term *surety* is employed. As noted, surety refers to a lowering of the probability that a negative event will occur. Surety does not promise perfection, but rather improvement, and takes into account that to live is to have risk in one's life. Classically, we can apply the same factors in tourism surety to sports security in at least six different areas of protection. These are:

- *Protection of spectators and visitors*. Arena and team risk managers have to find ways to protect the visiting spectator from locals who might seek to do the visitor harm, from other spectators who may be in attendance for the purpose of committing crimes, and also, from less-than-honest staff members. Surety specialists also must protect spectators from unlawful sales of tickets (scalping) and even from unhealthy food and water products.
- *Protection of staff*. A tourism industry that does not care about its staff (workers) cannot survive long. The second aspect of a tourism surety program is to find ways to assure that honest staff members can work in an environment that is crime-free and not hostile. Tourism is a high-pressure industry, and at times, sports tourism (such as playoff games) is even more stressful. Under these circumstances, it is all too easy for staff members to be abused or for tempers to flare, leading to a hostile work situation.

- *Protection of the site.* It is the responsibility of surety specialists to protect not only the field of play, be that a major stadium, or even an ocean or some other venue for aquatic competition. Since athletic activities take place in a wide variety of circumstances, weather conditions, and locations, techniques that work in one set of conditions may not work at another location, time, or circumstance. The term *site* can mean anything from a place of lodging to an attraction site to an athletic venue. In an age of terrorism, when there are people whose purpose is to destroy or harm a specific site, site protection must also take into account the careless spectator (or when away from the game, possible traveler). Often, when people are excited about a sporting event, they simply forget to care for furniture, appliances, or equipment. Surety, then, also takes into account the needs of cleaning staff and hotel engineers, and seeks to assure that the site environment is both attractive and as secure/safe as possible. It must be emphasized that athletes, when off the playing field, or away from the sports venue, will also be subject to the same norms of travel and tourism and are as vulnerable to the same errors as are the fans, or any other travelers.
- *Management of ecological and logistical issues.* Closely related to, yet distinct from, site security is the protection of the area's ecology. Bringing thousands of people to a single site for a few hours presents a great deal of logistical and ecological problems. No tourism entity—and this includes sporting events—exists in a vacuum. The care of a locale's streets, lawns, and internal environment has a major impact on surety. In a like manner, the bringing of thousands of people together can be a logistical nightmare. Evacuation routes may not operate during a panic, or the removal of a person who has fallen ill from a crowded stadium or arena may provoke additional problems. Surety professionals cannot overlook climatic conditions such as blizzards, electrical storms, and lightning, or a possible, sudden tornado—all hazards that cannot be ignored. Such issues as bathroom usage and garbage disposal are essential to the well-being of the locale. Surety experts must also take into consideration issues of health. For example, having large numbers of people in close proximity means that the surety expert must consider the potential for the spread of communicable diseases, ranging from the common cold to a pandemic.
- *Protection of the economy.* Sporting events are a major generator of income on both the local and national levels. As such, these events are prone to attack from various sources. For example, terrorists may see a sporting event as an ideal opportunity to create economic havoc. Criminals, contrary to terrorists, do not wish to destroy a sporting locale, but rather view the event as an ideal "fishing" ground from which to harvest an abundance of riches. Sporting events bring in many visitors from out of town, both spectators and visitors. They

rarely distinguish between the treatment they are afforded by stadium personnel, by the local travel and tourism industry, and by people living and working in the community. As such, sports surety professionals have a special role in protecting a locale's economic viability. The way that security professionals act and the methods that they use can reinforce the marketing department's message or undercut it.

- *Protection of the host location's reputation.* We only need to read the newspaper to note that crimes and acts of terrorism against sporting events receive a great deal of media attention. The classical method of simply denying that there is a problem is no longer valid, and is counterproductive to a locale's best promotional efforts and the interests of both the sporting association and the athlete. When there is a lapse in security, the effect is long term. Some of the consequences to a reputation include the need to drop prices, the general deterioration of the state of the game, and the potential need for a major marketing effort to counteract the negative reputation.

A good sports security program, then, involves much more than simply hiring a few extra security guards. Sports surety, like other forms of tourism surety, is a highly professionalized plan that permits the protection of everything from the site to the visitor, and from the locale's ecology to its very reputation. While sports surety programs do not promise that nothing can or will happen, they do lessen the risk of negative events and prepare a locale to minimize negative effects, should an incident occur.

Since many sporting events contain both physical security and high levels of emotions, they also have some special issues that must be taken into consideration.

Examples include the following:

The potential for issues of litigation is ubiquitous. In today's society, where litigation has become a way of life, it is essential that a surety specialist check with his/her community's law enforcement offices about the need for waivers when conducting public tournaments, hosting major sporting events, or encouraging out-of-towners to visit your community for recreational reasons. In many cases, these waivers may not stand up in court, but if they are combined with a solid risk management program, then they provide at least some protection against unnecessary litigation.

Sports tourism, like other forms of tourism, requires that a locale and venue maintain good community lists and emergency numbers. All sporting events have an element of risk, and because athletics are physical in nature, the risk may be higher than in other forms of tourism. It is essential that the sports security professional or the person in charge of the athletes' logistics know where to go for medical attention, what restaurants serve pre- and post-game foods, and if hotel check-outs can be coordinated with sporting event timetables.

The following are two issues that locations seeking athletic events should consider:

- *Be age-sensitive.* Especially if you are promoting participatory athletic activities, know about the special needs with which you may be challenged. Businesses catering to older athletes might have to deal with different risks than those dealing with visitors or younger sports enthusiasts. Every sports-oriented tourism community should know the locations of 24-hour pharmacies, hospital emergency rooms, and doctors and dentists willing to take on emergency, out-of-town patients.
- *Know the difference between a safety concern and security concern.* Although we use the word *surety*, there are, at times, major differences between acts that deal with safety and acts that deal with security. Although no single definition distinguishes safety from security, we may assume that safety most often deals with such issues pertaining to health or wellness, while security often reflects causality, or the notion that someone intentionally does something that will cause harm to another person, or locale.

  As the author of this work noted in his book *Tourism Security*, "In a number of European languages, such as French, Portuguese, and Spanish, the same word is used for both security and safety. Security and safety experts do not always agree where one concept ends and another begins. For example, we speak of food safety, but if a person intentionally alters food so as to sicken someone else, then this act is no longer a food-safety issue but becomes a food-security issue. In the same manner, tourism specialists must worry about a traveler who deliberately carries a communicative disease from one locale to another for the purpose of harming others. Is such an act one of biological terrorism, a security matter, or an issue of safety?"[8]

SPORTS RISK MANAGEMENT

An industry as large as the sports industry is bound to need and attract a great number of professional risk managers, people whose behind-the-scenes efforts are essential to the economic and marketing side of the game.

---

[8] Tarlow, P. Tourism security: Strategies for effectively managing travel risk and safety. 1st ed. Amsterdam: Elsevier; 2014; 8–9.

Risk management is not easy, and must be carefully distinguished from its "sister" profession of crisis management. Risk managers have a wide range of issues to which they must attend. In the world of sports, these include:

- Crowd management, both inside and outside the sports venue.
- Control (when permitted) of alcohol sales and consumption.
- Traffic management to and from the venue. The "from" is especially difficult as people tend to leave the venue at the same time causing the potential not only for traffic problems but also rage. These issues include knowing which roads are closed and where road construction (repair) may be occurring, offsite parking and shuttles, and road confusion stemming from poor signage. A constant worry for risk managers is emergency ingress and egress. Egress management is especially challenging as thousands of people may need to be moved within limited times and under the possibility of panic.
- Gangs and criminal threats, both to fans and players, and also to the event's reputation.
- Structural defects or other problems at the venue, which can lead to tragedies.
- Control of spectators who see themselves as part of the event. Spectator control is especially important, as the risk manager must deal with an ever-changing set of people, yet many crowds have similar psychological profiles. For example, many European sporting matches, especially soccer, must deal with the issue of hooliganism. In this case, the individuals might be different, but the personality types are both similar and predictable. Crowd managers can make some predictions based on the fact that different sports tend to attract different crowds. Predictions based solely on past history, however, may be dangerous in an age of terrorism. Thus, there is a need to know the event's crowd history and also to use the best intelligence possible.
- Public health (food handling), medical care, and environmental risk.
- Fire safety. Although many venues are concrete structures, the potential for localized fires at venues is ever-present and can lead to panics, the need for emergency evacuations, and/or physical destruction.

These many challenges mean that people working in sports security will need to have information on some or all of the following aspects of the event.

- *Which types of sporting event are being held.* The type of event and the characteristics of the fans the event will attract is often the first guideline to determining the type of security that will be needed. Getting answers to questions such as whether the event is a major playoff game, or will celebrities be attending the match, is essential. It is important to know the amount and type of potential publicity that the sport event expects to generate. A good rule of thumb is that the greater the publicity generated by the event, or the more controversial an attendee (or some of the attendees), the great the likelihood of a demonstration or security incident.

- *The event's timetable.* Sports security must be developed in accordance not only with the event's demographic makeup, but also with its times and places: the "when's" and "where's." How much pregame time is needed? Will the players be in seclusion or on the streets? Are there after-game events, and if there are, what is the likelihood for the presence of drugs or alcohol? What is the length of the event? The longer the event is scheduled, the higher the chance that a mishap might occur. If the sporting event is a series, such as a World Cup or World Series, then added security might be needed as the event reaches its climax. If the event is an outdoor event where alcoholic beverages are served, then consider not only the problem of protecting event-goers from those who may seek to sully the event, but also protecting of the community from the event-goers.

- *How nonathletic workers are cleared for the event.* Concessions or clean-up crews are essential to the event's security. For example, how trustworthy are the people at the concession stands? What does security know about their backgrounds? In an age of terrorism, background checks are necessary for everyone working at a major event. If an incident were to occur, few people would know who the concessionaires were, so consider: Would you be able to withstand media scrutiny? Would the community receive unjust, negative publicity? The key here is to realize that no matter who is at fault in an incident, it is the local community that might well suffer. The same is true for private security firms. Some do an excellent job in vetting and training their employees, while others are much less reliable, so a great deal of caution should be used. Unfortunately, more expensive does not always mean better.

- *Sporting event risk managers must review all of the event's structural parts.* Event security is not only about making sure that others do not succeed in damaging the event, it is also about making sure that the venue is safe and that the structure can support the number of people at the event. There have been too many incidents in recent years of stages falling, fireworks setting off fires and causing panics, and people being trampled due to a lack of easy access to exits (as well as other structural problems) to simply assume that local fire departments or building inspectors will be able to anticipate all logistics and structural problems.

- *Building in redundancy.* Redundancy is a key concept in all security measures. It means having multiple systems (machine or human) overlapping each other so that if one system fails, there are other methods of protection in play. Sports security at major events redundancy is essential. Often, event managers and security personnel are the only people who have access to, and knowledge of, critical areas. The question to consider is, who will take over if these people become incapable of doing their job? Events demand backup teams and multiple forms of redundancy. It is essential that your backup team know how to access not only needed equipment, but also have a full list of contact and key people with whom they can consult.

- *Local authorities should have as much information as possible.* Not only do you want local authorities to be able to move into a situation quickly, but it is also essential that they understand the consequences of their actions. That means that in a tourism-oriented community, what is shown on television becomes the narrative that drives the event. In a perfect world, police and other first responders would not have to worry about being part of a marketing team, but in a world of 24-hour, 7-day-a-week news cycles, they unfortunately, have to be trained in how their words impact the community.

Sports risk managers must always be prepared for problems that they may not have considered. Issues such as vandalism, thievery, and health-related issues can easily destroy an event and/or its host community's reputation. Be prepared to deal with everything from cyber sabotage to identity theft, and from unintentional pandemics to intentional food poisoning. Given this, sports managers must do the following:

- *Determine who should be stationed where.* For example, entrances might need large, muscular men, while other parts of the event may need a different type of person. In tourism, we treat all people equally, but also know that physically, not all people are the same. The essential point here is finding the right person for the correct job.
- *Combine machines and personnel to get the greatest security for the least cost.* There are times when metal detectors make a great deal of sense, but in an age of terrorism, they are not enough. Trained personnel (and animals) are essential not only in making critical decisions but also in spotting problems not picked up by the metal detector.

In addition, use the land and event geography to your advantage:

Make sure you find high spots from which to see the crowd, easy ingress and egress areas, and control centers of communication. Also, have a way to clear spaces for first aid personnel and other medical personnel if they are needed. In making these determinations, be clear about the crowd's demographic makeup and what problems this particular population will present.

RISK MANAGEMENT VERSUS CRISIS MANAGEMENT

In the world of sports, there is no single definition of *risk, emergency,* and *crisis management.* Often, and as noted above, the best way to avoid an emergency or crisis is through good risk management. To understand the difference between risk and crisis management, study the chart below.

Note that risk management is always proactive. Risk management occurs prior to an unwanted occurrence. Crisis management and emergency management are reactive, coming into play after an occurrence, as seen in the chart, below.

Basic Differences Between Athletic Crisis and Risk Management		
	Risk	**Crisis**
Surety of occurrence	Uses a statistical system	Is a known event
Goal of management	To stop the event prior to occurrence	To minimize the damage once the event has taken place
Type of preparation to combat risk that can be used	■ Probability studies ■ Knowledge of past events ■ Tracking systems ■ Learning from others	■ Specific information, such as medical, psychological, or criminal ■ Developing a "what if" attitude
Training needed	Assume crises and find ways to prevent them	Assume crises and practice reacting to them
Reactive or proactive	Proactive	Reactive, though training can be proactive toward the reactive
Types of victim	Anyone: visitor, spectator, or staff	Can be visitors, staff members, or the site
Publicity	Goal is to prevent publicity by acting to create nonevents	Goal is to limit the public relations damage that might occur
Some common problems	■ Poor building maintenance ■ Poor food quality ■ Poor lighting ■ Fear of terrorism ■ Fear of a crime occurring	■ Rude visitor ■ Sick person ■ Robbery ■ Threat to staff ■ Bomb scare ■ Lack of language skills
Statistical accuracy	Often very low; in many cases, the travel and tourism industry does everything possible to hide the information	Often very low; in many cases, the travel and tourism industry does everything possible to hide the information
Length of negative effects on the local tourism industry	In most cases, short term	In most cases, long term unless replaced by new, positive image
Recovery strategies	■ New marketing plans; assumes short-term memory of traveling public ■ Probability ideals: "Odds are, it will not happen to you" ■ Hide information as best as one can	■ Showing of compassion ■ Need to admit the situation and demonstrate control ■ Higher levels of observed security ■ Highly trained (in tourism, terrorism, and customer service personnel

Risk managers face another—and at times, almost insurmountable—issue: job justification. In the case of crisis management, there is a defined problem, and the problem is either solved (success) or not solved (failure). Crisis management has clear-cut goals and outcomes. Risk management is more obscure in that there are no clearly defined objectives. If the risk manager is successful, then it is possible that management may wonder if the position is needed. If, on the other hand, the risk manager is unsuccessful, then management may easily question why resources were expended since a crisis still occurred.

In order to deal with this psychological and political challenge, it is important that the risk manager know his/her own personal strengths and weaknesses. Staff analysis is also essential. No matter what errors a risk manager's staff may commit, the results belong not to the staff member, but to the risk manager. For this reason, risk managers must be proactive as far as educating both management and the public. Some of the most important points that risk managers of sporting events must make are the following:

- No event is 100% free of risk. In the case of spectators, they choose to be at the event, they wish to see it, and to be seen at it.
- Risk management is statistical in nature. The risk manager is playing a probability game.
- To travel is to be insecure. In the case of sporting events, both the athlete and the spectator might be traveling and both are subject to the normal risks of travel.
- There is a distinction between allocentric and psychocentric risk. Allocentric risk refers (in this context) to people taking active risks. For example, running onto the field is an allocentric risk. Psychocentric risk (in this context) refers to passive risk. For example, a person sitting in his (or her) seat who is hit by a flying object dropped from the tier above.
- As world tension mounts, the demand for risk management increases. This is especially true of mega-sporting events such as Olympic Games, Super Bowl events, or World Cup events. In the case of the Super Bowl and World Cup events, there is a psychological connection between a team's success and a spectator's reaction. This relationship means that a team's loss may also be viewed by the spectator as his/her personal loss leading to a greater potential for crises, or even violence.
- From the perspective of publicity, the further one is from the incident (such as those learning about it in the media), the worse the event seems, and the greater the potential for reputational damage it may produce.

- The further we are from a crisis, the longer it lasts in the collective memory.
- Most spectators have little knowledge of the venues' layout or the locale's geography.
- Different types of guests require different forms of risk management.
- In sports risk management, be careful not to rely too heavily only on technology. A good rule of thumb is to combine human expertise with technology. The spectator is coming for the experience, and if the experience becomes too burdensome, then the joy of the event will soon fade.
- As we script events and try to rationalize them, we discover that irrationalities often become part of the event. No matter what we plan for, there always will be unplanned problems or combinations of problems. The best risk management results from a sense of awe and the realization that we must expect the unexpected. Creativity and flexibility are key.

CRITICAL RISK MANAGEMENT STEPS

Risk management, especially in the world of sports, is never easy. In reality, risk management can exist on all three of the following group levels, and also simultaneously: the micro level (that of the individual athlete), mezzo level (the team), and macro level (totality of those playing and those observing, plus the physical structure). On all levels, it is essential to enter into a risk management situation with the following knowledge:

- As much background information as possible.
- Number of attendees.
- Who the attendees are.
- The circumstances under which the event will occur, from politics to weather.
- The various risks that may occur, and how you would prioritize them.

ANALYZING RISK

The following chart presents four different risk potentials, valid on all the levels defined above (micro, mezzo, and macro).

What are the consequences of a mistake to the facility and the traveling public, as well as to the area's prestige and economy? Then, consider the following chart for each of these groups: risks to clients, risks to facilities, political risks, and economic impact risks.

Determining If There Is a Risk

	State the Risk	What Motivates the Risk?	Rank the Risk: High, Medium, or Low?	How Will You Identify the Risk?	What Are the Consequences Should the Risk Occur?
Weather					
Gangs					
Terror					
Food poisoning					
Fire					
Theft					

An easy way to classify risk is to follow the following simple steps:

1. Create a list of every possible risk that the event may hold.
2. Review the risks and classify them as follows:
   a. Type 1. Highly likely that the risk will materialize, but the consequences are limited.
   b. Type 2. Highly unlikely that the risk will materialize, but if it does, the consequences would be great.
   c. Type 3. Highly unlikely that the risk will materialize, but if it does, the consequences would be minimal.
   d. Type 4: Highly likely that the risk will materialize, but if it does, the consequences would be great.

The chart below reviews these first four steps.

Classifying Risks

Risk	Type 1 — High Probability, Low Consequences	Type 2 — Low Probability, High Consequences	Type 3 — Low Probability, Low Consequences	Type 4 — High Probability, High Consequences
Fire				
Natural disaster				
Bad publicity due to illness				
Crime wave				
Terrorism				

3. Estimate the chances that the materialized risk will have a short or long news cycle.

Determine the following:

   a. Would the risk have local or wide-ranging publicity?
   b. Would the materialized risk become a major news story?
   c. Would the materialized risk have a short or long life cycle?

ORGANIZATIONS DEALING WITH SPORTS SAFETY

In today's world, there is rightful concern for the safety and well-being of both sports participants and venues. A number of organizations seek to protect and serve athletes and venues. For example, in the United States these organizations include the National Center for Spectator Sports Safety and Security, better known as the NCS4, which exists not only to study sports security management but also to provide practical advice. The NCS4's website states the following purpose:

> The National Center for Spectator Sports Safety and Security (NCS4), at the University of Southern Mississippi, supports the advancement of sport safety and security through training, professional development, academic programs and research. NCS4 collaborates with professional leagues, open access events, inter-collegiate and interscholastic athletics, along with professional associations, private sector firms, and government agencies. It is a critical resource for sport venue managers, event managers, first responders, and other key stakeholders.
>
> In order to meet current and future needs and to advance the industry, NCS4 has Advisory Boards, committees and subject matter experts that provide strategic guidance, assistance, and advice on critical issues and trends. These individuals are recognized and respected experts from the world of sport safety and security.[9]

On the international front, we find the International Center for Sports Security, or ICSS, which is located in Qatar and dedicated to sports safety and security. Its president, Mohammed Hanzab has stated that:

> The essence of sport—integrity of competition and a safe, secure environment in which to watch and play—is precious. At the heart of the ICSS is the belief that we have a responsibility to protect this for present and future generations. From corruption to key safety and security risks, there are significant existing and emerging threats to these ideals that, if left unchecked, could cause significant damage to the fabric of sport. The ICSS' goal is to be a global hub of security, safety and integrity expertise, with the sole purpose of ensuring sport is equipped to overcome these challenges. I welcome you to the ICSS and hope you will share our vision and our passion for sport.[10]

---

[9] National Center for Spectator Sports Safety and Security. NCS4 Overview, https://www.ncs4.com/about/overview; 2015 [accessed 10.08.15].

[10] International Centre for Sport Security. ICSS Profile, http://www.theicss.org/profile/; 2014 [accessed 10.08.15].

DEDICATION

In a sense, this book is dedicated not only to the men and women who seek to compete not for political gain, but as signs of brotherhood (and sisterhood) and goodwill. The book is also dedicated to those who were not allowed to compete in the Olympic Games of 1936, either for having been born with the wrong skin color, or for having been born into the wrong ethnicity. Although the Munich Games are symbols of violence toward athletes, as the reader will see in this book, both professional and university athletes continue to face a myriad of physical, psychological, and health challenges that go far beyond the realm of sports. Athletes not only must compete against themselves and each other, but also against a numerous challenges that range from issues of air and water quality to acts of crime and terrorism.

The following table presents an overview of the world of sports as seen from the perspective of this book.

Some Forms of Inappropriate Behavior in Sports						
	Professional Team	Semipro Team	Amateur Team	Individual Proplayers	Individual Semipro Players	Individual–Amateur Players
Against players of other team	Yes	Yes	Yes	Yes	Yes	Yes
Against fan(s)	R	R	ER	Yes	R	ER
Against venue	R	R	ER	ER	ER	ER
Against locale	ER	Occurs	ER	ER	ER	ER
R, rare; ER, extremely rare.						

The idea of tourism security for professional athletes is much more complicated than it might first appear. The student and professional in the area of tourism sports travel surety and risk management must look at the problem not only from the multivariate nature of the individual (the macro level) but also from the mezzo level of the athlete's interaction with his or her teammates, and on the macro level of the interaction between the athlete and the environment.

Jim Fisher, the football coach at Florida State University (US), said the following in 2013:

How to Prepare Your Players for a Big …? Technical preparation is important, but also important is to focus on "the mindset, temperament, how the players perceive things, and the attitude of the team." Florida won that game and in understanding how athletes travel, not only between games but the road of life, we all learn something about how each of us travels through the journey called "life."[11]

---

[11] Soccer Drills and Games. Motivational Quotes for Coaches Sports Inspirational Motivational Quotes Motivating Players, Inspiring Players Motivational Coaching Quotes, http://soccerhelp.com/Motivational_Quotes_Coaches_Sports_Inspirational_Coaching_Quotes.shtm; 2015 [accessed 04.09.15].

CHAPTER 2

A Review of Literature

Reviewing the literature that already has been published in the case of sports travel is not easy. In fact, it could be said that conducting a literature review is problematic, at best. The field is so diverse that without some overall framework, the reader is not sure where to go or what to consider.

Not only is the literature dispersed, but there is also no single accepted definition of sports travel or its various components. The student of sports travel, then, needs to ask multiple questions. For example, does sports travel consist of teams going from place to place, or does it consist of fans visiting stadiums or playing fields around the world? Is this a single academic field, or does it break down into multiple subfields? Are there principles that unite all athletes, or do different types of athletes need different methods to ensure their safety and security?

To make the matter still more complex and daunting, different authors have differing opinions on how to define security, safety, travel, problems in travel, and risks, so the field tends to be wide open. The term *sports* or *athletics* tends to cover a wide range of options. For example, when we think of *sports*, are we thinking about formal or professional sports, or about amateur athletics? There is also the question of who is an athlete and into which social groups the athlete falls. For example, a review of the literature demonstrates that there is no one, single body of literature concerning this topic. Instead, a great variety of "literatures" address questions of sports travel according to such criteria as age groups, type of sport and location, gender, and media coverage. The wide spectrum of variables not only demonstrates the depth and breadth of the subject, but also calls into question if we must be thinking not about singular paradigms, but rather, multiple paradigms that coexist in multiple worlds.

Before we can even beginning to examine the literature in the field, we first need to understand whom we are protecting and from what. It is only from this point that we can begin to examine the existing literature.

For example, does the term imply the transporting of a team, or individuals? Does the security professional need to think in terms of major sports idols, or

25

Sports Travel Security. DOI: http://dx.doi.org/10.1016/B978-0-12-805099-6.00002-6

unknown persons? Although the great majority of people would not dispute the fact that each person has a right to life and freedom of movement, and to be free of harassment and of ill treatment, there are, unfortunately, differences in the way that human beings treat each other. Certainly, few would argue that a woman might need different forms of protection than a man. Older and younger athletes likewise have different travel challenges than do people in the prime of their lives, and athletes who represent nations at war or with many enemies are often vulnerable and require different types of security needs. The charts below provide a road map for some of the challenges in defining sports travel safety and in the literature that is pertinent to the field.

We can categorize sports travelers and athletes into the following:

- Issues of gender: Male, female, transgender.
- Age cohorts.
- Professional versus amateur.
- Well known (celebrity status) versus lesser or unknown.
- Team members versus individual players.

Some of these categories are discreet variables; i.e., the person falls into one category or the other (such as well known vs not well known). Some are changeable. For example, an unknown person might become a celebrity and thus move to a different category. Others are on a continuum. For example, we move from youth to elderly merely by continuing to live. Furthermore, none of these categories is exclusive. We can be a famous or unknown male or female athlete, as all athletes age over time, and human beings are capable of participating on several planes. Thus, an athlete may compete in more than one sport, or be well known in one and not in another.

Dealing with sports travel security, then, is a diffuse topic that changes with the person, the time, the type of sport, and the event's location. For example, in his article published on the ESPN website (November 30, 2007), Wayne Drehs makes the following statement that frames much of our discussion:

> No matter where professional athletes are—at home, out with friends, in their cars—they know they are targets, and they perhaps have never been more uneasy about their personal safety than they are right now. The slaying this week of Washington Redskins safety Sean Taylor during what investigators are calling a 'random burglary' at his house in Palmetto Bay, Fla., is the latest in a string of armed home invasions that has shaken the sports world since the summer (of 2007).[1]

---

[1] http://www.ports.espn.go.com/espn/news/story?id=3133995.

What Drehs writes about an athlete at home becomes even more complicated when we deal with athletes during travel. Despite these many subcategories of athletes per se, certain overarching issues touch all athletes.

Before we can even begin to explore the current literature on such a wide-ranging topic, it is important to list at least the major areas of risk facing athletes and where these risks especially apply to professional versus amateur athletes.

STEREOTYPES

Athletes suffer from a number of stereotypes that often influence that athlete's personal security during travel. For example, Jessica Kiss, writing for the online journal *the Eagle*, states that "Athletes all over the world are stereotyped based on race, height, gender, and several other reasons. Being stereotyped is awful no matter what it's for."

She then lists 10 common stereotypes about athletes. These include that only African-Americans are good at basketball, soccer players tend to be overly emotional, women's sports are inferior to men's, and all athletes have to be muscular or bulky. One of the biggest stereotype that a majority of student athletes face is that they all are jocks. Not all of us are jocks! Student-athletes have to maintain certain grades to be eligible to play sports, so they still have to do their academic work. Even if they miss classes, their professors have the same expectations from them.[2]

Antiathlete stereotypes have also gained significant support in the academic world. For example, writing in the scientific journal *Science Blogging*, we read the following: "There is a common belief that some schools, high school and college, are giving athletes an easier time because they have physical skills but not academic ones, for example, and so all athletes become considered 'dumb jocks'."

The article goes on to state the following:

'Coaches spend a lot of time with their players, and they can play such an important role to build academic confidence in student-athletes,' said Deborah Feltz, University Distinguished Professor of kinesiology at Michigan State University and lead author of the paper in the Journal of College Student Development. They wanted to see what factors influence student-athletes' susceptibility to the 'dumb jock' stereotype. It's well-documented

[2] http://www.obamaeagle.org/creative-writing-opinion-and-poetry/2013/12/11/10-stereotypes-athletes-face/.

in the literature that many student athletes hear prejudicial remarks from professors who say things like, 'This test is easy enough that even an athlete could pass it,' Feltz said. "They're kind of the last group of students who can be openly discriminated against." Well, no. White people, men, southerners, Republicans and Catholics are still okay to ridicule at every university in America. There is no liberal guilt at all in stereotyping any of those six. The researchers surveyed more than 300 student-athletes representing men's and women's teams from small and large universities and a range of sports, from basketball and football to cross-country and rowing.[3]

Casey Gane-McCalla noted this problem when he stated the following:

The problem with stereotypes in sports is that they often lead to general stereotypes. If you say, 'white men can't jump,' why not 'black men can't read defenses?' And if black men can't read defenses, maybe they can't read books either? Sports stereotypes have a real effect in the real world. Most employers are not concerned with employees' natural athletic abilities, so stereotypes of African-Americans being athletically superior for the most part do not help blacks in the real world. However, the stereotypes of whites being hard working, disciplined and smart are helpful to them in finding employment.[4]

Stereotyping is an important issue because we soon discover that combining stereotypes with the problems associated with travel creates multiple problems and dangers. For example, does the travel industry take advantage of athletes because it believes that athletes do not have the intellectual power to fight back? Is less protection given to athletes, despite the fact that they are consistently exposed to risk, because of the stereotype that all athletes are strong and therefore, close to invincible? It is in this context that we begin to review the literature concerning athletic travel safety and security.

ATHLETES AS TARGETS OF ATTACK

As Drehs noted above, athletes live a life in which the threat of some form of violent or other criminal attack is ever-present. The reasons for this constant threat are varied. For example, professional athletes attract media attention, turning them into known quantities who are both loved and hated. Often, an athlete's actions have less to do with a negative response than his or her celebrity status. Although the potential for violence against athletes is ever-present, both professional and amateur athletes face other risks. These include the following.

---

[3] http://www.science20.com/news_articles/are_athletes_biggest_victims_stereotype_threat_college_campuses-109975 [accessed 08.03.16].

[4] http://www.huffingtonpost.com/casey-ganemccalla/athletic-blacks-vs-smart_b_187386.html [accessed 08.03.16].

FINANCIAL FRAUD OR OTHER FINANCIAL LOSSES

Many athletes, just as most people, are not deeply schooled in the world of finance. The difference is that, in general, most people go through life anonymously. In the case of professional (and even university) athletes in major sports, however, many are often in the media, and are well-known personalities. This notoriety makes athletes more vulnerable to people who would take advantage of their fame and (supposed) fortune.

Additionally, when we combine a potentially limited knowledge of finance with athletes who earn high salaries, there is a great potential for unscrupulous people to attempt to take advantage of these people.

Often, the public tends to take two contrary positions on the public lives of well-known athletes. One school of thought is that they are immune from the problems of the common man (or woman) and the second school of thought is that, that athletes have strong bodies but are not necessarily bright. Of course, neither is correct. Muscles do not equal economic strength or financial knowledge. In reality, athletes, despite their physical dexterity, fall along a financial spectrum. Some handle money well; others tend to allow money to go to their heads or manage it poorly. The perception, however, among some financial charlatans is that this group is easy prey.

Furthermore, many athletic careers may be well-paid, but only for a short duration. Career brevity means that earning potential can be seductive and lead those who may have risen in the world of professional sports with little financial knowledge to believe that there is little or no reason to save.

The understanding that athletes are vulnerable to financial abuse was recognized at a special panel discussion of the Sports Lawyer's Association on September 10, 2015. According to the association, the topics discussed included the following:

- How an athlete's financial health impacts contract negotiations.
- How best to prepare an athlete for on-field success through appropriate representation.
- How to handle off-the-field endeavors to best enhance financial health.
- How an athlete's insurance coverage and liability exposures can affect their overall financial portfolio.[5]

Although financial problems of the type listed above do not impact the amateur athlete, other financial travel-related issues might have a greater impact

---

[5] https://www.sportslaw.org/events/09-10-15_cleveland.pdf.

on the amateur than on the professional athlete. In many cases, professional athletes do not need to make their own travel arrangements. This fact is especially true of athletes who play on a team sport. Instead their travel plans are often set by a tournament's timing or by a team travel specialists. What is true of the professional is most likely not true in the case of the general amateur athlete, especially if he or she is not playing for a university team. In his or her case, travel might not only involve the normal risks of being on the road, but may also require bringing equipment, rearranging schedules and being subjected to normal travel risks that range from pick-pocketing to fraud, as well as issues of fire safety and food safety. Both stress and fatigue are a normal part of travel, and athletes who travel are subjected to both. Once at the destination, they are expected to perform at a level superior to that of the average person, thus causing additional issues of stress and anxiety.

ISSUES OF HEALTH

Most laypeople assume that athletes are in better shape than the population as a whole. The general assumption is that perceived strength is a sign of organ health, and that a person with muscles is therefore healthier than the average person. As we shall see later in this book, athletes are not only vulnerable to health problems, but in many cases, due to heavy travel schedules, are also considerably more vulnerable.

In an article entitled "Why Do Healthy Athletes Die of Heart Attacks?" the author states:

> Why does it seem that so many healthy athletes suddenly die of a heart attacks—while their overweight peers outlive them? Or is it a case of complete anecdotal blindness? It appears that the data support the fact that exercise, along with diet is good for you. J. N. Morris, D. G. Clayton et al., published the study, "Exercise in leisure time: coronary attack and death rates."

> And noted: "*Nine thousand three hundred and seventy six male civil servants, aged 45-64 at entry, with no clinical history of coronary heart disease, were followed for a mean period of 9 years and 4 months during which 474 experienced a coronary attack. The 9% of men who reported that they did vigorous aerobic activity experienced less than half the non-fatal and fatal coronary heart disease of the other men. In addition, men aged 55-64 who reported the next lower degree of this vigorous aerobic exercise had rates less than two thirds of the others. When these forms of exercise were not vigorous they were not protective against heart disease, nor were other forms of non-aerobic exercise or high totals of physical activity per se. A history of vigorous sports in the past was not protective. In addition, men with exercise-related*

reduction in coronary heart disease also had lower death rates from all other causes compared to the other men." (Italics found in the original article).[6]

There is a big "but" to this statement. Some sports, such as US football, require very large players who carry a great deal of extra weight. An ESPN article, "Heavy NFL Players Twice as Likely to Die Before 50" (January 31, 2006), notes that "The heaviest athletes are more than twice as likely to die before their 50th birthday than their teammates, according to a Scripps Howard News Service study of 3,850 professional-football players who have died in the last century."[7]

The article goes on to note that:

The bone-crushing competitiveness of professional football is spawning hundreds of these behemoths—many of whom top the scales at 300 pounds or more—and the pressure to super-size now extends to younger players in college and even high school. Health problems are not however limited only to the physical brutality of football. For example, in an article in the *Sports Performance Bulletin* Owen Anderson states: "About 1 in 50,000: if you run marathons or participate in other forms of exercise which last for three hours or more, that's your approximate risk of suffering an acute heart attack or sudden cardiac death during—or within 24 hours of—your effort. For every 50,000 athletes, one will be stricken during such prolonged activity (1). Running a marathon or cycling intensely for three hours is riskier than taking a commercial airline flight, even in these troubled times!

It is not only the contact sports athlete who may put his or her body under undue stress. Many practitioners of the non-contact sports also suffer from many of the same issues. The truth is that marathon runners, ironman triathletes and long-distance cyclists, swimmers, rowers and cross-country skiers are all in the same boat. In fact, any athlete who participates in a strenuous test of endurance lasting about three hours or more has an increased chance of dying during—and for 24 hours following—the exertion, even when the athlete's chance of a death-door knock is compared with the risk incurred by a cigarette-smoking, sedentary layabout (sic) who spends the same 24 hours drinking beer and watching TV. The reasons for this are not entirely clear, but the heightened risks of a visit from the Grim Reaper are unsettling to most athletes, especially those who exercise in the hope of improving cardiovascular and overall health.[8]

---

[6] http://www.diet-blog.com/07/why_do_healthy_athletes_die_of_heart_attacks.php [accessed 03.02.16].

[7] http://sports.espn.go.com/nfl/news/story?id=2313476 [accessed 08.03.16].

[8] http://www.pponline.co.uk/encyc/heart-attack-risks-are-greater-for-athletes-who-compete-in-endurance-sports-263# [accessed 08.03.16].

EATING DISORDERS AND ATHLETES

Physical ailments are not the only health issues that impact both professional and amateur athletes. For example, in an article entitled "Protecting Athletes from Disordered Eating," from the Canadian Centre for Ethics in Sports, the authors note that: "For an athlete, disordered eating can often start with the belief that only one body size is acceptable for a chosen sport. This belief may cause the athlete to want to 'lose a few pounds' to improve performance, or follow a strict exercise or eating regimen to maintain current body size. Disordered eating can be identified when an athlete develops eating and/or exercise habits that are harmful to her well-being, such as being very concerned with the fat and calorie content of food, skipping meals, cutting out certain foods, or exercising to 'burn-off' calories to make a body look a certain way. In more extreme cases, this obsession with losing weight or 'maintaining' a certain body size may lead to an eating disorder (anorexia, bulimia, or binge-eating)." The article then states that: "Simply put—athletes are under more pressure than non-athletes in the area of body weight and shape. In addition to the harmful messages that many girls and women receive about how their bodies should look, athletes in some sports must also deal with the weight or aesthetic demands that go along with their participation. Athletes sometimes get the message that only certain body sizes and shapes are acceptable for their sport, whether that means being assigned to a certain weight category or having to wear clothing that emphasizes their body shape."[9]

It is also assumed that eating disorders are a particular problem for females. In the world of athletics, however, eating disorders impact both men and women, often arising from the mistaken tendency to "bulk-up" (add weight) or "trim down," resulting in alternative eating disorders.

Athletes can suffer from multiple forms of eating disorders, from overt dieting to overt eating; however, athletes in some sports seem to have a greater propensity for eating disorder problems than others. For example, athletes in the sports listed below tend to have a higher risk of developing eating disorders:

- US football
- Boxing, wrestling, rowing, and the martial arts
- Equestrian sports
- Running (all forms) cycling and swimming
- Gymnastics
- Track
- Volleyball and ski jumping

---

[9] http://bodysense.ca/protecting-athletes-disordered-eating [accessed 08.03.16].

It should be emphasized that although a relationship might exist between body image, the sport, and eating disorders, there is not necessarily any form of statistical causality. In other words, simply because a person chooses to become a football player or gymnast does not mean that the person will necessarily develop an eating disorder. The basic rule to remember is that correlations never demonstrate statistical causality.

IMMIGRATION ISSUES IN REGARD TO ATHLETES' SAFETY AND SECURITY

The current debate regarding who is a proper immigrant or how one distinguishes immigrant from "illegal migrant" and "legitimate refugee" is an area often overlooked from the perspective of security. In most cases, the question regards issues such as, do athletes from other countries deprive local athletes of their "fair share?" That is to say, do foreign athletes "steal" jobs from native athletes? The second issue that is often raised is that of integration of the foreign athlete into the host culture. In countries such as the United States or Israel, this complex issue is much less complicated than in the European Union, where it is unclear exactly who a foreign athlete is, or if he or she is a part (or not part) of the host society.

The recent flood of refugees to Europe from the Middle East and Africa, however, now raises multiple, additional problems, given that the issues surrounding sports have both a political and a security aspect. Sports have long been a mechanism for athletes to "escape" from what they consider to be "oppressive regimes." For example, in his 1992 article entitled "Freedom in Sports," H.D. Hemphill argues that "sport is an 'extension of alienated capitalist labor.'" He states that: "It is hard in some instances for a country to see a beloved hero leave for the United States to become rich and famous. On the other hand, some countries embrace the idea that their athletes have made it to the pinnacle of professional sports."[10] Not all immigrant athletes are rejected. For example, National Basketball Star Amar'e Stoudemire's move to Israel has created a great deal of excitement throughout the country.[11]

Furthermore, there is often no way of knowing the political affiliation or perspective of an athlete. Is the person loyal to the country, or does he or she represent an undercover threat to national security? So far, no foreign athlete has been involved in an act of terrorism. However, foreign athletes are often

---

[10] Hemphill, D. A. (1992). Sport, political ideology and freedom. *Journal of Sport & Social Issues*, 16(1), 15–33.
[11] http://www.breakingisraelnews.com/73235/nba-star-amare-stoudemire-moving-israel-live-actual-scriptures-watch/#jwCHmREcFKrw4Mu7.97 [accessed 08.03.16].

resented for numerous reasons—often prejudicial—and they, too, may be victimized by local residents who seek to take advantage of the foreign athlete's ignorance of local customs and/or laws.

The fact that athletes are often "known figures" means that they could be victims of a host of secondary issues, such as when an athlete changes not only countries, but also climates. For example, an athlete from a warm country who must play in a colder, outdoor environment could be subject to a number of new physical problems to which the body is not accustomed.

Foreign or immigrant athletes are potential victims of a myriad of potential weather-related safety issues. For example, heat and heat-related illnesses are a potential threat to athletes playing out-of-doors and in hot weather. Both humid and dry climates present risks. Foreign athletes are also subject to issues of anomie, language confusion, and homesickness. These psychological problems may lead to a number of other issues, ranging from alcoholism to suicide.

ISSUES OF WEATHER AND ATHLETES' SAFETY AND SECURITY

Weather issues impact sports players in multiple ways. For example, the following headline comes from the July 16, 2012 issue of the *New York Daily News*: "Lightning kills two soccer players, wounds another in Texas." The article describes a sudden lightning storm that struck players who were on the field. The newspaper article then goes on to state that:

> Houston holds this year's record for most deaths caused by lightning or damage caused by lightning with three. Eleven people have been killed by lightning strikes in the United States overall this year. Lightning was also what sent 17 people to the hospital in Canada on Sunday after lightning struck an outdoor food festival in Whitby, Ontario, according to the Canadian Broadcasting Corporation. The injuries were not life threatening, but victims said the strikes were intense. 'It was so painful, yet the pain was gone so fast. The pain didn't linger,' attendant Bill Sandiford told the CBC.[12]

The fact that lighting strikes injure more players in soccer than other sports should be seen as merely a correlation, and not cause. There is no statistical reason for causality. According to the (US) National Weather Service article published on June 24, 2013, in the *Medical Daily*, "Much to the surprise of experts from the NWS, 41 percent of sports-related lightning fatalities were

---

[12] http://www.nydailynews.com/news/national/lightning-kills-soccer-players-wounds-texas-article-1.1115306 [accessed 08.03.16].

attributed to soccer, compared to 28 percent that were attributed to golf. Of course, fishing was considered the most dangerous activity during a lightning storm, contributing to 26 deaths between 2006 and 2012, io9 reported."

The article then goes onto state that, according to the National Weather Service's lightning specialist, John Jensienius, "When people think of lightning deaths, they usually think of golf. NOAA has made a concerted effort to raise lightning awareness in the golf community since we began the campaign in 2001, and we believe our outreach has made a huge difference since lightning-related deaths on golf courses have decreased by 75 percent."[13] It should be emphasized again that these are mere correlations and do not imply causality. The reason for this phenomenon simply may be that soccer players have a habit of staying on the field longer than they should during the onset of an electrical storm.

ISSUES OF HEAT AND COLD ON ATHLETES

Both heat and cold have their roles in sports injuries or illnesses. The most common forms of heat-related illnesses are heat cramps, heat exhaustion, and heat stroke. Athletes often practice in full uniform in very intense heat conditions, especially where the climate does not cool down during the earlier part of the autumn. Many athletes, especially younger ones, do not drink enough water during practice (although the opposite—over drinking—could be just as dangerous). In hot climates (or on hot days), acute perspiration leading to dehydration is an ongoing threat. Doctors have noted that: "Heat plays a large part in sport and everybody is affected differently. As we are performing any sport or activity our body temperature rises due to an increase in our metabolism. Also we lose or gain heat depending on the air temperature around us, or, our body changes temperature if we have a warm bath or cold shower. When we sweat it is our bodies' way of keeping cool."[14]

HEAT EXPOSURE

A sad, but all-too-common item in today's news media deals with athletes and their exposure to excessive summer temperatures. The death of Minnesota Vikings player Korey Stringer, (he died of heat stroke in 2001) brought the topic to national prominence in the country (United States), and a number of other serious heat-related incidents since then have reminded the

---

[13] http://www.medicaldaily.com/all-athletes-soccer-players-most-likely-be-struck-lightning-national-weather-service-study-reveals [accessed 08.03.16].
[14] http://www.commonsportsinjuries.com/heatrelatedinjury/ [accessed 08.03.16].

public that this is a topic deserving of the attention of parents, coaches and team administrators. In the summer months of 2011, as much of the country has (United States) seen record-breaking periods of extreme temperatures, at least three heat-related deaths on practice fields has been reported, as high school football season approached. These included two high-school football players from Georgia and a coach in Texas, who have died amid sweltering temperatures.[15]

COLD WEATHER ISSUES

Cold weather presents different problems and issues. Depending on the sport, athletes may see cold and snow as either a blessing or a curse. For example, Kansas City (USA) television station KMBC, in a special report on athletic activity in cold weather, noted that:

> Doctors at the University of Kansas Hospital said some athletes are showing up with cold-related problems, and it's not just the risk of frostbite. A specialist told KMBC 9 News that even healthy, well-conditioned athletes dressed in layers of protection are taking a risk working out in extreme temperatures. "You're stressing the system by inhaling all that cold air, and it may even lead you to the emergency room to be evaluated with chest pains or discomfort or shortness of breath," said Dr. Bill Barkman of the University of Kansas Hospital. Not only does outdoor exercise in extreme cold put extra stress on the body, athletes need to be extra diligent about staying hydrated.[16]

The Cox Health system has written about the impact of cold-weather issues on athletics. They state that:

> Runners and other athletes from colder climates brave the elements every day to pursue their passion, some looking for a competitive edge or preparing for the spring and summer seasons. Experts say that with the right clothing and sound judgment, it's okay to keep running or exercising outside even at 20 below. But they also tell athletes to know their personal limits.

The article goes on to note that other factors that can impact an athlete's ability to handle cold are "inadequate winter hydration and nutrition, dehydration, alcohol consumption, certain medications and health conditions such as diabetes and heart disease, which can significantly decrease a person's ability to exercise outdoors in the cold."[17]

---

[15] http://www.hanover.com/risksolutions/athletes-risk-hot-weather.html [accessed 08.03.16].
[16] http://www.kmbc.com/news/athletes-running-outside-in-cold-take-extreme-risk/30579184 [accessed 08.03.16].
[17] http://www.coxhealth.com/SportsandExerciseintheHeatandCold [accessed 08.03.16].

Similarly, the Better Health Channel notes that:

> Sport and exercising in cold weather places extra demands on the body. Common cold-related injuries include muscle sprains and strains, hypothermia and 'snow blindness'. Many of the risks can be reduced with planning, adequate preparation and proper equipment. Be alert for signs of hypothermia and frostbite.[18] There are a number of cold weather related injuries.

According to *Better Health*, most cold-related injuries fall into the following categories:

- *Blisters*. The friction of wet socks and badly fitting footwear can cause blisters on the toes, feet, and heels.
- *Sprains and strains*. Both ice and snow can lead to falls even in the most dexterous athletes.
- *Hypothermia*. This can result from being outside too long, or from lying down to rest and allowing one's body temperature to fall below 35 °C.
- *Frostbite*. This could be especially hard on an athlete who is not used to cold weather and/or does not have adequate protection.
- *Head injury*. Snow sports are high-speed, and impact injuries to the head can have serious consequences. For anyone sustaining a head injury, seeking medical advice is essential. Be safe, not sorry.
- *Sunburn and other sun-related injuries*. Ultraviolet radiation causes sunburn and snow blindness (sunburn of the eye's cornea).[19]

The key here is that many of these problems are exacerbated when we travel. Thus, weather difficulties that are a challenge when the athlete is in his own environment become even more difficult when the climatic conditions of the host area are very different. These environmental changes, such as altitude, humidity, change of food, time zones (and jet lag), and poor eating habits while traveling, impact not only performance but also the athlete's health.

AIR POLLUTION AND ATHLETIC TRAVEL HEALTH

Air pollution is hard on everyone's lungs, and especially hard on athletes, who must exert a great deal of physical energy. What is dangerous for people exercising in their own locale is even more challenging for visitors. For example, Gretchen Reynolds, writing in the *New York Times* (Thursday, July 12, 2007) noted that: "While air pollution affects exercisers at all levels in cities

---

[18] http://www.betterhealth.vic.gov.au/bhcv2/bhcarticles.nsf/pages/Snow_sports_and_cold-related_injuries?open [accessed 08.03.16].

[19] http://www.betterhealth.vic.gov.au/bhcv2/bhcarticles.nsf/pages/Snow_sports_and_cold-related_injuries?open [accessed 08.03.16].

around the world, elite athletes and their retinues are also looking with trepidation toward Beijing, the site next year of the Summer Olympic Games and one of the most polluted cities in the world."

The article then goes onto to state that:

> Dr. Kenneth Rundell, the director of the Human Performance Laboratory at Marywood University in Scranton, Pennsylvania, said, 'Athletes typically take in 10 to 20 times as much air,' and thus pollutants, with every breath as sedentary people do. He was the chairman, in May, of a scientific session on air pollution and athletes at the annual meeting of the American College of Sports Medicine.[20]

Although no one is suggesting that people stop exercising, athletes who must travel from one locale to another might not have acclimatized their bodies to the added stress that comes from what we may term *travel pollution*. Many people assume that the only athletes who suffer from pollution are those who practice an out-of-doors sport, but pollution also impacts athletes in indoor settings. For example, only three states—Minnesota, Massachusetts, and Rhode Island— regulate the air quality at ice rinks.[21] Brooke De Lynch notes that: "The EPA has standards for emissions from ice resurfacers (*sic*) designed to reduce hydrocarbon emissions by about 71 percent, nitrous oxide emissions by about 80 percent, and carbon monoxide emissions by about 57 percent, but does not set air quality standards for indoor rinks."[22] The results can be seen in a February 2011 *Today Show* Investigation that found carbon monoxide and particulate levels at one neighborhood rink in Pennsylvania [that were] well above safe levels for children, and, even an hour after ice resurfacing, the levels were so dangerously high that the tester recommended that the Today crew leave the building. According to *Today* investigator, Jeff Rossen, news reports show that over 250 people have been poisoned at indoor rinks in just the past two years."[23]

DEEP VENOUS THROMBOSIS

Deep venous (or vein) thrombosis (or DVT) is a specific health travel risk to athletes. This does not mean that others do not suffer from DVT, but as Tom Isbell for Active.com, quoting the website Airhealth.org, noted, 85%

---

[20] http://www.nytimes.com/2007/07/12/health/12iht-air.1.6628800.html?pagewanted=all&_r=0 [accessed 08.03.16].

[21] http://www.momsteam.com/ice-hockey-poor-air-quality-pollution-health-concern [accessed 08.03.16].

[22] http://www.momsteam.com/ice-hockey-poor-air-quality-pollution-health-concern [accessed 08.03.16].

[23] http://www.momsteam.com/ice-hockey-poor-air-quality-pollution-health-concern#ixzz3nWJ45blU [accessed 08.03.16].

of air travel thrombosis victims are athletic, usually endurance athletes.[24] Furthermore, "No other risk factor comes close to this. Age over 60 is supposed to be a risk factor, but these victims are younger, 82% of them under 60."[25]

The reasons why so many victims of DVT are athletes directly have to do with the following travel-related issues:

1. Athletes often must take long flights.
2. Many athletes are larger or taller than other travelers.
3. Airline continue to reduce both the size of seats and the space between rows.
4. Athletes often travel as a team in coach class on commercial flights where space is limited and the opportunity to stretch one's legs is minimal.

DVT is a serious problem for many athletes who need to travel. According to Clinical Advisor (June 2004, p. 53), the condition affects more than two million people in the United States alone each year. It is estimated that around 100,000 of these victims will do more than suffer; they will die as a result. Although doctors recommend that passengers on flights of 4 hours or more stretch their legs at 15-minute intervals, in many cases, this precaution is physically impossible. Thus, it is noted that:

> Athletes should flex their legs at fifteen minute intervals during air travel. If other risk factors are present, such as a personal or family history of clots, more frequent flexing would be advisable, and wearing compression stockings. Avoid sleeping. The English soccer team flying to the World Cup games in Japan broke the trip into two segments with a two-day rest stop and wore compression stockings during the flights.[26]

> The following is one example of the problems that DVT can cause: "Tim Hentzel, 26, a competitive triathlete, was recently diagnosed with DVT, deep vein thrombosis, a blood clot in the leg, after a flight from Minneapolis to San Francisco. His life has been difficult since then, revolving around pain, swelling, warfarin (rat poison) tablets, and blood tests."[27]

It is beyond the scope of this chapter to go into the medical reasons for DVT. The basic principle is that athletes are

> at greater risk because, with lower resting blood flow to the large muscles, they are more prone to stasis, stagnant blood subject to clotting. A large

---

[24] http://www.active.com/articles/hidden-danger-dvt-in-endurance-athletes [accessed 08.03.16].
[25] http://www.airhealth.org/athletes.html [accessed 08.03.16].
[26] http://www.airhealth.org/athletes.html [accessed 08.03.16].
[27] http://www.airhealth.org/athletes.html [accessed 08.03.16].

majority of air travel thrombosis victims contacting Airhealth.org are athletic, usually endurance-type athletes like marathoners. No other risk factor comes close. Age is supposed to be a risk factor for DVT, but 83% of these victims are under age 60.[28]

Athletes often take undue risks. Many believe that DVT will not happen to them because:

1. They are physically fit and often, being younger, are convinced that they are invincible.
2. Older people are typically affected by DVT, yet the statistics do not bear out this fact.
3. First class passengers are less likely to get DVT. Although first class does offer more legroom, from a medical perspective there is not that much difference. For example a "Japanese study (of DVT) victims) found 70% of victims in coach class, 25% in business class, 5% in first class, and one pilot."[29] At first, this statistic would seem to indicate that there are fewer DVT victims in first class (or the cockpit); however, it is not the raw number that is important, but rather, the percentage of DVT suffers within each section (class) of the airplane. It should be noted that the ratio of victims is the same in all sections of the aircraft, including the flight deck.
4. Stretching is not enough and we do not become acclimatized to the danger. Pilots are also at risk of DVT, and cold weather exacerbates rather than reduces the problem.

The most complete and scientific study we were able to locate is the LONFLIT study, which examined the incidence of DVT occurring as a consequence of long flights. These are typical of the flights that athletes take not only around the United States, but also around the world.

The authors report that:

> In the Lonflit2 study the authors studied 833 subjects (randomized into 422 control subjects and 411 using below-knee stockings). Mean age was 44.8 years (range, 20–80 yr, SD 12; 57% males). The average flight duration was 12.4 hours. Scans were made before and after the flights. In the control group there were 4.5% of subjects with DVT while only 0.24% of subjects had DVT in the stockings group. The difference was significant. The incidence of DVT observed when subjects were wearing stockings was 18.75 times lower than in controls. Long-haul flights are associated to DVT in some 4–5% of high-risk subjects. Below-knee stockings (the anti-embolism variety) are beneficial in reducing the incidence of DVT.[30]

---

[28] http://www.airhealth.org/athletes.html [accessed 08.03.16].
[29] http://www.airhealth.org/athletes.html [accessed 08.03.16].
[30] http://www.ncbi.nlm.nih.gov/pubmed/11437026.

JET LAG

To be an athlete in either university or professional sports is to travel. East–west/west–east flights across one or more time zones move quicker than the body can adjust. In the case of nondiagonal north–south/south–north travel, there is less time zone crossing, but a potential change of climate. In all cases, travel is hard. In fact, the English word *travel* is derived from the French word *travail* meaning work. Jet lag is "a recognized sleep disorder that is experienced after rapid travel across multiple time zones (transmeridian travel). It affects a large proportion of travelers who cross multiple time zones." The American Academy of Sleep Medicine defines jet lag as a syndrome involving insomnia or excessive daytime sleepiness following travel across at least two time zones. It is associated with impaired daytime function and general malaise and may include other somatic complaints, such as gastrointestinal disruption in the days immediately following travel.[31] Athletes who travel a great deal and then must exert a great amount of physical energy are subject not only to lack of sleep, but also to mood swings and issues of exhaustion. The change of one's internal clock, combined with in-cabin poor air quality and the fact that alcoholic beverages tend to be two to three times more powerful in the air than on the ground, can create both mental and physical problems for the athlete.[32]

ISSUES OF PHYSICAL SECURITY

We can divide the issue of athletes, crime, and security into various categories. Owing to fame and public exposure, many athletes are open targets for criminals. In an age of terrorism, athletes may be either the target of a terrorist attack (such as in the Munich Olympic Games) or the even the perpetrator of a criminal act. Unfortunately, in the case of the latter, numerous athletes have found themselves on the wrong side of the law. It should be noted that, despite the high level of publicity that professional athletes receive when they break the law or are caught breaking the law, reality is quite different. The high publicity around athletes and crime has led to two very different perceptions regarding sports (often, but not always, linked to US football) and crime. There are those who clearly see a relationship between the two.

For example, in his August 9, 2013, CNBC article, Michael McCarthy writes:

> Sports, crime and money have long been intertwined. Babe Ruth once said, 'If it weren't for baseball, I'd be in either the penitentiary or the cemetery.' In more

---

[31] http://www.ncbi.nlm.nih.gov/pmc/articles/PMC3435929/[accessed 08.03.16].
[32] https://www.medco-athletics.com/education/jetlag.htm [accessed 08.03.16].

recent years, well-known sports figures have been convicted of serious crimes, from ex-heavyweight boxer Mike Tyson (rape, road rage) to NFL (National Football League) quarterback Michael Vick (dog fighting) to former Penn State defensive coach Jerry Sandusky (child sex abuse). But the pace of athletes making the police blotter seems to have sped up dangerously in 2013.[33]

On the other side of the argument, we find newspapers such as the *Boston Globe* questioning the CNBC conclusions and stating, on July 2, 2013, after the highly publicized Aaron Hernandez case that: "According to crime reports, NFL pros are not, on the whole, more prone to behaving badly than the rest of us. If anything, they are more law-abiding."[34]

The *Boston Globe* then continues by quoting the Statistical Academic Journal *Chance*:

> Two researchers writing in the academic journal Chance (published by the American Statistical Association) several years ago went through reams of data about crime and NFL players. Their perhaps startling conclusion: The rate of arrests of pro athletes for assault and domestic violence was less than half that of the general population. In other words, the football players were not more violent and in truth were markedly less so. That finding applies to other crimes as well. NFL players commit property crimes at a far lesser rate than does everyone else (perhaps not unexpectedly, given their relatively high incomes). And despite the image of NFL players as wild and crazy partiers (over 624 have been arrested for drunken driving since 2000), the drunken driving arrest rate for pro footballers is about half of that for all young men ages 20 to 29.[35]

Going against the ideas expressed in the *Boston Globe,* Bethany P. Withers writing in the June 12, 2015 edition of the *New York Times* writes that:

> Domestic violence is an obvious indicator of violent tendencies. While there is not conclusive evidence that professional football players are more likely to commit violence against women, there is evidence that they are not punished by the league, teams or the criminal justice system as harshly or consistently as a member of the general public would be. Professional athletes are not the only individuals with careers that are enhanced by certain aggressiveness or that require brute strength. But they may be the only ones for which we— the teams, the leagues, the fans—justify it. It is no wonder that conviction rates are astonishingly low for professional athletes.[36]

---

[33] http://www.cnbc.com/id/100942614 [accessed 08.03.16].

[34] https://www.bostonglobe.com/opinion/2013/07/01/the-myth-about-crime-and-pro-athletes/qlnKoSMkbhuImiS4pO87WJ/story.html [accessed 08.03.16].

[35] https://www.bostonglobe.com/opinion/2013/07/01/the-myth-about-crime-and-pro-athletes/qlnKoSMkbhuImiS4pO87WJ/story.html.

[36] http://www.nytimes.com/roomfordebate/2013/07/01/should-character-matter-in-pro-sports/athletes-get-off-easy-when-they-are-violent.

In other words, she argues that fewer athletes (in this case, professional) are convicted, and therefore, crime rates appear to be lower.

When we examine crimes against athletes, the picture changes completely. There is a whole body of literature, both academic and nonacademic, about women athletes who are victims of male crime. In most cases, the article refers to males (often, but not always, athletes) who commit violence against women athletes, most commonly, sexual assault. Below is a partial list (alphabetical, by title) of scholarly articles on the topic of assault against women.

- "Androgen Abuse by Athletes," by Jean D. Wilson.
- "Creating Lasting Attitude and Behavior Change in Fraternity Members and Male Student Athletes: The Qualitative Impact of an Empathy-Based Rape Prevention," by J.D. Foubert and B.C. Perry.
- "'He Owned Me Basically . . .' Women's Experience of Sexual Abuse in Sport," by Celia Brackenridge.
- "Intentional Fouls: Athletes and Violence Against Women," by Ellen E. Dabbs.
- "Male Student-Athletes and Violence Against Women: A Survey of Campus Judicial Affairs Offices," by T.W. Crosset, J. Ptacek, and M.A. McDonald.
- "Masculinities, Violence and Culture," by Neil Websdale.
- "Complex Mapping: TheMargins of Intersectionality, Identity Politics and Violence Against Women of Color," by A.F. Kimberlé Williams Crenshaw.
- "Penalties, Fouls, and Errors: Professional Athletes and Violence Against Women," by C.A. Moser.
- "Public Heroes, Private Felons: Athletes and Crimes Against Women," by J. Bennet.
- "Sex, Violence & Power in Sports: Rethinking Masculinity," by Michael A. Messner, and Donald F. Sabo.
- "Rethinking Violence Against Women," by R.P. Dobash.
- "Understanding Violence against Women," by Nancy A. Crowell and Ann W. Burgess (editors).
- "Violence Against Women By Professional Football Players: A Gender Analysis of Hypermasculinity, Positional Status, Narcissism, and Entitlement," by W. Welch.

There is, of course, no excuse for male violence against women athletes, or any women. It also should be noted that male-on-male or female-on-female of violence is either not reported or not considered worthy of academic or journalistic articles. Despite the dearth of material found, we can assume that male athletes suffer from issues of assault, blackmail, economic robberies, muggings, and theft, both in the clubhouse and/or locker room and whenever they appear in the public eye. At the time of this writing, there is also minimal literature concerning violence against gay or transgendered athletes. Often this violence must be inferred as in the article that appeared in the October 14, 2014 *Hoffington Post* entitled: "LGBT Athletes Still Face Harrasment and Decrimination."[37]

Eric Anderson's book, *In the Game: Gay Athletes and the Cult of Masculinity*, even states: "… this research found no overt violence against gay athletes. That is to say that none of the athletes in this study were beaten or harassed" (Anderson, p. 8).[38] On the other side of the coin, Michael Nassar has noted the number of antigay laws promulgated in Russia and their impact on gay athletes who wanted to (or did) participate in the 2014 Winter Olympic Games in Sochi, Russia.

Although there is some literature regarding the problems of gay athletes, the great majority of the literature is about who is, or might be, a gay athlete.

At the time of this writing, there was a dearth of literature regarding violence against transgendered athletes, with the majority of the articles dedicated to issues of implementing inclusion. Often, this literature is connected to literature describing acts of legal, physical, psychological, or social violence or nonacceptance against other members of the gay and lesbian communities. For example, in her book, *The Penalties of Puppy Love: Institutionalized Violence Against Lesbian, Gay, Bisexual and Transgendered Youth*,[39] Elvira R. Arriola writes about transgendered people, but only as part of a larger cohort. One article that does address the issue squarely is "On Transgendered Athletes, Fairness and Doping: An International Challenge," by Sarah Teetzal. Teetzal maintains that the real issue is one of biology in that there remain questions regarding whether the transgendered athlete has maintained some of his or her original sexual characteristics that give men who have transgendered to women an unfair competitive advantage.[40]

ISSUES OF STADIUM SECURITY AND TERRORISM

Brent Schrotenboer, writing in the May 2, 2013 edition of *USA Today*, questions the security of US stadiums. He writes:

---

[37] http://www.huffingtonpost.com/ken-reed/lgbt-athletes-still-facin_b_5648282.html [accessed 08.03.16].

[38] Eric Anderson, In the Game: The Cult of Gay Athles, State University of New York Press, 2005.

[39] http://heinonline.org/HOL/LandingPage?handle=hein.journals/jgrj1&div=24&id=&page= [accessed 08.03.16].

[40] http://www.tandfonline.com/doi/abs/10.1080/17430430500491280 [accessed 08.03.16].

Experts call it 'security theater' at stadium gates—a show of uniforms and bag searches that does little to protect fans from what we witnessed in Boston. After that attack in broad daylight, they say the entire system needs an overhaul, from security guard regulations to the public's awareness at major events.[41]

Almost every Saturday afternoon, tens of thousands of people attend college football games. Schrotenboer notes a major flaw, but stadiums also have a great number of secondary issues. Among these are:

- Crowd control and evacuation plans
- Number of ambulances
- Police Department integration with private security and multiple police forces
- Triage centers
- Vetting of concessionaires

Many small-town colleges have large stadiums, and these communities could double their population during game days. They might not, however, have sufficient infrastructure to handle such large temporary increases in populations. These rapid population shifts combined with poor stadium security put players as well as the public at risk. In fact, in some ways the players might be more at risk. Should there be an active shooter, or a terrorist attack, the public would panic, making it almost impossible to evacuate the athletes. Furthermore, athletes are in full view of the general public, giving an active shooter a clear line of sight with the added protection of shooting from a location where those nearby might panic.

An additional problem is that many stadiums do not have barriers between the players and the public. For example, during the last World Cup games, there were no physical barriers separating the public from the playing field. The field was protected only by a string of security guards.

We can subdivide the issue of athlete security at stadiums into the following categories:

- Athlete evacuation
- Protection from fans
- Security both on the field and in the locker room
- Weather issues while athletes are at play

---

[41] http://www.usatoday.com/story/sports/2013/05/02/stadium-security-boston-marathon-kentucky-derby/2130875/ [accessed 08.03.16].

NEW SECURITY CHALLENGES

Security is a constantly changing subject, and one area that is only now being considered is the relationship between drones and stadium security. Jacob Molz, writing in *Athletic Business*, has noted that: "Unmanned aerial systems pose a legitimate threat to sporting events in America. These devices are not only becoming cheaper and easier to own, but technology has advanced to such a point that virtually anyone—hobbyist or terrorist—can fly one."[42] The Federal Aviation Administration (FAA) also considers drones a potential threat to stadiums. At the time of this writing, FAA regulations prohibited unauthorized aircraft or drones over a stadium with a seating capacity of 30,000 or more starting one hour before the event and continuing until one hour after the event. Although the FAA is to be commended (see full policy in footnote), the policy contains a number of potential loopholes. In today's 24-hour news cycle, the policy does not affect attacks against smaller stadiums or against multiple stadiums at the same time.[43]

Thus, to quote the *Bismarck Tribune* in North Dakota:

> Operators who fly drones or model planes near or over large sports stadiums and auto racetracks are breaking the law and can be fined and imprisoned for up to a year, the Federal Aviation Administration warned in a notice posted on the agency's website.[44]

The notice marks the first time the FAA has sought to criminalize the use of drones and model planes, attorneys representing drone users said.

---

[42] http://www.athleticbusiness.com/stadium-arena-security/drones-emerging-as-security-threat-at-domestic-sporting-events.html [accessed 08.03.16].

[43] Any person who knowingly or willfully violates the rules pertaining to operations in this airspace may be subject to certain criminal penalties under 49 usc 46307. Pilots who do not adhere to the following procedures may be intercepted, detained and interviewed by law enforcement/security personnel. Pursuant to 14 cfr section 99.7, special security instructions, commencing one hour before the scheduled time of the event until one hour after the end of the event. All aircraft operations; including parachute jumping, unmanned aircraft and remote controlled aircraft, are prohibited within a 1410271420-perm end part 1 of 3 fdc 4/3621 fdc part 2 of 3 special 3nmr up to and including 3000ft agl of any stadium having a seating capacity of 30,000 or more people where either a regular or post season major league baseball, national football league, or ncaa division one football game is occurring. This notam also applies to nascar sprint cup, indy car, and champ series races excluding qualifying and pre-race events. Flights conducted for operational purposes of any event, stadium or venue and broadcast coverage for the broadcast rights holder are authorized with an approved airspace waiver.

[44] http://www.athleticbusiness.com/more-news/faa-flying-drones-by-stadiums-can-mean-fines-prison.html.

STADIUM PERSONNEL AND EQUIPMENT FOR ATHLETES' SAFETY AND SECURITY

Good stadium security revolves around security layers and the use of redundancy. The security of a stadium, then, needs both human beings and machines, and both the human factor and machines must be so programmed to work in sync. Below are some of the basic tools in assuring that the physical plant (the stadium or arena) is kept secure.

Security Personnel. This means both the training and vetting of people working in and for the stadium event. Personnel refers to private and public security agencies, along with those who are there to serve the public.

Equipment. These devices often include video surveillance, systems for access control, devices to scout the stadium's perimeters, control of data (data centers) securing the power supply and IT security software. Since stadiums and players must be protected both from fan hooliganism and potential terrorist attacks, CCTV systems are an integral part of security networks. However, CCTV systems are only as effective as the personnel overseeing them, and their real-time integration with active security personnel.

Legal Protections. The best security systems must be integrated not only with law enforcement, but must also align with policies that allow security personnel the flexibility to do their job without fear of frivolous lawsuits or other liabilities.

For example, in a Fox News interview with Daniel DeLorenzi of MetLife Stadium in Rutherford, New Jersey, DeLorenzi noted that:

> If someone is ejected from MetLife Stadium, that person is banned for all events until completing a readmittance (*sic*) program. That program entails having the barred person fill out a form that basically is an ejection report; explain to DeLorenzi what his or her actions were; and take an online conduct course vowing to act responsibly. Once that person has a certificate of completion, readmittance is granted. 'We've had no repeat offenders from people who have taken the class,' says DeLorenzi.[45]

Policies might cover anything from a suspicious package, to alcohol and drugs, to unruly behavior. In call cases, security personnel must have the backing of both law enforcement and the law itself, along with the knowledge that they are acting in accordance with management policies.

---

[45] http://www.foxnews.com/sports/2014/10/24/nfl-lauds-metlife-stadium-security-system-and-programs-as-trendsetting.html [accessed 08.03.16].

LEGAL ISSUES

Athletes, like all human beings, are subject to all sorts of wrongful injuries. These injuries may result from negligence during travel, at a place of lodging, at a dining facility, or at the stadium. As noted, players might be subjected to unfair weather conditions, such as extreme heat or cold, leading not only to injury, but also to lawsuits. The Hoover insurance group has noted that:

> The injury or death of an athlete will almost inevitably raise questions about the team's program, which may result in a lawsuit against the team, the coaches, administrators and others. The nature of such a lawsuit will likely find its genesis in a claim of negligence against the defendants. Allowing for various jurisdictional differences, a successful claim for negligence will require the plaintiff to prove that the defendant(s) had a duty to the athlete, the defendant(s) breached that duty, the breach of the duty caused the injury (or death) to the athlete, and the plaintiff has suffered damages.[46]

On April 22, 2015, CNN reported the settlement between football players and the NFL over concussions and head injuries. CNN reported the following:

> A federal judge has given final approval to a class-action lawsuit settlement between the National Football League and thousands of former players, the league said. The agreement provides up to $5 million per retired player for serious medical conditions associated with repeated head trauma. While the lawsuit was a combination of hundreds of actions brought by more than 5,000 ex-NFL players, the settlement applies to all players who retired on or before July 7, 2014, according to Judge Anita Brody's 132-page decision. It also applies to the family members of players who died.[47]

Although this settlement has more to do with play on the field than with travel to the field, the principle that injured players have a right to class action law suits means that travel agents, tour providers, hotels, and other travel-related business have been put on notice that the legal principles of "foresee-ability" apply to all travelers, including athletes.

The right to sue, however, does not mean that athletes do not have to have personal social responsibility. For example, Kwame J. A. Agyemang, PhD, writing for the Huffines Institute, notes that:

> While many think the life of a professional athlete is all 'glitz and glamour,' it can be difficult at times dealing with the numerous responsibilities asked of the athlete. Thus, having a management strategy in place can be invaluable. To further this framework, athletes should hire capable, respected managers

---

[46] http://www.hanover.com/risksolutions/athletes-risk-hot-weather.html [accessed 08.03.16].
[47] http://www.cnn.com/2015/04/22/us/nfl-concussion-lawsuit-settlement/ [accessed 08.03.16].

to help manage their careers and activities. In the end, well-developed social responsibility prolongs the athlete's career, thus keeping fans and other stakeholders happy.[48]

Travel, however, has a tendency to lessen social responsibility. When people travel, they tend to enter into a specific travel mindset. Tarlow[49] has written extensively on psychological and social problems in the field of travel. Among the problems inherent in this mindset are the following:

- Travelers often tend to leave their common sense at home. Most vacationers tend to assume that the place to which they are traveling is safe. This concept is certainly true not only of vacationers, but often of business people, and a traveling athlete is essentially a business professional. Many travelers tend to believe that they are in a closed and protected environment. As such, there is a tendency to leave one's worries at home, to assume that someone else is looking out for the traveler and that nothing bad will happen. Tarlow notes that the word *vacation* gives insight into this phenomenon, as it is derived from the French word *vacances*, meaning *vacant*. A vacation, then, is a time of mind-vacancy when we relax and tend not to think.

- It is often easy to identify cruise travelers at a port of call. They often fail to blend in with the local culture. They may use neither local dress nor speak the local language. Cruise travelers' time frames are a great deal shorter than those of other tourist cohorts, and therefore, these tourists have less time to adjust to a place. Land-tourism is based on a place (or group of places) that acts as the destination; in the world of cruise tourism, the cruise itself is the destination, and in the world of sports, it is often the concept of the competitive game that becomes the destination.

- Travelers are often in a state off anomie. To travel is to be confused. There are many reasons for this anomic state. Athletes who must travel long distances often suffer mentally and physically from cramped quarters, and some might (especially after a game) take personal liberties that result in both social and reputational damage. The French Sociologist David Emile Durkheim, in 1893, was the first to identify this sociological state of disorientation, naming it "anomie." Anomic cruise travelers are likely to make silly travel mistakes, to let down their guard, or simply to be careless, and predators are well aware of this state.

---

[48] http://huffinesinstitute.org/resources/articles/articletype/articleview/articleid/178/special-issues-of-social-responsibility [accessed 08.03.16].
[49] See Tarlow's writings in *Tourism Security: Strategies for Effectively Managing Travel Risk and Safety,* Elsevier (2014) Chapter 2.

- Tourists often drop their inhibitions when they travel. People tend to do things on the road that they might not try at home. This lowering of inhibitions might result in experimentation, be it with drugs or sexual, or simply being ruder than usual. For many, the cruise is a place where inhibitions can be safely lowered.
- To travel is to be stressed. Athletes are under a great deal of stress, and the travel experience often amplifies it. Stress-related issues when traveling often mean that the athlete and his or her entourage may tend to enter into higher levels of anomic states, tend to think in less rational ways, and are often become more prone to anger.
- Closely related to stress is the issue of time—perhaps an athlete's most challenging issue. The athlete must have sufficient time to rest, must arrive at practices and game locations on time, and unconsciously knows that time will, in the end, diminish his or her abilities. Athletes thus live in a continual competition against time. One merely has to observe how people line up for athletic events and become frustrated if an event begins later than scheduled. In such situations, the anger, disappointment, frustration, and stress on passengers' faces reflect the power of time in travel.

These concepts are of extreme importance, because no matter how much protection we offer athletes, no one can protect them continually, and any person can defeat a system meant to protect him or her if good judgment is not used.

CHAPTER 3

Sports as a Tourism Attraction

There is little doubt that around the world, sports and sporting facilities not only are major attractions, but they are also an important contributor to many local economies. In fact, it is often almost impossible to separate local economies from local sports cultures. College towns often have prefootball events, called tailgating. Prosports cities' bars and entertainment districts are often filled both before and after a game, and major victories might result in parades or other forms of local celebrations. Usually, these celebrations are peaceful and good-natured, but there are times when victory celebrations have turned ugly and resulted in a loss of property. Although sporting and athletic events are cultural events, they are also important parts of the local economy. For example, in the case of a tailgate party, fans might purchase a great deal of local products or frequent local eating and drinking establishments as part of their postgame celebration. Likewise, after a professional game fans often visit bars and restaurants.

These activities result in the local community earning not only additional revenue, but also gaining revenue from sales and sales taxes, from the hotel–motel tax on room rentals, and from transportation or parking. What is true of college athletic events is also true of professional sports and, to an even greater degree, of international, mega sporting events such as the Olympic Games or soccer's World Cup.

Sports' social and economic impacts have been with the world for thousands of years. For example, as far back as ancient Greece, we note that the Olympics were much more than a chance to win a medal; they were also a center of socialization that provided the local economy with an economic boost.

In his book *A Visitor's Guide to the Ancient Olympics*, Neil Faulkner describes the party atmosphere of the ancient Olympic Games held in Olympia, Peloponnese, Greece, stating that:

> Directed to the 'Olympic village,' they [the attendees] would find a vast, partly tented, partly open-to-the-skies encampment, with inadequate water supplies, heaps of stinking refuse and huge improvised latrines. The air was

51

Sports Travel Security. DOI: http://dx.doi.org/10.1016/B978-0-12-805099-6.00003-8

alive with millions of flies, mosquitoes and wasps. The dumps were overrun with rats. By the end of the five-day festival, no one had washed properly for a week, and you could smell the games a mile away.

Faulkner then goes on to write that:

In the Olympic stadium, you sat on a grassy bank under the searing heat of the midsummer sun. It was the same in the nearby Hippodrome, where the equestrian events were held. Naked athletes participated in foot races; the pentathlon; horse and chariot races and in three combat sports—wrestling, boxing and the almost-no-holds-barred *pankration*. That was the crowd's favorite, because there were virtually no rules and it was all blood and pain.

Finally, according to Faulkner:[1]

the ancient Olympic games were a time for male bonding. Men spent time with family and (male) lovers. Both the athletes and the attendees partook in a wide range of spiritual and physical experiences. As we shall see at a later part of this chapter, just as in the case of the modern Olympics: 'the real added attraction of the games was not the cultural Olympiad but the sexual one. At the Olympics, parties went on through the wee hours, and hundreds of prostitutes, both women and boys, touted their services until dawn.'[2]

Faulkner could be writing about many modern athletic events. In fact, spectators and athletes at the modern Olympics, and at other mega events, share certain character traits with the ancient Olympic Games. Among these are:

1. These athletes tend to be young and have well-cared-for bodies.
2. Youth is a time when sexual hormones tend to be most active.
3. The athletes live in close quarters and only a few of the hundreds who participate will have a chance at winning a medal. Close quarters offer the possibility of breeding intimacy on many levels.
4. Athletes have a good deal of downtime, and few participate in more than one competitive activity.
5. Many athletes report that they practice abstinence during their training period. Once at the Olympic Games, and after their event, however, there may well be a downturn in personal discipline. In fact, once the athlete has competed, there might be little to do until the closing ceremonies.
6. As at the ancient Olympics, there is a party atmosphere where all can easily obtain alcohol and those not participating in the actual games might well be able to obtain other, illegal, substances.

[1] Faulkner, N., A Visitor's Guide to the Ancient Olympics" (Yale University Press) 2012.
[2] http://www.wsj.com/articles/SB10001424052702303448840457741043148794 6516 [accessed 08.04.16].

SPORTS TOURISM

Although multiple writers and commentators use the phrase *sports tourism*, in reality, there is no one definition of *sports tourism*. Most people, however, accept some form of a definition that refers to the act of traveling from one locale to another for the expressed purpose of viewing or participating in a sporting event. People travel not only to see major events, such as the World Series, World Cup, or National Football League Super Bowl, but also to see their children compete in Little League or to support their favorite team. Sports tourism might be the primary motivation for travel, or an add-on to an existing trip or vacation. Sports tourism also has an active side, in that people travel to participate in an athletic activity. These activities range from team sports to individual sports, and include competitive activities, such as a bowling tournament, or personal, recreational activities, such as skiing or scuba diving. Since sports tourism is so wide-ranging, there is no one type of sports tourist or "consumer." Sports tourism attracts people of all ages to a location to participate in anything from senior Olympic Games to viewing their grandchildren or children at a tournament. The sports tourist also might be both participant and spectator.

In all cases, the athletic event is the "attraction." From this perspective, sports tourism most closely resembles cultural tourism. Just as in fields such as theater or dance, rarely does the visitor come to see the venue, but rather what occurs within the venue. Just as in the world of cultural tourism, once the event has finished, then the attraction disappears. In that way, sports tourism is a form of ephemeral tourism.

Charles Pigeassou, writing in *The Journal of Sports Tourism*, defines this as

> a human experiment in which is focusing on a set of services necessary for the realization of non professional temporary journeys towards specific destinations to experience sport culture. The experience of sport culture influences the choice of the destination. It is essential to dissociate sport whilst on holidays and sport tourism. In one case, sport practice is likened to any activity, which can be undertaken whilst on holidays. In the other case, the desire to experience sport culture drives the tourist activity.[3]

MAKING THE SPORTS TOURISM EXPERIENCE ENCHANTING FOR BOTH ATHLETES AND GUESTS

As we shall see in the coming chapters, travel often is not an easy or pleasant task. In fact, the word *travel* is derived from the French word *travail*, meaning

---

[3] http://www.tandfonline.com/doi/abs/10.1080/1477508042000320205?journalCode=rjto20 [accessed 08.04.16].

work. Throughout the entire travel and visitation system, there are numerous challenges, many of which spawn additional, unforeseen challenges. Athletes and spectators often have to put up with numerous hurdles, ranging from transportation delays to long waits on lines, and from travel problems caused by inclement weather to issues of safety and security, including potential acts of terrorism. For these reasons, people who look after athletes, communities that seek athletic events, and athletic event planners try to do everything possible to create as enchanted an environment as possible. The last thing that any of these professionals want is for the magic of sports to become a sports travel nightmare, or to have the mundane conquer the special moments that transform mere physical activity into the grace of athletic competition. Below are a number of factors for sports travel professionals to consider in order to eliminate, as much as possible, the drudgery of the travel experience and turn what for many athletes is nothing more than into a business trip into a memorable experience.

Sports tourism specialists (STSs) need to find ways to create enchantment through product development. Successful sports tourism industries rely less on marketing and more on offering value. The worst thing a sports tourism center can do is not meet the expectations of athletes and their fans. Therefore, one must learn what these expectations are and find a way to exceed them. Rather than overstating the STS's case, make it known that the staff and the STS professionals care especially about the smallest of details and providing outstanding interpersonal actions. The best form of marketing is a good product and good service. Provide what your community promises at prices that are reasonable. Athletes and fans well understand that sports communities are seasonal locations where workers have to earn their year's wages in just a few months. Pricing with this in mind might be acceptable, but gouging is never in fashion. Enchantment-oriented sports communities realize that everyone in the community has a part to play in creating a positive tourism experience in a unique and special environment.

Enchantment in tourism does not have to be grounded in absolute reality. Although the world of sports is based on statistics and numbers, the community in which the sporting event is located can create a balance between fantasy and real. Often, the further away from reality we are, the greater the enchantment. Cities with colorful characters or unique locations can provide an extra measure of "simulata" for the spectator. A community can even create enchantment by emphasizing a particular, successful film or book set in that space. If the literary work is about a sporting experience, then there is a powerful overlapping of the athletic experience with the enchantment experience.

It is essential to be sure that staff understands the importance of making the athletic experience one of enchanted memories. Staff members need to understand that no matter how good their STS's policies are, the public judges them based on the staff's actions. People attend athletic events in order to have fun. Even the players, despite all their hard work, have to have fun at their job if they are to be successful. If employees project an image that they do not like tourists, then the message they are giving to the public destroys the public's sense of being special or participating in a special experience. When tourism professional are more interested in their own ego trips than in the vacationer's experience, then the experience turns from fun into hassle. An employee who is unique, funny, or makes people feel special is worth thousands of dollars in advertising.

Similarly, tourism professionals or hotel general managers (GMs) must always remember their particular roles. To aid in this pursuit, they would benefit from performing every job in their industry at least once a year. Often, tourism managers focus so much on the bottom line that they forget the humanity of their employees. Hotel managers create enchantment by playing the role of visitors and seeing the world through their eyes. Perhaps the number one way to create an enchanted experience is to make staff members so happy that they want to come to work everyday. No tourism locale, including a sports tourism locale, can ever afford to cease emphasizing that tourism and travel personnel exist to serve the public. Without the public's approval, tourism and travel jobs simply fade away.

We can also turn a sports event into a community of enchanted sports events. Few cities and communities can cater to every need. Rather than claiming that a community offers something for everyone, it is best to focus on experiences and places that represent something special. Ask: What makes our community or attraction different from our competitors (or even better, unique)? How does our community celebrate its individuality? Who in our community is special or unique and could add value to the athletic experience? A good rule of thumb is for community leaders to ask themselves: If I were a visitor to our community, would I remember my experience a few days later, or would this town simply be one more place on the map? Sports tourism does not stop when the sun sets or the game is over. Evenings can be used to create new forms of enchantment. If your community lacks nightlife, then create special moonlit walks, star gazing experiences, or moments of solitude.

The STS should identify and improve those aspects of a tourism experience that destroy enchantment. If the community has an attraction with lines that are too long, then find ways to entertain people while they stand in line. If service is not too satisfactory, then provide extra training for personnel; if airports and traffic are negative experiences, then seek ways to provide "feasts for the eyes" that compensate for the hassles of travel. Perhaps nothing destroys the enchantment of tourism as much as poor signage! Make sure that your signage is clear and precise, use international symbols, and provide translations when necessary.

One can also create enchantment through beautification and environmental projects. Sporting events are not only about athletic power, but also about the ambience in which the event takes place. That is why sporting venues must be both practical and also eye-catching. It is essential to work with specialists in such areas as lighting, landscaping and "streetscaping," color coordination, exterior and interior decorations, street appearances and city themes, parking lots, and internal transportation service. Even utilitarian devices, such as subway cars or airports, can become vehicles of enchantment. The subway in Santiago, Chile, is filled with classical music, and the airport in Monterrey, Mexico, is a museum in motion, while the airport in Vancouver, Canada, guides visitors through the world of Inuit culture.

Enchantment dies in a location that does not exude a sense of safety and security. One must create a safe and secure atmosphere. There can be little enchantment if people are afraid. Sporting events are places "to be" and "to be active," and to see and to be seen. Events such as the Kentucky Derby are as much about the visitor's experience as about the racing of horses. To create a positive atmosphere, local security professionals must be part of the planning from the beginning. Tourism security is more than merely having police or security professionals watching over a site; it requires psychological and sociological analysis. Remember that no matter how good our security hardware may be, it is only as effective as the people who use it. Creating a safe and secure sports venue not only protects athletes and visitors, but also those who live in the community.

No matter what, STS professionals must never forget that they dare not take customers for granted. The visitor does not have to attend a sporting event. Spectators are customers, and just as in any business where there are no customers, the business either closes or moves to a new location. Enchant your customers and you will enhance your greatest asset: your reputation.

SPORTS, TOURISM, AND SOCIAL BEHAVIOR

Tourism is, first and foremost, a business. Although the tourism industry has many components, each aspect must produce more income than outflow if it is to survive. The one exception to this rule may be that the industry, often represented in the United States by Convention and Visitor Bureaus (CVBs) or local governments, might invest in events or other programs designed to increase the number of people who come to a locale. We call these "moving attractions" in the sense that they are ephemeral events intended to enhance a locale's reputation. Sporting events fall into this category. For example, nations and cities compete to host a mega event such as a Super Bowl, (Soccer) World Cup, or Olympic Games. Vast quantities of money are invested both in local infrastructure and marketing efforts in the hope that these events not only will enhance a locale's image, but also produce a great deal of extra revenue. Often the mega issues of safety and security are overlooked by marketers, but they have a major role in shaping a locale's perception and set the stage for a location's long-term image.

THE TRAGIC CASE OF RIO DE JANEIRO[4]

There is a Brazilian saying that God must have been drunk when He created Rio de Janeiro (often called simply Rio). Rio is a city known for beautiful beaches and mountains that almost seem to kiss the sea. Rio's beauty, however, is not merely confined to landscapes. There is another, dark side, a side of the city that its promoters wish the world would not seem but at which hundreds of media personnel are shining a light.

Rio de Janeiro in some ways is more than a city in Brazil; for much of the world, Rio *is* Brazil. It not only holds the nation's most important monuments, such as Corcovado, the statue of Jesus with open arms stretching across Guanabara Bay, and the Maracanã stadium, perhaps soccer's most hallowed ground, but it is also the nation's cultural and tourism capital. Also, like much of Brazil, Rio de Janeiro has the reputation of being a place where beautiful bodies intermingle—a sensuous city, best known for Carnival, where human sexuality is set against the beat of samba.

Yet there is also a darker side, the side that Rio promoters prefer not to mention and on which the light of media attention during the prelude leading up to the 2016 Olympic Games was being shined. Brazil invested millions of dollars into both the 2014 World Cup and the 2016 Olympic Games. The hope is that these investments will produce:

- Jobs
- Large numbers of visitors
- Long-term tourism
- Positive publicity that will enhance the city's image, both as a tourism locale and a place in which to invest.

At the time of writing this chapter, it is still too early to determine the long-term impact of the Brazilian Olympic Games. The full data may not be known for months, or even years. What we do know is that by May 2016, Brazil had already received a great deal of negative publicity, the impact of

---

[4] The city of Rio de Janeiro and the Olympic Games in this chapter are used as "symbols" or paradigms for problems that can take place at any mega sporting event. The goal of this section is not to analyze the problems at the 2016 Olympic Games nor to analyze Rio de Janeiro but to use these as examples of problems that can take place at any large event in any venue around the World. It should be noted that the chapter was written prior to the games being held.

which might shape the city's (and nation's) image for years to come. This negative publicity revolves around two key factors: questions about the city of Rio de Janeiro's security situation, and questions about the city's health and sanitation problems. Even if the Olympic Games is determined to be a success, the negative prepublicity will still haunt the city.

From the perspective of security, perhaps nothing could have been more negative than the CNN (among the many media outlets) headline of May 11, 2016, that read "Former Brazilian Soccer Star: Don't Come to Rio Olympics." One of the great Brazilian soccer stars, Rivaldo, posted on social media that Rio is simply too dangerous to visit. The CNN article goes on to note that: "The message is likely to frustrate the country's leaders, who have been trying to dispel the notion that Brazil is not ready for the games and Rio is not safe for tourists." The CNN news report tried to balance the negative by quoting the city tourism secretary: "'We are waiting for everyone to come so we can showcase our city,' Rio de Janeiro Municipal Tourism Secretary Antonio Pedro Viegas said. 'People already know our problems, but they will be surprised by Rio's beauty and the warmth of its people.'" The article, however, demonstrates the interconnectivity of safety and security when it goes on to state:

> But violence is just one problem that Brazil is facing ahead of the games. The coastal city of Recife is considered ground zero for the deadly Zika virus. A host of countries have issued travel warnings for areas affected by the virus, which is carried by mosquitoes.[5]

Placed at the bottom of the article are the words: Then there's concerns about the physical spaces.

It's not clear if all the venues and infrastructure will be ready. And water quality is also a concern for those who will compete in Rio's Guanabara Bay, which has been polluted by sewage. This final sentence demonstrates that safety and security are not only about caring for spectators and visitors, but that the athletes, too, are human beings who also fear for their well-being. The issue of competing in contaminated waters then becomes a problem of tourism sports security. It is not only a health problem, but also a marketing problem. The ESPN: "The Promise Rio Couldn't Keep" (ESPN, February 18, 2016), exemplifies how both athletes and local Olympic organizations are worried. For example, the article, read around the world, notes that:

> The USOC [United States Olympic Committee] does not have the authority to order water athletes to withdraw because of the conditions and is focusing instead on providing information along with beefed-up medical counsel, according to CEO Scott Blackmun. 'The water's still dirty and it stinks some

---

[5] http://www.cnn.com/2016/05/11/sport/rivaldo-brazil-olympics-2016/index.html [accessed 08.04.16].

days, and, I don't know. You don't need to study a lot to understand that it's not going well.'

The article goes on to state that:

'The water in Rio is dirty,' Blackmun told *Outside the Lines* in an interview last week. 'We need to do everything we can to prevent our athletes from getting sick while they're down there. But our athletes have competed in difficult conditions around the globe on many, many, many occasions in the past, and it's just a matter of making sure our preparations are specifically targeted to the conditions we're going to find in Rio.'

Statements such as the following do not exactly convey the image that Rio de Janeiro wants to show the world as it sells itself as a premier destination: "Raw sewage. The athletes do not talk about it. They are not there to challenge the world's environmental issues. But the athletes are all concerned and deeply worried."[6]

If tourism is as much perception as reality, then the Rio Olympics may turn out to be a very costly exercise in negative marketing, a marketing that could impact the city's reputation for years. For example, a headline in the popular, online website, "Travel and Tour World," in its May 13, 2016 edition reads: "Could traveling to Rio Olympics cause global heath disaster?" The article asks if, in a location where the Zika virus is prevalent, sexual mores are loose and there is the potential for tens of thousands of foreign tourists to be present, might Rio de Janeiro be the perfect incubator for a world pandemic. The article notes that: "Rio de Janeiro is all set to welcome its international delegates and other tourists from all across the globe for its 2016 Olympic Games. Unfortunately, the doctors have warned that it could spark a 'full-blown public health disaster'."[7] Zika would be connected to Brazil's image, and this negative marketing would take years from which to recuperate. Rio, then, not only has a crime problem, but its Olympic Games represent more than mere sport, and are a gamble on which the entire reputation of Rio de Janeiro is riding.

SOCIAL AND MORAL CHALLENGES

Although the 2016 Olympics will take place in one of the world's most beautiful cities—Rio de Janeiro, known for beautiful scenery set against lush rain forests—Brazil also is a land where prostitution and child trafficking are

---

[6] http://espn.go.com/espn/feature/story/_/id/14791849/trash-contamination-continue-pollute-olympic-training-competition-sites-rio-de-janeiro [accessed 08.04.16].
[7] http://www.travelandtourworld.com/news/article/could-traveling-to-rio-olympics-cause-global-health-disaster/?utm_source=iContact&utm_medium=email&utm_campaign=Travel%20And%20Tour%20World&utm_content=Could+traveling+to+Rio+Olympics [accessed 08.04.16].

rampant and (adult) prostitution is legal. While legalized prostitution does not mean that child prostitution is legal, sex managers often give young girls a variety of drugs and send them onto the street to earn their keep.

It is in this environment of sexuality, disease, and crime that the 2016 Olympics will take place. Unfortunately, Brazil also has a reputation for a sex tourism, which exists throughout the country, with major concentrations in coastal resort towns and major tourist destinations such as Rio de Janeiro and Fortaleza and Ceara, as well as in the wildlife tourist areas of the Pantanal and Amazon. Likewise, slavery is not unknown there. For example, women are trafficked (for sexual purposes) from all parts of the country. The (Brazilian) National Research on Trafficking in Women, Children, and Adolescents for Sexual Exploitation Purposes identified 241 international and national trafficking routes. It is estimated that Brazil is responsible for 15% of women trafficked in South America, a great majority of these unfortunate souls being from the poorer parts of the nation.

Brazil is trying to tackle the problem. For example, just prior to and during the World Cup games, Brazil set aside $3.3 million to fund advertisements on the penalties for sex with a minor. Rio, then, will have to face a number of sexual problems, including the following:

- Child trafficking (both female and male).
- Legal adult-to-adult prostitution that may spread sexual diseases.
- Issues related to the spread of the Zika virus through sexual transmission.
- Sexual activities by athletes, staff members, media members, and visitors that may result in sexually transmitted diseases.
- The potential use of sexually transmitted diseases as a form of asymmetrical bioterrorism.

To make matters worse, at the time of this book being written, doctors believed that the Zika virus is spread not only through mosquito bites, but also through sexual contact. That means that Rio de Janeiro must control the Zika virus in the midst of an event where both participants and spectators often engage in sexual contact. At the time of this writing, it is not known how the city's social problems will impact the Olympic Games and its athletes. In the case of the city of Rio de Janeiro, just as at other major sporting events, we may expect "social" issues to emerge at the Olympic villages, which are filled with young men and women with sexy bodies at the prime of life housed in close quarters where physical contact or chemistry might well occur. Often, these athletes, many of whom led lives of abstinence during periods of intensive training, now come to the Olympic villages to compete and (although not explicitly stated), also to have fun. In the village, athletes have large amounts of downtime coupled with pent-up energy. It is not surprising, then, that it is also a location of great amounts of sexual activity. To complicate the situation, athletes are not isolated from the larger world. They might well interact with adoring fans, people working at the games, and media personnel. Furthermore, the Olympic Games, used here as a symbol for a great many mega sporting events, attract visitors and locals who seek to exploit each other. The Olympics Games are not only about what takes place on the playing fields or other competitive venues, but also about both the pre-events and after-event parties and the surrounding ambiance, which, although not officially part of the Olympic Games, has a symbiotic relationship with the games. In a location such as Rio, where sensuality is part of the culture and sexually transmitted disease are never far away, security and safety personnel will have to find ways to mix good prevention with liberty, and caution with fun. Furthermore, it is almost impossible to separate international spectators from local residents who might not even attend an Olympic event, but nevertheless are impacted by others who do attend or work at the games.

PROSTITUTION AND THE RIO DE JANEIRO OLYMPIC GAMES

If Rio de Janeiro did not have enough problems, the city also has a "live and let live" attitude toward prostitution. Although prostitution in Brazil is not legal, it is also not against the law. Since prostitution is mixed with extreme poverty and an open attitude toward sexuality, it does not come as a surprise that Rio is a center for prostitution and also, at the time of this writing, might be one of the world's capital for sex trafficking. This is the other side, the second side, of a mega sporting event, a world where sexually transmitted diseases can create new pandemics and the line between health, asymmetrical warfare, and sexual activity blurs. It also means that athletes, young and often good looking, and the center of attention, might well become involved in "extracurricular" activities that could cause a lifetime of damage. Prostitution often involves both adults and children. Brazil is considered to have the second-worst levels of child sex trafficking (Thailand being number one), with an estimated 250,000 children involved. Many sociologists believe that this phenomenon is closely related with high levels of poverty and inequality. Various official sources agree that there are between 250,000 to 500,000 child prostitutes in Brazil.

Along with sexually transmitted diseases and multiple forms of unregulated sexual activities, there also is the health issue of the Ebola virus, which apparently can survive in sperm for up to nine months. Other health threats to both spectators and athletes are the dengue virus and H1N1.

BLURRING ATHLETIC-SEXUAL LINES AROUND THE WORLD

What is fascinating is that this merging of sexuality with athletic games is not a new phenomenon, but is as old as the games themselves. As we saw at the beginning of this chapter, the Olympics Games some two thousand years ago combined sociability, sexuality, and athletic abilities. This merging of two physical activities has continued right into the present.

The following is a brief summary of what is known about sexual activity that took place at some previous mega events, such as the Olympics and World Cup. It should be noted that gathering data on sexual activity is not easy. Direct observation in most cases is impossible, and conclusions must be drawn either from statistical inferences or anecdotal evidence.

THE BARCELONA 1992 OLYMPICS

Within Olympic history, Barcelona marks the first time that public authorities accepted the health threat posed by sexual activity. Having accepted this premise, Barcelona officials provided athletes with condoms to encourage safe sex during the event's nonathletic moments.

THE SYDNEY 2000 OLYMPICS

Since ancient times, events such as the Olympic Games have provided a party atmosphere that continues well past the event's conclusion. Athletes reported that the Sydney Olympics were filled with extracurricular postgames activities that were close to pure debauchery. It is believed that nonathletes, such as visitors and staff, also joined in the "fun." The international nature of the event meant that a subsequent sexual epidemic would have made it difficult to trace all those who might be have been infected or infected others.

LONDON 2012 OLYMPICS

The athletes' village at the London Olympic Games was a unique Olympic environment, with nearly 3,000 tightly packed apartments, housing more than 10,000 of the world's finest athletes from more than 200 countries. These thousands of young men and women, in the same place, at the same time and cordoned off from the outside world, now found themselves with new opportunities. Although we might assume that they arrived with a love of sports, they no doubt also brought differing sexual attitudes and customs.

Many of the athletes reported that these weeks brought a smorgasbord of opportunity. Others saw the village as a place to be "liberated" from their home countries' more conservative cultures.

The media reported that the Olympic village became a mixture of heterosexual and homosexual activity. For example, during the London Olympic Games, the iPhone app called Grindr, which connects gays, nearly crashed when more than 350,000 people tried to log in. Initially, each athlete was given 15 Durex condoms, but athletes ended up using some 150,000 condoms—50% more than the number reportedly used at the Beijing games.

London also serves as an example that sexual activity is not confined solely to athletes. Since thousands of nonathletes also were present, it is impossible to determine the percentage of people who took part in sexual activity. We can only determine that this many people in a party atmosphere leads to sexual activity, some of which is unprotected.

SPORTS AND ECONOMICS

No matter what the reason for attendance at a major event such as a World Series, World Cup, or other professional sporting event, several economic or business realities emerge. Including the following:

- Sporting events function as ephemeral attractions, rather than consistent or permanent attractions. In almost all cases, the event is the attraction, rather than the venue. From this perspective, a sporting event is no different from a cultural event or of a festival. Once the event ends, its "attraction-ness" disappears.
- Sports and athletes are intertwined with the local economy. Sports is a business and from the perspective of tourism, any activity that draws people from one location to another is a commercial undertaking.
- Sporting events are also social events. Although people come for the "game," they also want to see and to be seen under what John Urry calls the "tourist gaze."
- Athletes, like other people, might choose to participate in unofficial and unsanctioned extracurricular activities that surround an event. This means that athletes, being young men and women, need both guidance and protection when on the road.

These social phenomena merge with the business of tourism and sport. To understand how to protect athletes in a world in which they might be victimized as much (and at times, more than) anyone else, it is first necessary to understand the economic impact of sporting events.

SPORTS AS AN ECONOMIC PRODUCER

The sporting industry is both a direct and indirect economic generator, and also produces multiple side economic benefits. That is to say, sports and sporting events provide direct contributions to a local economy as well as numerous indirect contributions, many in the form of multiplier effects.

In terms of direct impact, sporting events of all types bring a local economy such added benefits as hotel and restaurant revenues. Sports tourism also produces employment and tax revenue. In fact, sporting events are so important that the tourism industry sees them as a subcategory of tourism called "sports tourism." In reality, there are several subcategories of sports tourism.

PARTICIPATORY SPORTS TOURISM

Participatory sports tourism occurs when people travel from one place to another (the usual definition being a trip of at least 100 miles with at least one night spent at a taxable place of lodging) for the purpose of participating in an athletic activity. Usually included under the label of participatory sports tourism are people who travel with the athlete. They may be guardians (parents or grandparents), fans or supporters, or part of the support staff (coaches, team bus drivers, and chaperones). In all cases, the goal is for an athlete (or an athletic team) to participate actively in some sport, either as part of a formal competition, or to improve athletic skills. Participatory sports, such as skiing, swimming, or jogging, may or may not have a competitive side, but in call cases force participants to increase their skills and physical stamina. In this latter category, success in one is not dependent on the other, but rather on the skill and luck of the actor. Participatory sports are beneficial for any community and are especially sought by communities that either do not have a major sports team or can use already existing facilities as a means to enhance revenue.

SPECTATOR SPORTS

If participatory sports and athletics play a major role in tourism, spectator sports that also include major or mega events play an even greater role. As will be seen, there are questions regarding how much, and even if, the local community profits from these large events as much as many in the spectator sports industry might want the local community to believe. Despite these controversies, there is no doubt that sporting events and sports figures play major roles for the public. For example, in much of the world, newspapers devote more space to sports news than foreign news. Major sporting events, such as World Cup soccer, or the Olympic Games, World Series, and Super Bowl, have become more than national pastimes and are official or quasi-official national holidays in many nations. Both young and old alike idolize sports figures as role models, so much so that when a sports figure ends up on the wrong side of the law or faces a moral crisis, that, too, becomes major news. It can be argued that spectator sports are really part of the entertainment industry; in fact, some call the university sports system in the United States "edutainment," as college athletes are as much entertainers as students. These athletic games exist as emotion releases and permit people to discuss "safe" and "noncontroversial" subjects. Both spectator and participator sports can play a major role in a community's tourism industry and quality of life.

AMATEUR LEAGUE SPORTS

Midway between professional and academic sports and participatory sports is what could be called amateur league sports. These tournaments can be especially helpful to a tourism industry during an off-season. It is not uncommon for players to bring their entire families to these localized series. These amateur league sports attract people from all ages and ethnic groups. They range from little league baseball to senior citizen bowling leagues. Their impact is felt not only in large urban areas but also in small rural settings.

Both forms of the athletic experience are major tourism generators. Thousands of people attend major sporting events such as Super Bowls or Olympics Games, and this generates a great deal of revenue, not only for the teams, but also for the tourism industries that serve these athletic spectacles. If participatory sports add to a community's bottom line, major event athletic events generate even more for the local economy, through hotels, restaurants, nightspots, and transportation facilities. Not unlike the major professional sports, sports connected to education, such as university-based athletics in the United States, bring thousands of loyal fans to the host community, where pregame and after-game activities produce a great deal of economic revenue. Sporting events not only bring athletes (and attention) to a specific locale, but also (depending on the size and importance of the event), many spectators. From the tourism perspective, athletes, members of their entourage, and spectators must be fed, housed, and transported. From the perspective of local community, there may also be pre- and postevent activities that provide additional revenue-generating opportunities. Sports tourism runs the gamut of event sizes and prestige. Smaller cities, with less-sophisticated venues, might concentrate on anything from soccer tournaments to Little League tournaments. College and university communities derive a great deal of revenue from college athletic games. In many cases, universities have constructed stadiums that more than rival national stadiums, and the income generated by these games is seen as an essential part of that community's income and, through sales taxes, local tax base. Major League sports not only provide constant publicity and act as an economic generator, but also become part of the locale's economic development offerings. Mega-sporting events often produce not only worldwide publicity, but also add millions of dollars to the local economy. Sports also add major sums of money to nondirect expenses. For example, a major event may require new construction, including new roads, parking areas, hotels, and hospitals. Each of these will produce a local multiplier effect as new employees begin to purchase needed services and their currency begins to circulate throughout the local economy.

In all cases, communities that seek these forms of competition need to consider their local infrastructure and the challenges that any major participatory league or sporting events present to their community, including the following:

- Determine what facilities the community already has and build a sports tourism program around the best that community can offer. For example, if a town is building its sports program around participatory activities, then it should make sporting equipment easily available. A golf course that does not rent clubs might be well suited for the local population but might fail to become a tourism attraction if visitors cannot rent clubs easily.
- Sports is more than an activity; it is also an environmental experience. For this reason, it is essential for athletic facilities to have pleasant surroundings, not only to develop a sense of *ésprit de corps*, but also to encourage people to stay in town after the athletic event ends. This need for ambience is true not only for outdoor athletic events, but also for the land and community surrounding an indoor venue.
- If a community is seeking some form of tournament, then it needs to know the conditions under which tournament teams are going to have to compete. There is perhaps nothing more destructive for a community's sports tourism reputation than taking guests by surprise. Athletes have a right to know what difficulties or challenges the environment will produce, and what they should expect in terms of playing conditions and weather challenges. Athletes are human and face issues of cold, rain, and allergies the same way as the general population.
- As will be seen in later chapters, sports tourism, like other forms of tourism, requires that a locale maintain good community lists, including emergency numbers. In the case of spectator sport teams, the team might travel with a full staff, but participatory sporting events might need a great deal more local support. All sporting events have

an element of risk. It is essential to make sure that visiting athletes know where to go for medical attention, what restaurants have service before and after games, and if hotel check-outs can be coordinated with sporting event timetables. Communities, then, need to know the risks that go with each type of sporting event.

- Officials in communities promoting sporting events should be age-sensitive. Especially if a locale is promoting participatory athletic activities, it needs to be aware of any special needs that may turn into sports tourism challenges. Businesses catering to older athletes might have to deal with different risks than those working with visitors or younger sports enthusiasts. Every sports-oriented tourism community should provide lists of 24-hour pharmacies, hospital emergency rooms, and doctors and dentists who willing to take on emergency, out-of-town patients.

- Sport experiences offered as a means to teach new skills also can be ways to keep visitors in the community for longer periods and increase the community's profit margins. Many people love to combine travel with skill enhancement. Sports-oriented tourism communities may be able to create lists of athletes, formers professional athletes, or educational centers willing to accept visitors for the purpose of teaching them or helping them to improve a particular athletic skill. Learning a new athletic skill might not only benefit a person's stress levels, but also can teach teamwork and help the participant develop a new outlook on life. Therefore, community leaders might want to establish centers where individuals can learn how to incorporate the art of a particular sport into a person's private or business life, along with a chance to destress over a glass of wine and/or relaxing dinner.

- Sports tourism communities should always seek the counsel of their legal team and understand their legal liabilities. A good team of event staff and risk managers is essential, and the community should not solely rely on a team's risk managers. In much of the world, and especially in the United States, litigation has become a way of life. For this reason, tourism and event management teams should always check with the community's law specialists. For example, it is essential to understand the need for waivers when conducting public tournaments, hosting major sporting events or encouraging out-of-towners to visit your community for recreational purposes.

- Sports tourism can change a community's image. Athletics provides a community with a sense of sizzle and a dynamic image. Sports tourism, both the participatory and spectator variety, can help create what is called a halo affect that spills over into every aspect of a community's social life and thus can be a major tool in self-image enhancement.

ECONOMIC IMPACTS

The economic impact of sporting events can extend beyond the local community to impact both local and out-of-town athletes. For example, athletes will need special services in the guise of additional training centers and sports venues will have to provide additional, personalized services, such as medical treatments. Outside the athletic venue, out-of-town athletes might need a host of other services, ranging from medical care to entertainment, and from food services to transportation. The benefits of sports tourism to athletes was noted by Mary Helen Sprecher and Peter Francesconi when they wrote:

> For many cities, sports tourism has gained serious momentum over the past decade and has even become an economic engine. Major college and professional seasons and events rake in millions for their host locations while providing spectators with one-of-a-kind entertainment. On the amateur/recreational side, hundreds of communities around the country are providing athletes and their families with solid, high-quality tournament experiences that have the ability to change and influence young lives.[8]

Additionally, sports travel, even on a subminor league basis, tends to play an increasingly important economic role, be the games being held even in smaller communities. Mary Helen Sprecher and Peter Francesconi, in *Sports Destination Management*, note that:

> many events—whether for youth or adult, amateur, college or professional— must take place every year, so the demand for venues stays high. In fact, that demand appears to be continually increasing, as we constantly hear about CVBs and sports commissions looking to expand, improve or build more facilities.

The authors then go on to state that:

> Often cited is that families will travel to attend tournaments and events to support their young athletes, frequently turning the trip into a mini-vacation. Finding quality "family time" continues to be more and more important in American life, and we should expect this factor to increase in the future.[9]

If sports tourism plays a major role in smaller cities, its impact on large cities is often many times greater. In the case of major events such as an Olympic Games, these sums might be sizable. For example, the summer Olympics is a major revenue generator. The 2008 Beijing Olympics brought more than

---

[8] http://www.sportsdestinations.com/management/economics/2015-champions-economic-impact-sports-tourism-10249 [accessed 08.04.16].

[9] http://www.sportsdestinations.com/management/economics/2015-champions-economic-impact-sports-tourism-10249 [accessed 08.04.16].

11,000 athletes from 204 nations to China to compete in some 302 events, and it is estimated that they generated US $42 billion in additional revenue to the local economy. In reality, these figures should also account for the millions of dollars spent in preparation and construction.

The Olympic Games are not the only large revenue generator.[10] For example, the International World Cup for football (soccer) has had a major impact on host nations. South Africa reported that the 2010 World Cup generated a positive economic impact. According to government sources, these games contributed US $509 million to the 2010 real GDP. The government further noted that the World Cup also created some US $769 in household benefits, along with some 130,000 jobs in the construction and hospitality industries.[11] About 360,000 tourists went to South Africa to attend the World Cup, spending more than US $444 million while there. In reality, this figure was lower than the hoped-for 450,000 spectators.[12]

There is a persistent question regarding whether university sports play a major role in the campus and local economies. There can be little doubt that college communities benefit from major sporting events. University athletic events, such as men's football and basketball, fill hotel rooms and provide major boosts to the local restaurant industry. As with all statistical analysis, however, data or facts are somewhat determined by what the researcher decided to place into the economic pie. For example, those who promote sports tourism as an economic generator often fail to look at questions of leakage (money exiting the locale so as to purchase goods and services), infrastructure damage to roads and parks, and additional labor costs, especially in the form of overtime that must be paid to city workers such as law enforcement, firefighters, and sanitation service providers. Considering this, it is not certain that college (or professional) sports provide the economic boost that their supporters claim. In their study titled "Big Men on Campus," Robert A. Blade and Robert Baumann write that:

> Of course, colleges, leagues, team owners, and event organizers have a strong incentive to provide economic impact numbers that are as large as possible in order to justify heavy public subsidies. In professional leagues, the prospect of large economic benefits is highlighted to minimize the team or league's required contribution to the funding of a new stadium or arena. For universities, large economic impact estimates are used to justify public expenditures on athletic programs or improvements to playing facilities.

---

[10] http://www.economywatch.com/world-industries/sports [accessed 08.04.16].
[11] http://scholarworks.wmich.edu/cgi/viewcontent.cgi?article=3609&context=honors_theses [accessed 08.04.16].
[12] http://scholarworks.wmich.edu/cgi/viewcontent.cgi?article=3609&context=honors_theses [accessed 08.04.16].

In addition, the majority of the largest college football and college basketball programs are public institutions. In 2009, for example, the University of Minnesota will open a new $288 million stadium, 55% of which was paid for with state funds (although the precise line between what constitutes state and university funds is admittedly unclear when dealing with a public university)[13]

From these authors' perspective,

if a college football game that attracts 80 or 90 thousand fans to a relatively small community only generates small identifiable economic gains, there is no reason to place any serious credence in economic impact estimates in other sports that can easily range into the hundreds of millions of dollars. Furthermore, a $2 or $3 million bump in taxable sales per home game does not justify large public handouts for sports facilities. The results show that cities would be wise to view with caution economic impact estimates provided by sports boosters, who have an obvious incentive to inflate these estimates.[14]

The debate over the economic value of sporting events is not an easy one to bring to a final resolution. Part of the reason for the ongoing discussion might lie in the fact that many of the components of a sporting event are intertwined, and a statistical analysis depends not only on which factors are included, but also on how these factors are statistically weighted, as well as the time frames and afterlives of these factors. On one side of the debate, we see statements such as the following by the British researchers Chris Gratton, Simon Shibli, and Richard Coleman, who state:

The economic benefit of the Games is often overestimated in both publications and economic analyses produced by or for the OCOG [Organizing Committee of the Olympic Games] multipliers tend to be too high and the number of tourists is estimated too optimistically (Preuss, 2004: 290).[15]

A good understanding of the event and its economic value rests on such factors as:

- The sporting event's ability to attract tourists from outside the local area and create the need for places of lodging and restaurants.
- The size of the event and the fact that larger events tend to draw more people from outside the local area and may receive greater media coverage.

---

[13] http://web.holycross.edu/RePEc/hcx/HC0704-Matheson-Baade-Baumann_CollegeSports.pdf.
[14] http://web.holycross.edu/RePEc/hcx/HC0704-Matheson-Baade-Baumann_CollegeSports.pdf [accessed 08.04.16].
[15] Gratton article, page 3: The economic impact of major sports events: A review of 10 events in the UK. Chris Gratton, Simon Shibli, and Richard Coleman.

- The event's duration. The longer an event lasts, the more rooms and food sales it generates.
- The amount of media coverage the event will receive. Media coverage for a locale is more than name recognition; it is perhaps the best and least expensive form of advertising.

Does the event draw participants who are major sports figures, and does it attract celebrity spectators? Celebrities create a "gaze effect," in which other people want to be associated with the event, increasing the locale's prestige. The problem with these factors is that their value not only changes with the statistical weight (importance or effect) we choose to give each, but also with the longevity of each. An event might garner a great deal of prestige and media coverage, but both of these are time-sensitive. If the event has a long "afterlife," then its economic impact may spill over into other events that the first event attracted. If on, the other hand, the event has a short publicity life-cycle, then it could be compared to a shooting star and have only minimal long-term economic impact.

Other factorss with both positive and negative economic aspects are the following:

- *First responders' presence*. First responders cost money, and a locale that hosts a sporting event must provide and pay for extra police, ambulances, first aid stations, and road crews. These are all additional costs to the host community. On the other hand, these extra costs can be translated into additional salaries that might circle back into the economy. This recirculation of money back into an economy is called a multiplier effect. Exactly how much importance we should give to a multiplier effect depends on the size of the community, its ability to provide basic services and supplies, and its physical location relative to other communities.
- *Negative publicity*. If nothing goes wrong, then a major sporting event should expect to generate positive publicity. However, as we have noted earlier, Rio de Janeiro received a great deal of negative preevent publicity, and it is impossible to determine how much this has hurt the city.
- *Physical damage*. Physical damage is not only caused by unruly fans; it is also is a by-product of wear and tear on a community. Major sporting events might produce a great deal of garbage or refuse. Roads may be inadequate and traffic jams may occur.
- *Local departures due to the event*. In some cases, locals may not desire to be present at the event due to their perception of crowding, fans' unruly behavior, or traffic congestion. It is important to weight the amount of income acquired by a community versus the amount of income lost.

ISSUES OF QUALITY OF LIFE AND NEIGHBORHOOD INTEGRITY

There is perhaps no single-best way to measure the impact of a major sporting event on a community's quality of life. This is also true of lesser events in smaller cities. Those who both enjoy sports and/or attend events might see this as a major addition to their community's quality of life. Those who do might see the increased pressure on community services as quality of life detractor. This bifurcation is especially noticeable in university towns that host major sporting events, but the same impact may also be felt in smaller or nonathletic event-oriented locations. Large sporting events often cause major problems between the "cap and the town," and have led to issues of neighborhood preservation, especially in areas where there has been an infusion of students or other groups into residential neighborhoods, bringing issues of noise, large numbers of cars on the streets, and rowdy postgame behavior. For example, the Danbury (Connecticut) *News-Times* of February 15, 2016, reports the following problem:

> 'You had all-day athletic events going on with cars all over the neighborhood and people selling food and alcohol,' said Robert Melillo, a former zoning commissioner, at a hearing last week. 'This was in a residential neighborhood, and there was nothing in the regulations to allow the zoning enforcement officer or any other official in Danbury to put a stop to it.'

The article goes on to note that:

> The city last week passed an ordinance requiring a permit for anyone in a residential neighborhood who wants to build an athletic court in the yard. And within two weeks, the city will propose changes to its noise ordinance making it easier to cite people who blast music, whether from a nightclub or from a car equipped with concert-sound speakers.[16]

Not only are there issues of neighborhood integrity, but large stadiums also might have a major sociological impact on a community. Issues that need to be considered regarding neighborhood impacts not only include noise, but also traffic control, drainage, environmental codes, needs for buffer zones, and issues of light pollution surrounding evening events. In a 2014 study of the impact of Yankee Stadium on the local neighborhood, Natalie Hernandez of Pace University concludes that:

> Clearly living in an area like Yankee Stadium can improve the quality of your life, especially if you are a Yankee Fan. Most of the residents deal with the

---

[16] http://www.newstimes.com/news/article/Danbury-aims-to-curb-noise-neighborhood-athletics-6827507.php [accessed 08.04.16].

nuisances such as the constant crowds and parking issues. But having the stadium in their back yard AND being a Yankee Fan almost adds a slight happiness to their life according to this research, they just deal. Arguably if you have lived in the area long enough you can appreciate the added safety and decrease in crime that many residents feel has happened since the new stadium, and for any South Bronx resident this definitely is an upside that comes with having the stadium.[17]

LAND SPORTS VERSUS WATER-RELATED SPORTS

This chapter has mainly focused on land-based sports and venues. Terrestrial sports, versus aquatic sports, make up the great majority of athletic experiences. However, there is a whole set of aquatic sports and sporting events, ranging from swimming to sailing, and from water skiing to scuba diving that also must be mentioned. Classically, these sports are divided into activities that take place: in the water, on top of the water, and underwater. Some of these sports attract spectators, and some involve individual practitioners and/or rarely attract visitors. The following chart provides a brief overview of examples of some of these aquatic athletic activities. To simplify, we list here only some of the aquatic sports that are part of the Rio de Janeiro 2016 Olympic Games.

Sport	Aquatic Location	Individual or Team	Sport Has Spectators?
Canoe	On water	Individual	No
Diving	In water	Individual	Yes
Rowing	On water	Team	Yes
Surfing	In/on water	Individual	Yes
Swimming	In water	Individual	Yes
Synchronized swimming	In water		
Water polo	On water	Team	Yes

The table above lists no underwater spectator sports. Rowing and perhaps synchronized swimming are the only real team sports. In other cases, the athletic event might have a team component, but in reality is a one-person event that in some cases operates as a marathon event. As in the case of most land sports, aquatic sports spectators are along the sidelines, either observing from a beachfront position or, in the case of diving and swimming, often

---

[17] http://digitalcommons.pace.edu/cgi/viewcontent.cgi?article=1013&context=dyson_mpa, page 62 [accessed 08.04.16].

from stands that overlook a swimming pool. There is also a major difference between athletic activities that are pool-oriented (where conditions are controlled), and those that are nonpool oriented. In the latter, athletes might need to deal with everything from unexpected sea animal attacks to underwater currents, both charted and uncharted.

The website "Sporty Ghosts" list the following 10 most dangerous sports:

1. Whitewater rafting
2. BMX (bicycle motocross)
3. Mountain climbing
4. Street luge
5. Big wave surfing
6. Bull riding
7. Cave diving
8. Scuba diving
9. Heli-skiing
10. Base jumping[18]

It is noteworthy that four major aquatic sports are listed. With the exception of athletes who perform in artificial environments, such as swimming pools, aquatic athletes tend to face a greater number of uncontrollable or unpredictable security challenges. For example, a worry with the Rio de Janeiro Olympic Games is the issue of ocean pollution. Reuters, in a February 20, 2016 dispatch, noted this when it wrote:

> A report into potential health risks for swimmers and sailors at the upcoming Olympic Games in Brazil has concluded that athletes will compete in conditions that could make them seriously ill. Rio de Janeiro's waterways are notorious for their high levels of pollution, and making them safe was one of the main promises from the host nation after being awarded the global sporting spectacle. However, only months out from the start of the Games, an in-depth investigation by ESPN has shown that Brazil has not delivered on its promise. Swimming, sailing, rowing and kayaking events will be hosted in venues such as Guanabara Bay, which remains infested with unprocessed waste.[19]

A headline in the July 30, 2015 Business Insider read: "Rio's waters are so filthy that 2016 Olympians risk becoming violently ill and unable to compete." The article then goes on to note that:

> Athletes competing in next year's Summer Olympics in Rio de Janeiro will be swimming and boating in waters so contaminated with human feces that they

---

[18] http://www.sportyghost.com/top-10-dangerous-sports-world-extreme-sports-list/ [accessed:08.04.16].
[19] https://www.rt.com/sport/333100-rio-olympics-water-pollution/ [accessed 08.04.16].

risk becoming violently ill and unable to compete in the games, an Associated Press investigation has found.

An AP analysis of water quality revealed dangerously high levels of viruses and bacteria from human sewage in Olympic and Paralympic venues—results that alarmed international experts and dismayed competitors training in Rio, some of whom have already fallen ill with fevers, vomiting, and diarrhea.[20]

The headlines once again show the interrelationship between an event and the hosting city's reputation. Rio spent millions of dollars preparing for the Olympic Games, but headlines such as the one above undercut the city's marketing efforts, and in the end, the efforts of city leaders might prove to be counterproductive. In addition to polluted waters, aquatic athletes must deal with everything from unstable weather conditions to sunburn or stroke. There is also the issue of proper internal hydration for athletes in saltwater aquatic sports.

Perhaps even more at risk than the knowledgeable aquatic athlete is the person who occasionally enters into the water. Understanding and following simple rules would save many lives. These include the following: do not enter the ocean when there is a red flag; do not swim alone, especially in the ocean; know what equipment is proper and how to use it; protect yourself from the sun; watch for boats; avoid alcohol and drugs; and always remember that human beings are guests in the water.

---

[20] http://www.businessinsider.com/rios-filth-is-already-spoiling-the-2016-summer-olympics-2015-7 [accessed 08.04.16].

CHAPTER 4

How Athletes Travel

Sports enthusiasts often hear about the so-called "home team advantage." In reality, there is a less of a home team advantage than a "visiting team disadvantage." This point is made clear in an article on the Teague website that reads in part: "As any sports fan knows, 'home-field advantage' is significant." But studies prove that home-field advantage is actually a lot less about the effects of raucous crowds and a lot more about the negative effects of travel, which create an "away disadvantage." The article then goes on to state:

> A 2008 study conducted by the Martha Jefferson Hospital Sleep Medicine Center showed that Major League Baseball teams traveling to game sites three time zones away lose 60% of those games. German researchers in 2002 confirmed that motor function measurably deteriorated in athletes after air travel and then lingered for roughly the same number of days as the number of time zones crossed. That's bad news if you're an athlete traveling from the West Coast to the East Coast on a Friday for a Sunday game.[1]

As we have seen in Chapter 1, Understanding the Issues, and Chapter 2, A Review of Literature, unless you are a billionaire, with the privilege of having your own private plane and boat, plus a chauffeured car on both ends of a trip, travel is not easy. Even under these best of circumstances, there still are issues of weather, sky-congestion, traffic jams, health issues, and wear and tear on the body resulting from changes in time zone and climatic conditions. Human beings are human beings, and this simple fact means that even the rich and powerful suffer from jet lag, change of climates, and fatigue. Likewise, so far, no one has been able to "buy" the weather or stop a tropical storm.

If travel is difficult for the extreme wealthy, it is even harder for the average man or woman. Those of us who are older can remember when air and train travel were elegant experiences. People "dressed up," meals were served on fine china, and smiling attendant served wine and drinks in a crystal glass.

---

[1] Teague. Steiner, P. Home-team advantage at 40,000 feet, http://teague.com/latest/home-team-advantage-at-40-000-ft; 2016 [accessed 01.08.16]

Sports Travel Security. DOI: http://dx.doi.org/10.1016/B978-0-12-805099-6.00004-X

Today, travel is more democratic in the sense that it is more affordable for the masses, but 21st century travel is often little more than a bus-in-the-sky or a bus-on-the tracks.

Not only is travel no longer elegant, but additionally, when we take into account the time the traveler must spend at the terminal, the need to pass through layers of security, and trip delays or cancellations (often with little or no information given), gate changes, missed connections, and lost luggage, we understand why so many people hate to travel. Furthermore, many rail, bus, and air companies have made point-to-point travel difficult and expensive. Owing to the "hub and spoke system," used by airlines, travelers often can go from point "A" to point "B" only by traveling through various other locations. These added stops not only increase travel stress, but can result in added delays, missed connections, and general frustration. The basic rule for most travelers is, the more connections there are, the higher the probability that something will go wrong.

Likewise, the drive for efficiency has replaced the romance of the train, and the need to show a profit has replaced the idea of elegance. This reduction in elegance is certainly true for domestic travel in the United States, and in the case of foreign travel, the passenger must also deal with cross-border issues and the fact that nations are seeking to tighten their visa policies due to fear of terrorism. Additionally, foreign travel has other challenges, such as immigration formalities. Furthermore, once the traveler has gone through both immigration and customs offices, there are the additional challenges that come from not knowing the local language, laws, and/or customs.

These travel problems are not new. While these particular issues did not exist centuries ago, travelers had to deal with other challenges such as poor roads, an often-hostile environment, pirates, robbers, and substandard lodging. When we examine the many travel challenges, we can understand why we derive the English word *travel* from the French word for work (*travail*), which in turn is derived from the Latin word for pitchfork. To travel, then, has been and remains an "experience in stress." Most people do not like the stress but succeed in absorbing this stress into their travel routine. Before we examine the issues of athletes traveling, it behooves us to list just some of the stressful situations that travel presents to anyone who takes a journey, whether for reasons of pleasure or business.

Here are just a few of the reasons that the average person experiences stress when traveling.

Before travel (pretrip): Travel stress begins the moment one decides to take a journey or is informed that for reasons of employment she or he will have to take a trip. Prior to embarking, stress arises from:

- Dealing with family issues.
- Packing for trip and leaving one's home in order.
- Dealing with multicity trips and multiple climates on the same trip.
- Making sure that health issues are in order, both at home and while traveling.
- Dealing with personal issues, from going to the bank to remembering to pay bills.

AT THE TERMINAL OR STATION

If prepreparatory stress is a challenge, time at an airline, bus, or terminal can test even the calmest of us. Here are just a few of the challenges that the traveler faces once she or he arrives at the terminal:

- Dealing with lengthy lines.
- Dealing with cancellations or flight or travel delays.
- Finding a bathroom—much less, a clean bathroom.
- Dealing with long lines and poor loud-speaker systems.

WHILE TRAVELING

Travel is more than work; it is hard on the body and on the mind. In today's world of practicality versus elegance, practicality wins almost always, and that means "un-delightful" consequences for the traveler. For example, the traveler must deal with the following:

- Seats that offer consistently less leg room and personal space.
- Poor air quality.
- Rude fellow passengers.
- Lack of hydration and food.
- Lost luggage.

UPON ARRIVAL

In today's world, a safe arrival is not enough. There are challenges from the moment we deplane or leave the bus or train. Among these are:

- Arriving at a strange city and locating a hotel.
- Dealing with poor road signage, or at night, driving when fatigued and navigating with poor signage.
- Dealing with inconsiderate or dishonest taxi drivers.
- Not knowing the language.
- Dealing with rental car agencies and the hidden costs in car rental contracts.

AT PLACE OF LODGING

Unless the traveler is staying with friends and/or family, the average traveler will have to spend the night(s) at a public place of lodging, be that a hotel, motel, inn, or bed-and-breakfast. Each has its own challenges, and the traveler will have to deal with at least some of the following:

- Late hotel check-in times and early hotel check out times.
- Trying to sleep with noise in corridors.
- Getting used to unfamiliar beds.

Dealing with jet lag, tense muscles, insomnia, poor food quality, poor air quality, and lack of exercise.

THE NOT-FOR-PLEASURE TRAVELER

The list above refers to all travelers, whether by air, bus, rail, or ship, and for business or pleasure. When we turn to the person who is not traveling for pleasure, the situation becomes even more difficult. For example, in a CNN news article published in 2012, Laura Miller wrote that: "Traveling for business presents particular dangers of a stress overload, according to experts … Missing out on sleep, working non-stop on the plane or train, and eating unhealthy foods are all common habits of the business traveler lifestyle." She then noted that:

> All this (travel stress) can create havoc with stress levels at a time when the pressures of preparing for presentations and making meetings mean business travelers are already on edge. 'There is absolutely added stress for business travelers,' says Neil Shah, director of The Stress Management Society. 'Unlike leisure travelers they are more likely to have no down time and will be working constantly, unable to switch off.'[2]

SPORTS TRAVEL AND TRAVEL STRESS

Sports travel may be a combination of the worst of leisure and business travel stress. Many fans and media representatives tend to forget that athletes, first and foremost, are human beings. This reality means that no matter what the athlete's talent might be, or how physically fit the athlete is, he or she must deal with many (if not all) of the same problems listed above. Although the super-famous athlete might have the advantage of a travel counselor, even the

---

[2] CNN. Miller, L. Beating the stress of business travel, http://www.cnn.com/2012/09/03/travel/beating-the-stress-of-business-travel/; 2012 [accessed 01.08.16].

most famous, wealthiest, or best athletes must deal with issues such as a sick child, poor air quality, and consistent change of venue.

Some athletes have the advantage of being part of a team that provides or makes many of the necessary arrangements. In some cases, professional teams and athletes at some large universities have the luxury of traveling via private or chartered planes. While helpful, these added perks do not eliminate the stress of travel or many of the personal problems that all travelers face. Athletes, however, have additional problems that more than compensate— but in a negative way—for the travel perks they receive.

STUDENT ATHLETES AND TRAVEL STRESS

In order to begin to understand the stress placed on athletes we should understand that the term *athlete* has several subsections. Professional and university athletes are expected to perform. There is a difference, however. Student-athletes are expected, at least in theory, to be students first and foremost. This often-overlooked fact means that although they are expected to perform on the playing field, they are also expected to perform in the classroom. Student-athletes must develop the skill for compartmentalized thinking or face stress-related issues.

This stress–travel–study combination is not easy to separate, and as research has shown:

> Because athletes often represent an 'at-risk' student group in terms of college academic success, it is important to identify the unique sources of stresses experienced during the first semester freshman year for the student-athlete. University athletic departments need to be cognizant of the time demands that are placed on their athletes during this crucial period of adjustment. Additionally, prevention programs need to be implemented that help assist the freshmen athlete in dealing with potential sources of stress.[3]

Multiple other studies have reinforced this idea. For example, in a study done by J. H. Humphrey and D. A. Yow, the researchers noted that: "0.95% of male athletes and 86 percent of female athletes were stressed by factors like making up missed assignments, preparing for tests and examinations, and missing consecutive classes because of travel." They also found that many athletes felt unprepared for college academics. The article goes on to quote Jesmine Hines, a Michigan State center, who said, "I feel like every athlete feels stressed or pressure when we travel; missing class and playing catch-up can be

---

[3] Athletic Insight: The Online Journal of Sport Psychology. Wilson,G, Pritchard M. Comparing sources of stress in college student athletes and nonathletes, http://www.athleticinsight.com/Vol7Iss1/StressAthletesNonathletes.htm; 2015 [accessed 01.08.16].

very stressful, but we have a great support system that helps us out and makes sure we get what we need to get done, done."[4]

There does not seem to be a consistent pattern regarding athlete requirements when it comes to travel. Many universities follow the practices set by Texas A&M University, in which student-athletes are given some slack, but are expected to work with the instructor/Professor to make up exams and missed work. The Texas A&M handbook states that: "If the absence is excused, the instructor must either provide the student an opportunity to make up any quiz, exam or other work that contributes to the final grade or provide a satisfactory alternative by a date agreed upon by the student and instructor. If an instructor has a regularly scheduled make up exam, students are expected to attend unless they have a university approved excuse. The make-up work must be completed in a timely fashion, working closely with the Professor."[5]

Not all universities, however, follow the Texas A&M model. For example, the Michigan State Student Athlete Handbook and Planner clearly states on page 14 that:

> An instructor is not under obligation to give you a make-up assessment and/or assignment. In addition, each instructor has the right to establish a class attendance policy which (sic) should be expressed in the course syllabus.
>
> When you travel with your team and miss an assignment, exam, quiz or participation points, faculty are not required to allow you to make-up those assessment opportunities.
>
> It is your responsibility to inform faculty of your status as a student-athlete and request an opportunity to make-up missed assessment opportunities due to team travel to away competitions.[6]

The professors and instructors of student-athletes may be either flexible or challenging, and often, student-athletes cannot predict which path the professor will follow. For example, in 2013, East Central Community College qualified for the NJCC National Volleyball championships. One of the players had had too many excused absences according to her professor, who informed her that should she miss another class she would fail his class. The decision sparked a great deal of controversy and prompted a local writer to note that:

---

[4] http://www.athleticinsight.com/Vol7Iss1/StressAthletesNonathletes.htm [accessed 08.06.16].
[5] http://sidearm.sites.s3.amazonaws.com/tamu.sidearmsports.com/documents/2015/8/26/handbook_2015_16_Edited.pdf, page 18, 2015.Texas A&M University Student-Athlete Handbook, http://sidearm.sites.s3.amazonaws.com/tamu.sidearmsports.com/documents/2015/8/26/handbook_2015_16_Edited.pdf, 2015 [accessed 01.08.16].
[6] Michigan State University Student-Athlete Handbook and Planner, http://sass.msu.edu/academic/documents/FS12handbook.pdf, 2015 [accessed 01.08.16].

"It's absolutely mindblowing (*sic*) that a junior college bio prof (*sic*) thinks s/he should deprive a student-athlete of her opportunity like this."[7]

It is beyond the scope of this chapter to determine or recommend professorial absentee policies regarding student-athletes. Furthermore, many schools still hold to the policy of academic freedom, which means that many academics have minimal oversight. If we add all of the stress that normally applies to people traveling, however, we can see that the student-athlete also must handle another level of stress to his/her travel plans. Not only must athletes perform at sports, but they also must be mindful that once back on the university campus, they must return to the role of student and face the potential of hostile faculty members, or even fellow students.

The pressure of travel stress can be a major factor in the life of a student-athlete. For example, the problem was heatedly discussed at the University of Maryland during its transition into the Big Ten football conference. Both students and faculty expressed concern about the additional stress that would fall on athletes as a result of travel. In discussing the issue, it is reported that at least one faculty member stated opinions such as:

> University policy states students 'participating in university activities at the request of university authorities" may be excused from class if they provide proper documentation. This policy applies to all students, from athletes to band members to chess club participants. and there is no policy specifically for athletes.'[8]

Another faculty member and student athlete advisor framed the problem in the following manner: "A course is an extended intellectual conversation, and for students to miss significant parts of it can create big problems."[9] It is essential to take into account that student-athletes not only are students, but also flesh-and-blood human beings with the same range of needs and wants as any other. Travel stress often bleeds into other forms of stress. This can touch on every aspect of the athlete's life, from his or her social life to his or her spiritual life. Not only does travel stress manifest itself in missed classes, late-night returns back to campus, and lack of sleep, but also, student-athletes who are traveling are subject to all of the other travel problems noted above.

---

[7] Deadspin. Burke T. Prof threatens to fail athlete for missing class for championship game, http://deadspin.com/Prof-threatens-to-fail-athlete-for-missing-class-for-ch-1468316908; 2013 [accessed 01.08.16].
[8] The Diamondback. Big Ten move could impact athletes' class attendance, http://www.diamondbackonline.com/news/campus/big-ten-move-could-impact-athletes-class-attendance/article_7e5ba66e-c9df-11e3-9fb4-0017a43b2370.html; 2014 [accessed 01.08.16].
[9] The Diamondback. Big Ten move could impact athletes' class attendance, http://www.diamondbackonline.com/news/campus/big-ten-move-could-impact-athletes-class-attendance/article_7e5ba66e-c9df-11e3-9fb4-0017a43b2370.html; 2014 [accessed 01.08.16].

For example, Gregory Wilson (University of Evansville) and Mary Pritchard (Boise State University) noted that:

studies also suggest that athletic participation itself can become an additional stressor that traditional college students do not experience (Kimball & Freysinger, 2003; Papanikolaou, Nikolaidis, Patsiaouras, & Alexopoulos, 2003). Athletes experience unique stressors related to their athletic status such as extensive time demands; a loss of the 'star status' that many had experienced as high school athletes; injuries; the possibility of being benched/red-shirted their freshman year and conflicts with their coaches, among other factors (Humphrey, Yow, & Bowden, 2000; Papanikolaou et al., 2003).[10]

The researchers then note that:

> The interaction of these multiple stressors presents a unique problem for the college student athlete, and evidence suggests that the combination of these stressors has a negative effect on their well-being. For example, a recent investigation found that almost half of the male athletes and slightly more than half of the female athletes interviewed indicated that stresses associated with sport participation, such as pressure to win, excessive anxiety, frustration conflict, irritation and fear significantly affected their mental or emotional health (Humphrey et al., 2000).[11]

When we combine these stress-related issues to those of travel, it becomes clear that many young people may suffer multiple short-term and perhaps long-term problems due to the combination of sports stress and travel stress placed within the framework of a university setting. It is also essential to take into consideration that student athletes travel a great deal more than the average student. In their academic study, Aimee Kimball and Valeria J. Freysinger noted that: "The interpretive study reported here examined a particular leisure activity—collegiate sport—and individuals' experiences of stress because of their participation in this type of leisure. (The study's) results indicate that collegiate sport is perceived to be both a buffer and experience of stress."[12]

---

[10] Athletic Insight: The Online Journal of Sport Psychology. Wilson,G, Pritchard M. Comparing sources of stress in college student athletes and nonathletes, http://www.athleticinsight.com/Vol7Iss1/StressAthletesNonathletes.htm; 2015 [accessed 01.08.16].
[11] Athletic Insight: The Online Journal of Sport Psychology. Wilson,G, Pritchard M. Comparing sources of stress incollege student athletes and nonathletes, http://www.athleticinsight.com/Vol7Iss1/StressAthletesNonathletes.htm; 2015 [accessed 01.08.16].
[12] Leisure Sciences: An Interdisciplinary Journal. Kimball A, Freysinger V. Leisure, stress and coping: The sport participation of collegiate student-athletes, http://www.tandfonline.com/doi/abs/10.1080/01490400306569;2003 [accessed 01.08.16].

PROFESSIONAL ATHLETES AND TRAVEL STRESS

Although professional athletes do not have the same forms of stress associated with having to deal with professors, exams, and academia, this does not mean that professional athletes do not suffer from other forms of travel stress. Professional athletes have a great deal of travel stress, although it may be of a different nature than that of the student-athlete. Professional athletes may be divided into what we may call the "worker bees" and the "stars."

Most professional athletes do not obtain star status. These men and women are talented and hardworking. They put in long hours of practice and being on the road, they often must spend a great deal of time away from family and friends. Athletes have all of the travel stress that other travelers have, but they have the additional problem that they must perform physically, often while lacking sleep, with time zone changes, and under the watchful (and not always kind) eyes of coaches, owners, the general public, and the media.

Athletes, despite the public perception of their being in a "romantic" or dream job, suffer from both physical and mental anguish. For example, the British newspaper *The Independent* has written that:

> Increasing numbers of elite British sports stars are falling victim to depression because of stress, leading psychologists warned this week. Pressure to perform at high levels, round-the-clock media attention and the huge amounts of money at stake have added to the mental and emotional toll, said Dr Barry Cripps, chairman of the sports and exercise division of the British Psychological Society.[13]

The article goes on to note that:

> 'Team players face an added burden: the expectations of their colleagues. For the footballer who misses a penalty or the fielder who drops a catch, the sensation of failure back in the changing room can be excruciating,' said former professional cricketer Richard Doughty. 'You're not just playing for yourself, you're playing for the rest of your side,' said Mr. Doughty, who bowled for Gloucestershire and Surrey bowling team in the 1980s. 'If you've under-performed, a dressing room is a very small place to be. It can be a very isolating and lonely experience,' he said.[14]

---

[13] Independent. Hodgson M. Pressure and the pro: Why do so many of our top athletes suffer from stress? http://www.independent.co.uk/life-style/health-and-families/health-news/pressure-and-the-pro-why-do-so-many-of-our-top-athletes-suffer-from-stress-424937.html; 2011 [accessed 01.08.16].
[14] Independent. Hodgson M. Pressure and the pro: Why do so many of our top athletes suffer from stress? http://www.independent.co.uk/life-style/health-and-families/health-news/pressure-and-the-pro-why-do-so-many-of-our-top-athletes-suffer-from-stress-424937.html; 2011 [accessed 01.08.16].

In other words, professional athletes must justify their job performance not only to themselves and to their "owners," but also to their teammates, their public, and the media.

Few people who have been caught in a tight connection or suffered from a travel delay will question the premise that travel produces anxiety. Kevin Gray, writing in *Men's Journal*, noted that many athletes suffer from issues of (professional business) anxiety. When we add anxiety-producing travel, the potential for canceled trips, long nights on the road, and often poor eating habits, we note a multifold increase in the problem of athletic anxiety. In other words, we now deal with a combination of already existing anxiety added to normative travel anxiety and impacted by underperformances due to stress and anxiety. Gray stated:

> For athletes competing in triathlons, marathons, and events in the Olympic Games, an anxiety rush can derail their gold medals or their careers. And yet, most cannot compete without having to deal with travel anxiety. 'Nervousness is your friend,' says JoAnn Dahlkoetter, a Stanford Medical Center sports psychologist who's treated Olympians as well as Fortune 500 businessmen. 'It's a normal reaction to an important moment in your life.' Anxiety is basically an adrenaline dump, your body's fight-or-flight response. It's telling you that you are ready to compete—or that you'd better get the hell out of there. This natural response goes off the rails when the body gets run down or is already ridden with stress. Hangovers are a known trigger for panic attacks: A heavy night of drinking can lead to fatigue, dehydration, too much caffeine, and not enough food. But piling on the stress—say, playing a PGA tournament after being up with a newborn all week—is the most common trigger.[15]

Stress is not the only travel problem faced by athletes. Athletes put a great deal of physical pressure on their bodies. Travel also creates additional body stress. For example, athletes' bodies use up many times more minerals than do people who are sedentary. This added pressure means that athletes lose both water and minerals from physical exertion and from natural body phenomenon such as sweating. The loss of minerals in the body, however, is more than a mere loss of bodily fluids, and over a period of time, can result in a wide variety of degenerative diseases. The pressure on the body has resulted in deaths of supposedly healthy athletes on the playing field, and when we add to these any changes in climate, altitude, and the mineral content in the local water supply, we can begin to understand the health risks that travel imposes on athletes.

Since athletes put a great deal more stress on their bodies, it is essential that they stay up-to-date with their immunizations. Travel to sporting events and

---

[15] Men's Journal. Gray K. The pro athlete's anxiety relief, http://www.mensjournal.com/health-fitness/health/the-pro-athletes-anxiety-relief-20130405; 2013 [accessed 01.08.16].

competitions also means that athletes might be exposed to diseases that they would not face at home, and against which they have little or no immunity.

To make matters even more complicated, not only does each nation have its own policy regarding immunizations, but immunization policies also change on an as-needed basis. Furthermore, the need or lack of need for a specific immunization rarely is determined by the athlete's nationality, but rather by the places where the athlete has been during specific periods of time.

Most nations tend to determine their required vaccination policies by both the host nation's local medical conditions and those found within the athlete's country of origin or locales visited during a specific incubation period. Immunizations, however, often cannot be given on an overnight or immediate basis, and often, a vaccination needs time before the recipient is protected. This "gray period" means that, should an athlete be traveling to a place that, for example, requires a yellow fever or malaria vaccination, plans for such vaccinations must be made well ahead of time, and the athlete must have sufficient time not only for the vaccine to take effect, but also to recover from any physical side effects that the vaccine might cause.

The effects of travel on an athlete's body are often more complicated than many believe. For example, in a study conducted by the *British Journal of Sports Medicine*, scientists and doctors discovered that athletes who crossed five time zones have a much higher incidence of getting sick while "on the job" than do those who take shorter trips. Joshua Wortman reported that the study looked at 14 elite rugby teams from such diverse places as Australia and South Africa. Owing to Australia's geographic location, its team members are forced to cross multiple time zones to participate in international competitions. South African teams, when playing in Europe, have less of a time zone (east–west/west–east) challenge, but to participate in international matches, must often cross the equator (north–south/south–north travel) and, therefore, experience change of seasons. During the study, teams of physicians traveled with the athletes and maintained careful notes regarding their health. The study not only examined the issue of time zone changes, however.

The physicians noted that athlete health is a highly complex topic, writing that:

> … many variables could be the reason for the differences in illness rates. Factors that could be influential are changes in altitude, pollution, temperature, allergens, humidity, as well as different food, bacteria, and culture. Athletes anticipating travel for competition would be well advised to factor in extra time for rest and acclimation to the environment before their event, as well as bringing items to combat as many of illness-causing factors as possible.[16]

---

[16] Breaking Muscle. Wortman J. Travel for competition puts athletes at risk of illness, http://breakingmuscle.com/health-medicine/travel-for-competition-puts-athletes-at-risk-of-illness; 2010 [accessed 01.08.16].

It would be a mistake to assume that any one variable is the sole reason for a particular athlete's medical condition. Human beings are simply too complex, and there are too many variables at play to assume any single set of conclusions. It should be noted that this study, then, examined only one variable among potentially multiple variables.

It is then necessary to emphasize the point that to the athlete who travels must not only put up with the physical strain caused to the body by strenuous activity, but also deal with this physical and mental stress under constantly changing conditions.

The conclusions of the study cited above are not unique. For example, A. C. Turner of the Air Corporations Joint Medical Service at London Airport reports in the *British Journal of Sports Medicine* the following problems, as noted below, for athletes resulting from long and/or multiple trips. It is of interest that the physicians pointed to the fact that not only does travel impact the body, but that this impact is based not only on comfort levels and length of travel, but also the direction of travel. We learn the following conclusions from this 2015 study:

- The study uses the term *trans time zones flights* to mean rapid (air) transit through several time zones. Flying forces us to travel across time zones in an unnatural manner and produce a shift in a person's physiological balance between the time at point of departure and the time at point of arrival. This is true of any traveler; athletes, however, need to physically react in the new time zone with little time given to their bodies for re-acclimatization to the new time zone reality. The study noted that an athlete needs about four full days for complete adaptation to the new time rhythms, a luxury that most athletes do not have. On the other hand, the return to the original time rhythms takes a great deal less time. This four-day period is crucial for an athlete to compete at his or her top form. Nevertheless, it is rare for athletes to have four days of rest prior to competition. Put into sports terms, and assuming all other factors as being equal, a home team or a team that has returned home ought to have the time-zone advantage over the team that has crossed numerous time zones.
- When flights cross seven time zones, the traveler's physical reaction time lessens. In the case of an athlete, this deterioration of the ability to react and make decisions might make the difference between winning and losing. Once again, on return to the original time zone, the athlete's performance loss is less than when traveling across multiple time zones. Often, sports require instant or immediate decision-making ability, and if the athlete is neither physically nor mentally in top shape, then this loss of physical and cognitive decision-making capabilities may have

an effect on athletic performance. Although the study did not examine the interaction between changes in body rhythms and loss of decision-making capabilities, the combined calmative impact ought to be greater than each individual loss. The study also noted that most people who cross time zones have fewer problems when their travel is from is east to west—for example, Europe to the United States—than when the travel is from west to east. Once again, in an evenly matched game, in most cases, those traveling east to west have the advantage. It should be noted that this study used as its basis "seven time zones" and to cross this distance means a great deal of travel. For example the trip to from New York to Hawaii entails, at most, six time zones, and from Texas to France, seven time zones.

- Athletes often are fatigued upon arrival at locations that are multiple time zones from the point of departure. Just as in other cases, the fatigue factor seems to have a greater impact on people traveling in a west–east (United States to Europe) direction than in an east–west direction. It also appears that as we age, we tire more quickly. As in other cases, these negative side effects are greatly reduced on return journeys.

The study noted that normal rectal temperatures tend to peak between 2 pm and 8 pm On west–east flights, it took about six days, and on east–west flights about four days, for rectal temperature patterns to return to normal. On the other hand, there were no recorded changes in north–south flights. Chronobiology studies (the study of a person's internal body clock) of travelers crossing multiple time zones demonstrate that body clocks took about eight days to return to a normal circadian state when the person was on a west-east flight and about four days after east–west flights. Again, with north–south flights there was no change. This "non-change" on vertical (north–south/south–north) travel may be due to the fact that there is minimal time zone adjustment. However, north–south travel during the summer–winter months (but not necessarily during the spring–fall months) involves some changes in sunlight due to the fact that the seasons are reversed upon crossing the Equator. Research has demonstrated that flights from north to south or vice versa involving no change in time zone produce some travel fatigue, but this has a minimal or nonexistent influence on a person's circadian rhythm or psychological performance. [17] All travel, to some extent, is trying. It appears, however, that travel primarily impacts our body rhythms when it

[17] BMJ Open Sport & Exercise Medicine. Turner AC. Some medical aspects of air travel, http://bjsm.bmj.com/content/3/3/112.full.pdf+html?sid=09042692-a00b-44e3-bb6e-413e292c45ea; 2016 [accessed 01.08.16].

involves crossing time zones, especially if the travel is from west to east. These normal body changes become highlighted in the case of traveling athletes whose success is very much body-dependent. There is also the fact although north–south flights (assuming the same, or almost the same, time zone) do not impact body rhythms, but the change in seasons might produce other physical effects.

For professional athletes in the 21st century, it is almost a foregone conclusion at least some travel will be part of their careers. In a sense, travel is as much of the athlete's work as the athletic event itself. Just as in any job, athletes travel not only for competitions but, at times, also for training and practice sessions (often called friendly matches). In all cases, added travel stress compounds the athlete's workload. Numerous trips not only put strain on the body, but also on the family structure. New environments mean a host of new exposures, from changes in schedule and exposure to different foods. The Australian Sports Commission noted that these changes can significantly affect usual eating habits. Major nutritional challenges faced by athletes while traveling include:

- achieving carbohydrate and protein requirements
- meeting daily vitamin and mineral requirements
- balancing energy intake and maintaining adequate hydration[18]

The continual stress of travel means that athletes must take special precautions. For example, the British medical study cited above offers a number of practical concepts that those arranging sports travel should consider. Among these are the following:

- Travel planners should attempt to choose flights, whenever possible, that allow the athlete to go to bed at usual bed times.
- Upon arrival at the new location, the athlete may consume a light meal, followed by sleep, but not a heavy meal.
- Athletes should avoid attending events or receptions on the day of their arrival.
- Clothing should be chosen that is comfortable to travel and at the same time suitable for the place of arrival.
- If the athlete smokes, smoking should be eliminated at least two days prior to departure. Needless to say, the best solution is to not smoke!
- Just prior, during, and immediately after the flight, alcohol consumption should be kept to a minimum.[19]

---

[18] Australian Sports Commission. Nutrition for traveling athletes,http://www.ausport.gov.au/ais/nutrition/factsheets/travel/nutrition_for_travelling_athletes; 2009 [accessed 01.08.16].

[19] BMJ Open Sport & Exercise Medicine. Turner AC. Some medical aspects of air travel, http://bjsm.bmj.com/content/3/3/112.full.pdf+html?sid=09042692-a00b-44e3-bb6e-413e292c45ea; 2016 [accessed 01.08.16].

- Should there be food on board, due to the airplane's altitude, athletes should avoid carbonated drinks, eat light food, and skip beer and hard alcoholic drinks.

Owing to the possibility of dehydration, it is important to hydrate and to avoid carbonate liquids.[20] The material above refers to a rapid change of time zones. There are other, slower forms of transportation that athletes use. Rail, bus, or car travel will not produce the same problems as airline travel. However, as is seen in this chapter, slower forms of transportation have their own set of travel challenges.

FOOD AND NUTRITION ISSUES

As noted, travel is not merely being in a vehicle that takes a person from place A to place B. Travel refers to the entire experience, from the time the person leaves his or her home until the time he or she returns. When traveling, athletes are on a business trip, but unlike most business trips, athletic competition places a great deal of strain on the body. In order for athletes to properly function and to do their jobs well, there is a need for proper nutrition.

Nutrition, however, for athletes is more than mere eating—it is the fuel that makes them function. Furthermore, because athletes are first and foremost human beings, food planners for athletes must take into account other issues, such as taste and cultural preferences. Eating problems or preferences, which also exist when the athlete is not traveling, become even greater when the athlete is on the road and away from comfort foods and a regular eating routine. When it comes to travel, the question might focus less on proper nutrition and more on the effects of malnutrition. In his article, Chris Daniels noted that:

> Athletic performance pushes your body to the edge. Progress is accomplished by progressively stressing your body and allowing it to recover. If you do not receive adequate nutrition from your diet, this recovery is not possible. As you continue to train, stress, fatigue and metabolic waste will accumulate in your body. If you are unsure if you are getting proper nutrition for your training, consult with your doctor or a registered dietitian.[21]

---

[20] BMJ Open Sport & Exercise Medicine. Turner AC. Some medical aspects of air travel, http://bjsm.bmj.com/content/3/3/112.full.pdf+html?sid=09042692-a00b-44e3-bb6e-413e292c45ea; 2016 [accessed 01.08.16].
[21] SF Gate. Daniels C. How can bad nutrition affect an athlete? http://healthyeating.sfgate.com/can-bad-nutrition-affect-athlete-2507.html; 2016 [accessed 01.08.16].

Daniels suggested that poor nutrition leads to the following problems in athletic performance:

1. Poor performance
    It is not easy to maintain a proper diet during travel. Eating times might be irregular, and most people only have a minimal understanding of what additives are found in restaurant-style food over which we have minimal control. From the perspective of the athlete, lack of proper foods, or foods not consumed in the right proportions, might lead to lower performance levels. The athlete or person in charge of the athlete's foods must know how to combine fats, carbohydrates, and proteins in the correct amounts. Furthermore, not all proteins and carbohydrates are the same. To add to the difficulties when a team is traveling together, the team might be treated as one unit, but it is a unit composed of individuals who have specific nutritional needs and tastes. Athletes might be allergic to specific foods, or tolerate some foods better than others. If the athlete does not like a particular dish, or for religious or cultural reasons chooses not to consume this dish, then even the most careful balancing of nutrients does the athlete no good. Both food managers and the athlete must know his or her own body and understand how altitude and climate differences might impact his or her food needs, and which foods the athlete is likely to eat and tolerate, and which have to be avoided.

2. Long recovery
    Daniels also notes that:

    Training induces controlled levels of damage in your muscles. Your body rebuilding stronger muscles is what leads to growth in muscle mass and increased strength and endurance. The first two hours after training are the most critical for exercise recovery, according to nutritionist Dr. John Berardi. The demand remains high for at least 24 hours after training. If nutritional demands are not met during this period, recovery will be prolonged over days or weeks.[22]

    There is, then, a need to coordinate training times with rest and eating periods so that these separate functions work together, rather than in opposition to each other.

3. Immune suppression
    Since athletic training and competition interact with an athlete's hormones, it is essential for the athlete to understand his or her physical and mental weaknesses. Food managers and the athlete must

---

[22] SF Gate. Daniels C. How can bad nutrition affect an athlete? http://healthyeating.sfgate.com/can-bad-nutrition-affect-athlete-2507.html; 2016 [accessed 01.08.16].

work with a qualified medical specialist to answer, on an individual basis, such questions as:

- Is there a problem with blood sugar levels?
- How does the stress of travel interact with the physical stress placed on the body due to rigorous exercise or athletic activity?

In the case of team sports, there might be a team doctor or medical professional who travels with the team. Not all athletes are part of a team that can afford its own medical advisor, however, and it is essential that the athlete not only understand his or her physical weaknesses, but also how to compensate for them. For example, "according to a study published in the *International Journal of Sports Medicine*, overconsumption of carbohydrates, protein and vitamins can also suppress the immune system. Eat a well-balanced diet attuned to the protein demands of your body mass and the carbohydrate demands of your activity level."[23] Each athlete, then, is an individual whose individual needs must be met in what is often a production line setting in which individual needs might not be taken into account.

WEIGHT CHANGES

In a healthy athlete, weight changes might be connected to poor eating habits. On the other hand, a person could appear to be healthy, but in reality might not be. A weight change, especially if it is sudden or does not reflect a change in eating habits, could be a sign of a more profound or serious medical problem. In the case of the healthy traveling athlete, there are other factors to consider regarding weight. These factors include issues of fatigue, climatic changes, times when food is consumed, and cultural habits.

Poor nutrition habits lead to the question of what is proper nutrition for a person participating in athletic activities and traveling. It must be emphasized that each person is different, and final decisions should be decided upon only after consulting with a person's physician. The following guidelines offered by the American College of Sports Medicine are meant to be nothing more than talking points between the athlete and physician. Below is a partial summary of some of the ACSM's nutritional recommendations.

> Athletes need to consume adequate energy producing foods during periods of high-intensity and/or long-duration training to maintain body weight and health and maximize training effects.

23 SF Gate. Daniels C. How can bad nutrition affect an athlete? http://healthyeating.sfgate.com/can-bad-nutrition-affect-athlete-2507.html; 2016 [accessed 01.08.16].

Body weight and composition should not be used as the sole criterion for participation in sports; daily weigh-ins are discouraged. Optimal body fat levels depend on the sex, age, and heredity of the athlete and may be sport-specific.

- Carbohydrate recommendations for athletes range from 6 to 10 $g \cdot kg^{-1}$ body weight $\cdot d^{-1}$ (2. 7–4. 5 $g \cdot lb^{-1}$ body weight $\cdot d^{-1}$). Carbohydrates maintain blood glucose levels during exercise and replace muscle glycogen.
- Protein recommendations for endurance and strength-trained athletes range from 1. 2 to 1. 7 $g \cdot kg^{-1}$ body weight $\cdot d^{-1}$ (0. 5–0. 8 $g \cdot lb^{-1}$ body weight $\cdot d^{-1}$).
- Fat intake should range from 20% to 35% of total energy intake. Consuming ≤20% of energy from fat does not benefit performance. Fat, which is a source of energy, fat-soluble vitamins, and essential fatty acids, is important in the diets of athletes. High-fat diets are not recommended for athletes.
- Athletes who restrict energy intake or use severe weight-loss practices, eliminate one or more food groups from their diet, or consume high- or low-carbohydrate diets of low micronutrient density are at greatest risk of micronutrient deficiencies.
- Dehydration (water deficit in excess of 2–3% body mass) decreases exercise performance; thus, adequate fluid intake before, during, and after exercise is important for health and optimal performance.
- Before exercise, a meal or snack should provide sufficient fluid to maintain hydration, be relatively low in fat and fiber to facilitate gastric emptying and minimize gastrointestinal distress, be relatively high in carbohydrate to maximize maintenance of blood glucose, be moderate in protein, be composed of familiar foods, and be well tolerated by the athlete.
- During exercise, primary goals for nutrient consumption are to replace fluid losses and provide carbohydrates (approximately 30–60 $g \cdot h^{-1}$) for maintenance of blood glucose levels. These nutrition guidelines are especially important for endurance events lasting longer than an hour when the athlete has not consumed adequate food or fluid before exercise or when the athlete is exercising in an extreme environment (heat, cold, or high altitude).
- After exercise, dietary goals are to provide adequate fluids, electrolytes, energy, and carbohydrates to replace muscle glycogen and ensure rapid recovery. A carbohydrate intake of approximately 1. 0–1. 5 $g \cdot kg^{-1}$ body weight (0. 5–0. 7 $g \cdot lb^{-1}$) during the first 30 minutes and again every 2 hours for 4–6 hours will be adequate to replace glycogen stores. Protein consumed after exercise will provide amino acids for building and repair of muscle tissue.

- Vegetarian athletes may be at risk for low intakes of energy (rich foods), protein, fat, and key micronutrients such as iron, calcium, vitamin D, riboflavin, zinc, and vitamin B_{12}. Consultation with a sports dietitian is recommended to avoid these nutrition problems.[24]

Most sources indicate that a person who has proper nutrition does not need supplementary vitamins. It also should be noted that in the United States, the Food and Drug Administration (FDA) does not regulate food supplements. It is advised that a person speak to not only a physician but also a dietitian, concerning nutritional needs while doing strenuous athletic activity in a specific locale.

TRAVEL CLOTHING

Before travel, especially if the team is traveling together and on public transportation, team managers must consider whether they want the team to wear a uniform, or prefer that each team member dresses according to his or her own needs. Although there are no overall regulations for sports travel, the following common sense rules should be considered:

- Use clothing that is appropriate for being seen in public. Be respectful of cultural and religious customs especially in the location to which the athlete is traveling.
- Avoid wearing fancy jewelry or other items that might draw undue attention.
- A good general rule of thumb is that if you cannot afford to lose something, either for financial or emotional reasons, then do not take it on the trip.
- Dress for comfort rather than fashion.
- If traveling between climates, use layered clothing.
- For reasons of safety and security, dress according to the customs of the place to which the athlete is traveling and avoid clothing that will call attention to the athlete or group of athletes. Female athletes should be careful of local customs and what is considered to be acceptable or unacceptable dress.

TRAVEL ARRANGERS

Since there are so many complications in the world of travel, and even more in the world of sports travel, an industry has developed around the needs of

---

[24] Medicine & Science in Sports & Exercise. Nutrition and athletic performance, http://journals.lww.com/acsm-msse/Fulltext/2009/03000/Nutrition_and_Athletic_Performance.27.aspx; 2009 [accessed 01.08.16].

athletic teams. Many large universities and professional organizations make their travel arrangement "in house." Individual players and less-wealthy organizations might seek to outsource this work.

THE SPORTS TRAVEL AGENT AND TRAVEL ARRANGER

These are professionals who specialize in travel for athletes. In many ways, they are similar to other travel agents and their commission structure does not vary greatly from that of a nonsports travel agent. A typical agent reimbursement structure consists of many of the following aspects:

- The development of standard and custom travel packages. Agents who design special packages tend to charge additional fees.
- Commissions are only paid when the trip occurs. Often, canceled trips result in no commission being paid.
- Often, commissions are not paid for unplanned championship games unless stipulated in the contract.
- Agents giving inaccurate information, including invalid IATA, CLIA, or ARC numbers, addresses, phone numbers, and so on, might experience a delay in receiving commissions.[25]

PLACES OF LODGING FOR ATHLETES AND ATHLETIC TEAMS

Specialists in sports travel are expected to know how to get their team or individual client the best hotel rates and airfares. Since teams often prefer to stay together, it is assumed that the travel professional or travel planner will know how to negotiate a block of rooms. During the regular season (or before the season), travel specialists have more time to negotiate and plan, but in the case of some forms of playoff games, neither the city nor the teams know who will need rooms or in which city they will need the rooms. Furthermore, sports teams and individual athletes might have special needs. Simply put, coaches are going to worry about the safety and security of their players, and issues such as cleanliness, quality of the rooms, and noise levels. The need to make arrangements at the last minute might cause additional problems, as many locations cannot handle a sudden, last-minute influx of people. The need for contingency planning, then, is ever-present.

Dealing with sports team travel has both advantages and poses difficulties. On the positive side of the ledger, the team occupies not only a block of

---

[25] Sports Traveler. Agent commission structure, http://www.sportstraveler.net/travel-planners.html; 2016 [accessed 01.08.16].

rooms, but also provides the place of lodging with a great deal of prestige. On the negative side, the team creates additional needs for privacy, security, and potential crowd control. Many hotels find that the positives outweigh the negatives, and sports travel specialists can use the positive side of the ledger to create competition and thus lower the price.

Athletes and athletic teams have special needs and oftentimes, these needs have little or nothing to do with price. Here are some additional things to consider when choosing a place of lodging. Choosing which hotel is best for an athlete or team depends on a number of factors other than mere price per room.

SPORTS TRANSPORTATION

There is no single-best methodology for sports travel. The choice of travel depends on a basket full of variables. Among them are the following:

- Distance to be traveled
- Number of people traveling in the athletic party
- The athletic party's demographic makeup
- Issues of safety
- Issues of insurance
- Issues of security
- Cost of travel
- Cost of travel in time
- Wear and tear on an athlete's body

NONAIRPLANE TRANSPORTATION

Since there is, then, no single means of transportation to athletic events, athletes and athletic teams may have to use a combination of modes of transportation. These combinations will depend on changing circumstances such as cost, safety, and convenience. It should be noted that all travel has some elements of risk and inconvenience. The right combination of travel depends on distance to be traveled, wear and tear on the athlete, cost of travel, travel schedules, and issues of comfort and safety.

Below is a discussion on several of these variables.

Travel by motor vehicle has numerous risks, discussed below, and it is essential that the transportation of the team, its staff, and its fans be carefully considered and supervised. For example, no one under 25 years of age should be involved in this driving a vehicle. Drivers should not only be competent and of good character, but also specially trained. Although land vehicle transportation might be less expensive and at times more convenient, it should be carefully balanced against other forms of transportation such as train, boats, and airplanes. Many university or smaller professional teams will, at times, transport their players via 15-seat vans. US government agencies such as the National Transportation and Safety Administration have questioned these vehicles' safety record and noted their instability on the road. LaVetter and Kim have written about the lack of safety of these vans.[26] Many athletic teams or individual athletes on short trips (usually defined as under two to three hours and/or less than 200 miles from the team's home base) tend to use either bus transportation or private cars. Teams can often rent buses relatively inexpensively and these provide the teams with a number of advantages, including the following:

- The team can set its own schedule.
- Bus travel allows for both camaraderie and team discussions while members are in transit.
- Snacks and nonalcoholic drinks can be provided during transit.
- Buses are less dependent on weather conditions and tend to cancel less often.
- The bus provider may assume issues of liability.
- There are fewer baggage and weight restrictions than on modes of transportation such as airplanes.

PRIVATE OR RENTED CARS OR MINI VANS

Buses work well for groups ranging between 30 and 40 people. The use of a bus for a relatively small number people might be extremely expensive. In these cases, athletes can turn to private cars, which have the advantage of no specific time schedules, but also have multiple disadvantages. Most people count private cars as anything from a minivan to a 15-passenger van. These forms of transportation might or might not have a hired driver. It should also be noted, as seen in LaVetter's and Kim's research, that larger private vehicles, such as 12- or 15-passenger vans, have been involved in rollover crashes involving athletic teams.[27] Rollovers tend to occur with higher weight factors and passenger loads. This fact means that although a larger van is more economical as a means of transportation, the risk factor is also greater, and increases when a nonprofessional driver is behind the wheel. When either private or rented vehicles are used, it is essential for the sports

[26] LaVetter, D. and Kim, H. D. (2010). Transportation practices in community college athletics. *Community College Journal of Research and Practice* 2010;34:449–61.
[27] Nohr K. Managing risk in sport and recreation. Champaign: Human Kinetics; 2009, pp. 10–11.

travel specialist to know such basic information as when the vehicle was last inspected, what its maintenance record is, and what safety and emergency equipment is on board. Transportation by motor vehicle also involves proper insurance. Team transportation providers should consult with both a lawyer, to understand who and under what conditions is there liability, and with an insurance agent, to be assured that both the driver and the vehicle are adequately and legally insured. Blanket answers such as, "The vehicle is fully insured" are not acceptable answers. Instead, the renter should ask what is and is not insured, and what is or is not covered as a result of paying for the rental with a particular credit card. Renters need to ask questions regarding whether the car/vehicle insured, and also questions about body liability, how medical damage is covered, and who is responsible when another vehicle is damaged. It is also important, when speaking to an insurance agent, to discuss umbrella policies, which might provide coverage if the at-fault driver is not properly insured.

Before using a car, or minivan, consider the following:

- Make a full list of all emergency and vehicle safety equipment needed. Make sure this list fits both the geographic and weather conditions to be encountered.
- Review all legal and insurance issues and liabilities.
- Review, with a qualified mechanic, what safety precautions need to be taken and what mechanical and maintenance items need to be inspected.
- Develop safety locations along the route.
- Make sure that you have safest routing possible, and know all road conditions.

Speak with local police or highway patrol officers, if necessary.

NONMOTOR-VEHICLE TRAVEL

Statistically, air travel is a great deal safer than private vehicles, and is necessary for cross-country or transoceanic travel, and is often also recommended for intermediate distances. Air travel, although safer, is not necessarily faster for shorter trips. Passengers not only must arrive at the air terminal at least an hour prior to flight time, but they also must pass through security clearances and pay add-on costs, such as checked-luggage fees. Air travel also means that once the team or athletes arrive at the destination, other forms of transportation will be needed to move the team from the air terminal to the hotel and sports arena or stadium.

SPORTS LODGING

The Athletic Niche Market

The fact that athletic and sports team travel is a niche market is underscored in a 2013 *New York Times* article, which noted that:

Serving guests is every hotel's mission, but professional sports teams represent a special opportunity. Their travel accounts for an estimated $100 million in hotel business every year and is almost immune to recession. Hotel stays for regular-season games, playoffs and championships like the World Series account for the substantial spending on blocks of guest and meeting rooms, food and beverages, and services like security.[28]

The article then goes on to state that: "'Sports teams are a niche market, like rock stars,' said Scott Berman, head of the hospitality and leisure practice at PricewaterhouseCoopers, which tracked the Super Bowl spending, 'but it's a very competitive travel segment'."[29]

In an article published in *Forbes*, Andrew Bender noted what many consider essential for National Football League lodging. Much of what Bender wrote is also true of other major athletic teams, so we can see his commentary as pertaining not only to football, but also to the wide gamut of professional (and major university) athletic travel. Bender noted that:

Success in the National Football League requires drive, dedication, professionalism and special teams. You could say the same for hotels that host NFL teams when they're on the road, which need all that and more: the right facilities, culinary skill, security, reliability and the ability to roll with the occasional oddball request.[30]

According to hotel managers and spokespeople interviewed by Bender, the following qualities are essential to win the business of a major team and to keep the team coming back:

Sports teams lodging means that places of lodging must show a great deal of flexibility and be aware if they are going after specific sports, types of athletes, and time of year. Although the economic benefits may be large, athletes often require special provisions. For example, in the *New York Times* article quoted above, Marla Miller, Major League Baseball's senior vice president for special

---

[28] The *New York Times*. Olson, E. For athletes, a home for away games, http://www.nytimes.com/2013/11/05/business/for-athletes-a-home-for-away-games.html?_r=0; 2013 [accessed 01.08.16].
[29] The *New York Times*. Olson, E. For athletes, a home for away games, http://www.nytimes.com/2013/11/05/business/for-athletes-a-home-for-away-games.html?_r=0; 2013 [accessed 01.08.16].
[30] *Forbes*. Bender A. What it takes to be an NFL host, http://www.forbes.com/sites/andrewbender/2013/09/08/what-it-takes-to-be-an-nfl-host-hotel/; 2013 [accessed 01.08.16].

events, noted that the hosting of professional athletes or athletic teams can provide the hotel with a great deal of prestige and/or publicity. However, hosting often involves a number of unusual demands. To be a successful host hotel, staff members must exhibit a great deal of fortitude and patience. Many star athletes have numerous "unusual" demands, quirks, or superstitions to which the hotel must attend. Demands are not necessarily food-oriented. For example, a team may demand a separate elevator from that used by the general public, special security guards, decorating parts of the hotel with the team's logos or colors, or assuring that the mini bars in the rooms are locked so that players do not drink alcohol prior to a game.

For fans, a football weekend is an outing, but for a football team, travel is merely part of business, and it is essential that hoteliers understand that the team's players and staff see their choice of a specific locale as merely a business matter. For this reason, teams do not tolerate mistakes well. Sports teams want a distraction-free experience in which they can get the rest needed to perform well. Below are a number of factors that provide the basis for a successful relationship between the place of lodging and the athletes or sports team:

- Food quality and consistency. Just as providing a good night's rest is essential for the athletic traveler, so is food: its quality, sanitation, and consistency. Most teams do not want to have to experiment with new foods just before an athletic event. They would rather have a known product that will provide them with the fuel needed to win games.
- Good safety and security. This means protecting players from unwanted mingling with the public. This means that athletes often will want private floors, special elevators, and a well-vetted and dedicated staff. In today's world, cybersecurity is as much a part of security as physical security.

Hotels, then, should never be booked without first being inspected. The most important factor is the make-up of the group. Certain groups will have demographic needs that may vary from other groups. For example, is the traveling group composed of one or both sexes? Does the group contain a well-publicized "star athlete" who may have special needs? Does the group have special food requirements or other cultural needs? Does the group contain someone who needs special protection or who may set off protests due to a political or cultural statement?

When booking a lodging site it is important to consider the following factors among others:

- The size of the group. Do not consider the size of the group to be merely the number of athletes. A number of other people often make up the group, such as coaches, support staff, and even media reporters.

- Hotel size matters for a number of reasons, including whether or not it is desirable to have teammates on the same floor, and how many people are to be housed in a room. Hotels usually have controlled entrances. On the other hand, most motels have greater ease of entrance and exit. Hotel reception areas might provide greater privacy, but also might create bottlenecks at locations such as elevators.
- A lodging property's capability to accommodate the size of a group and, if needed, whether there is a place for group activities, such as a press conference. Will the team need a "team" or meeting room for holding team sessions or merely relaxing?
- What other activities does the group plan for the place of lodging? Does it provide food services, and if so, can it accommodate your group in a single sitting? Who vets the chefs, and are you sure that all food personnel are healthy?
- Does the group want—or not want—in-room entertainment, and is a gym or swimming pool an extra or a liability? Create a list of needs, wants, and "don't wants," and compare that list against what a place of lodging has to offer.
- Location of the lodging. In real estate, there is a famous phrase: value is determined by three things: location, location, and location. Often, this same concept is essential for sports teams when choosing a place of lodging. Considerations are distance from stadium or playing field, traffic congestion problems, ability to enter or leave the site without incident, and in the case of air travel, distance to/from the local airport.
- In-room issues. Athletes (especially male athletes) are often larger than the general public. Will they be comfortable in the beds, and does the shower height work for them? Additionally, athletes, especially after a long trip, need quiet. How soundproof are the walls and the floors above the athlete's rooms? Will the athletes be kept awake all night due to screaming in the halls or children bouncing in rooms that are above their room? Many sports teams have two players in a room. That means that they need two beds per room. Make sure the hotel has enough rooms with two beds before you book your team.
- Nonsmoking policies. In the United States, many hotels are 100% smoke free, but this is not always the case. Even secondhand smoke is harmful to an athlete's performance. It is best to be in a location that is 100% smoke free.
- Ease of check-in/check-out. Large group check-ins can become a nightmare, especially when documentation such as passports must be shown. Is there a process for precheck-ins? Can one person handle the process for the entire group? Must mini-bars be checked prior to checkout, or can the mini-bar be sealed to avoid extra costs and delays?

- Wi-Fi access and and strength. Avoid hotels that charge for Wi-Fi and have Wi-Fi with weak signal strength. Wi-Fi is essential for the team's esprit de corps, especially when the team is traveling abroad. Make it clear that free Wi-Fi in the lobby is not good enough. If the hotel cannot provide in-room, free Wi-Fi with enough strength to allow emails and simple use of the Internet, it is the wrong hotel for a team, especially when traveling abroad.
- How will billing be accomplished? Checkout can also become a nightmare. Is the billing to the team or individual players? Is there a room inspection prior to check out? How are incidental expenses handled?

Below, you will find a simple lodging security checklist. This is merely a sample list.

Hotel Security Checklist for Sports Teams and Athletes	
Name of hotel	
Address	
(Rack rate) cost/night	
Discounts offered and cost	
Date of visit	
Bedrooms	
Type of lock(s) on main doors	
Are windows secure?	
Do bathrooms have windows?	
Is there a safe in the room?	
Noise level in room (per external noise)	
Is phone service available and easy to use?	
Is safety information provided?	
Services	
Is the city's promotional literature in room?	√
Is emergency information available?	√
Is a shuttle/taxi to the airport available?	√
Security points	
Are there rooms with interior entrances?	√
Is the room number on the key?	√
Key type: standard or electronic?	√
Who controls the keys? How often are keys changed?	√
Does the room door have a peephole?	√
Are security cameras in plain sight?	√
Are security cameras functional?	√

Hotel Security Checklist for Sports Teams and Athletes			
Are security cameras monitored?	√		
Does the entrance have a guard?	√		
Do guards regularly walk through the place of lodging?	√		
How safe is the facility's cybersecurity? Is personal information safe, and has the facility ever suffered a cyber-attack?	√		
Are elevators located within sight of the front desk?	√		
Are any of the hallways hidden?	√		
Is the facility in a safe neighborhood?	√		
Is there a secure parking area?	√		
Is access from the parking area to the lobby secure?	√		
Facilities			
Are there informal conversation areas?	√		
Is promotional material about the city available in the lobby?	√		
Are the following available?			
Indoor swimming pool	√	Outdoor swimming pool	√
Exercise room	√	Jacuzzi/sauna	√
Tennis court	√	Children's play area, and is it secure?	√
Gift shop	√		
Personnel			
Are the check-in personnel known?			
Are hotel personnel vetted? By whom?			
What is the personnel's attitude?			
Is the check-in process efficient?			
Are personnel knowledgeable about the city?			
Baggage			
Where are bags stored after check-out?			
Are unattended bags noticed?			
How is baggage handled?			
Is a security safe available in the lobby?			

CHAPTER 5

Travel and Terrorism

When we think of sports and travel security, the issues that first come to mind tend to deal with issues of safety and security vis-à-vis issues of crime. Unfortunately, the 20th and 21st centuries also present an additional security problem: acts of terrorism against athletes.

To begin to understand the relationship between sports and terrorism, it is first necessary to understand something of terrorism and why terrorism attacks both tourism and athletics. In fact, in the last quarter of the 20th century, tourism often has been a magnet for acts of terrorism. It behooves us to remember that spectator sports in particular are an integral part of tourism. Sporting events draw large crowds. The public not only follows sports teams and personalities, but events that happen to these people become major news items. Often, whole teams become tourism superstars. This interlocking relationship between the teams, their fans, the team's players, and even the sports venues, means that all four are potential magnets for politically and economically motivated acts of terror.

We often fail to consider that certain sports venues, such as Brazil's Marcanã soccer stadium, or New York's Yankee stadium, are icons in their own right, and as such are open to iconic forms of terrorism. If modern terrorism seeks publicity in order to produce public fear, then an attack on a stadium, a team, or a well-known athlete is bound to not only create economic problems, but also will have a great deal of negative propaganda value.

Mega events such as the Olympic Games or, in the United States, weekly university or professional sporting events such as football, basketball, or baseball tournaments, draw tens of thousands of spectators (tourists) who add millions of dollars (or whatever the local currency happens to be) to that locale's economy. A terrorist attack on athletes or their performance center (field, stadium, and arena) has a great deal of influence not only on the lives of everyone present, but also on the entire political and economic life of that community, region, or even nation.

Sports Travel Security. DOI: http://dx.doi.org/10.1016/B978-0-12-805099-6.00005-1

Before we can enter into a discussion of the impact of terrorism on sports, it is essential to clarify some of the differences between criminal acts and acts of terrorism. Tourism security often is divided between the criminal side of the field and the terrorism side of the field. These two aspects of tourism security should not be confused. Although the outcomes in both may be tragic, it is an error to confuse these two social and political societal diseases.[1]

Tourism crimes tend to be crimes of opportunities or passion. A partial listing would include hotel/motel invasions, crimes of distraction, such as the stealing of luggage and pick-pocketing, and site defacement. Criminals have a parasitic relationship with the tourism industry and depend on the industry's success in order to "succeed." Thus, there may be pickpockets at sporting events but if no one were to attend the event, however, the pickpocket would also become inoperative.

Terrorism, on the other hand, often seeks to destroy or do great damage to the tourism industry, including the spectator sports component within the industry. Terrorism's goals tend to be mass casualties, economic destruction, public fear, and publicity. (see Table 5.1).

The chart below[2] points out some of the differences between these two negative social events.

A BIT OF HISTORY

Terrorism has been part of society since ancient times although throughout the millennia the word has changed meaning. For example, we have the Sicarii, a first-century Jewish group that murdered collaborators with the Roman rulers of Israel and the Hashhashin, an 11th-century Islamic sect from whose name we derive the modern word *assassin*.[3] In fact, as the centuries have moved on, so has the meaning of the word *terrorism*.

If we consider terrorism from just a Western perspective and only during the last six centuries, we see that the word not only has taken on different meanings but symbolizes different stages of the West's history. For example, In *Tourism and Terrorism*, edited by Yoel Mansfeld and Abe Pizzam, Tarlow writes that:

> One of the earliest forms of terrorism may have occurred during the 15th century. "The Peasants' Revolt" of Germany is such an example of early

---

[1] When it comes to illegal drugs terrorists often sell drugs for the purposes of funding acts of terrorism. In this area there is an overlapping between acts of crime and terrorism.

[2] Tarlow, P. Terrorism and tourism. In: Wilks J., Leggat, P., editors. Tourism in turbulent times, first ed., Atlanta: Elsevier, 2006, p. 81.

[3] About News. Zalman, A. The history of terrorism, http://terrorism.about.com/od/whatisterroris1/p/Terrorism.htm; 2015 [accessed 08.02.16].

Table 5.1 Comparison of Crime and Terrorism

	Crime	Terrorism
Goal	Usually economic or social gain.	To gain publicity and sometimes sympathy for a cause.
Usual type of victim	Person may be known to the perpetrator or selected because he/she may yield economic gain.	Killing is a random act and appears to be more in line with a stochastic model. Numbers may or may not be important.
Defenses in use	Often reactive, reports taken.	Some pro-active devices such as radar detectors.
Political ideology	Usually none.	Robin Hood model.
Publicity	Usually local and rarely makes the international news.	Almost always is broadcast around the world.
Most common forms in tourism industry are:	■ Crimes of distraction ■ Robbery ■ Sexual Assault	■ Domestic terrorism ■ International terrorism ■ Bombings ■ Potential for biochemical warfare
Statistical accuracy	Often very low, in many cases the travel and tourism industry does everything possible to hide the information.	Almost impossible to hide. Numbers are reported with great accuracy and repeated often.
Length of negative impact on tourism industry	If single event, short-lived; if multiple events may be long-lived.	Medium to long.
Recovery strategies	■ New marketing plans, assumes short-term memory of traveling public. ■ Probability ideals: "Odds are it will not happen to you." ■ Hide information as best as one can.	■ Showing of compassion. ■ Need to admit the situation and demonstrate control. ■ Higher levels of observed security. ■ Highly trained (in tourism, terrorism, and customer service) security personnel.

terrorism in which the innocent were murdered as a form of social pressure. Led by radical theologians and second ranked knights and nobles the "revolt" occurred during a period of rapid social change in which thousands of people lost their social bearings. Its "Osama Bin Laden" was the radical cleric Thomas Muentzier. Peters has written of Muentzier: "Muentzier left a trail of devastation across the middle of the Germanys that only ceased when a coalition of the nobility and knights brought him to a final apocalyptic that ended with an uncompromising pursuit and massacre of the insurgents, followed by the ingenious torture and execution of their captured leaders" (Peters: 48). Despite the mass murders for the sake of murder, the Peasants' Revolt may have produced in the best Hegelian fashion, a counter theory of humanity. The rationalists who preceded the French revolution rejected the idea that some people are inherently evil and instead developed the position believed that humanity was perfectible through science and knowledge. The Enlightenment "philosophies" believed that history might be brought to its successful conclusion through social science and understanding.[4]

For example, in 18th-century France, during its post-revolutionary period the term *Reign of Terror* referred to the masses vengeance on those who had been part of the *ancien régime*. In a sense, this use of the term is not that different from the terminology used in the 21st-century Middle East. Just as in the world of modern Middle Eastern terrorism decapitation was often employed. Thus, in post-revolutionary France, the guillotine (decapitation) was the instrument of choice. It was used as the method by which revolutionaries would deal with those who were considered to be enemies of the state or counter-revolutionaries. The key element in the aftermath of the French Revolution is that "terror" was something imposed from the establishment as a form of producing fear by example, and therefore, social control. The French Revolution and its Reign of Terror was not unique. Many other dictatorial governments have employed the same methodology. For example, one of the reasons given for the second Iraq War was Saddam Hussein's use of state terrorism against the Kurds or Syrian President's Bashar al Assad's attacks on his nation's citizens.

By the 19th century, the face of terror had changed. It was no longer a control factor used by the ruling classes but rather a system of violence, perhaps inspired by Marxism, in which those out of power (or anarchists) created violence specifically against those in power. This was the age of political assassinations. Nineteenth-century terrorism targeted specific leaders and although others might have been hurt, the intention was not to harm the "innocent" bystander. To use a 20th-century term, innocent bystanders would have been declared "collateral damage."

The 20th century was even bloodier than ages past. It was a century marked by war and political violence. Terrorism now had a double face. As in the 18th century, Nazi Germany taught the world what state-sponsored terrorism was, and multiple nonstate terrorists groups brought suffering to people from the Americas to Oceania, from Asia to Europe, and from the Middle East to China. This new terrorism went from the specific or targeted killings of the past to an age of nondiscriminate killings. Both state and nonstate terrorism attacked people not for what they had done, but rather, for who they were or where they happened to be. Murder now would take place for the sake of murder.

---

[4] Tarlow, P. A social theory of terrorism and tourism. In: Mansfeld Y. and Pizam A., editors. Tourism security & safety. Atlanta: Elsevier, 2006, p. 35.

The 21st century has continued with the 20th-century's forms of terrorism, but has added the concept of mass media terrorism: "terrorism cum marketing" that seeks not only to murder, but also to destroy a locale's sense of safety through the deliberate use of violence aimed at "capturing" as wide an audience as possible. Perpetrators of media-oriented violence understand the use of both social and traditional media, the 24-hour news cycle, and when the maximum amount of publicity can be gained. Mass media terrorism seeks not only to destroy the enemy's citizens and economy, but also to destroy its soul and *ésprit de corps*. In the late 20th century and the first parts of the 21st century, there also have been not only alignments between crime and terrorism, but also new substrains of terrorism.

TERRORISM: WHAT IS IT AND SOME OF ITS BASIC PRINCIPLES

As noted above, terrorism, like any social disease, is not monolithic, but has multiple mutations. These strains of terrorism will have commonalities and also demonstrate differences. To understand these strains of terrorism, we first need to understand their commonalities. Only after we have a general sense of terrorism and the terrorist mentality can we begin to understand the threat they pose to sporting events and athletes.

As will be seen below, terrorism, as a social virus, has multiple stains and a varied history. For reasons of precision and clarity, this section will focus primarily on post-World War II terrorism. It is essential that we not confuse issues of tourism crimes with issues of acts of terrorism that either directly or indirectly impact travel and tourism. As has been stated, tourism criminals rarely want to destroy the local tourism industry. Much to the contrary, as the industry prospers, the number of potential victims grows.

Terrorists, on the other hand, rarely seek personal gain. In a sense, terrorists see themselves as modern-day Robin Hoods or a form of quixotic idealism. Despite what politicians like to state: terrorists are now cowards. They are evil, but evilness should not be confused with cowardness. Terrorists often are so sure of themselves, or of their cause, that they are willing to destroy property and lives for what they falsely believe is the righteousness of their cause. Terrorism attacks on tourism destinations in Australia, Colombia, France, Egypt, Kenya, Indonesia, Italy, Israel, Russia, South Africa, Turkey, the United Kingdom, and the United States—to name just a few of the nations afflicted with acts of terrorism—have made the tourism industry wake up to the fact that tourism venues are especially vulnerable to attack. In the years 2015–2016 the world has seen terrorists attack everything from sports stadiums to restaurants and from beach promenades to hotels, from airports to trains and airplanes.

In the modern world, acts of terrorism are not only a major security challenge, but also have created a great deal of discussion on the nature of violence, terrorism, and morality. Is an attack against a nation's athletes simply another form of war, or does it lay beyond the scope of "civilized behavior?" This issue has spawned a number of questions, such as:

- Is violence a part of the human condition? Is terrorism just another form of violence?
- Is a terrorist a freedom fighter using the only available tools that s/he may have, or a criminal who chooses violence under the guise of politics to destroy innocent lives?
- Is war terrorism, and how do we distinguish between the two?
- Are there legitimate forms of violence, and if so, how do we distinguish "legitimate" from "illegitimate" forms of violence?

As we have already seen in this chapter, terrorism (or the use of the word) is not a modern phenomenon. Have we, therefore, created a linguistic fog in which the word has come to mean so much that in the end it is meaningless? These are just a few of the many questions that we need to raise if we are to understand the interrelationship between terrorism and sport. In reality, these questions are so broad and at the same time so ephemeral that they might need entire books, not just a single chapter, dedicated to them.

Terrorists seek publicity. When they strike a tourism center, such as an athletic facility, they may well receive large amounts of media coverage that they seek by causing not only damage to life and property, but also creating a long-term negative economic impact on the local tourism industry and possibly that of neighboring cities, states, or even nations. Furthermore, the unique sociological make-up of tourists (i.e., they tend to be mentally on vacation, to assume they are safe, to be easily identifiable, and often function in anomic states of mind) makes tourist venues and the tourism industry's customers prime terrorist targets. While the probability of a terrorist attack in any single, specific location might be low, the media's hunger for news, and its tendency toward sensationalism means that were a terrorist attack or a bombing to occur at any tourism venue, and especially at a sporting event or center, the consequences would certainly be long lasting and highly destructive.

To further complicate matters, tourist centers and sports centers are vulnerable to other forms of violence that at first might appear to be acts of terrorism but occur for other reasons. For example, football (soccer matches) in many locales have a history of hooliganism among fans, and thus, bombings may take place as a form of revenge, extortion, or for reasons of sheer madness. In all cases, however, the negative consequences of such an act extend far beyond the "theatre of action." In a like manner a government or the media, for reasons of political expediency, may report an act of violence as something other than terrorism. Thus, the United States government called a terrorist attack at a military base "workplace violence" rather than terrorism for political reasons. A CNS report on December 7, 2015 stated: "More than six years after a Muslim army major shot dead 13 people at Fort Hood, President Obama on Sunday night—for what may be the first time—publicly identified it as a terrorist attack."[5]

Listed below are a number of general principles that touch on the multiple strains of terrorism. Although each is listed separately, they should be seen as interacting one upon the other and operating in concert. Each of the following principles in one way or another touches on sports travel and safety:

- Terrorism is a method and never a goal. It is a method whereby an inferior military force can take a battle to its enemy's home and through random acts of maiming and/or murder sow fear among the civilian population.
- Terrorism is the marriage of violence to political goals. It is not a crime, but an act of war. It works by the random wounding and/or murdering of innocent victims.
- The more random the violence, the more successful the terror.
- Terrorism connects the media to the public and to government realms. Terrorism is media-oriented, and the more attention an event has, the greater the terrorist sees his/her reward.
- Terrorism need not be directed against only people. Certain buildings or places are so iconic that they are targets. Examples would be places such as the Vatican, the Eiffel Tower, or the Statue of Liberty. Since sports venues have a "quasi religious" aura about them, stadiums such as Rio de Janeiro's Marcaná, or New York's Yankee Stadium, become iconic targets themselves.

SOME REASONS FOR THE INTERACTION BETWEEN TERRORISM AND TOURISM AND ITS IMPACT ON SPORTS TRAVEL

Terrorism generally falls into two major categories. Practical terrorism tends to be short term and concentrates on a single goal. Apocalyptic terrorism seeks to bring a new world (or return of an old world) order. It is often ideological in nature and sees itself as an important part of the current of history.

---

[5] http://www.cnsnews.com/news/article/patrick-goodenough/obama-six-years-later-calls-fort-hood-terrorist-attack, [accessed 08.07.16].

The following table notes the differences between these two forms of terrorism.

	Practical terrorist	**Apocalyptic terrorist**
Mental state	Hopes to change a policy through violence	Victim of self-rage and anger
Time frame for success	This-world-oriented	Next-world-oriented
Attitude toward religion	Tends toward secularization	Tends toward religious mystical experiences
Suicide	Rarely suicidal, not a key goal	Highly suicidal, seeing suicide is a means to a greater end
Goal	Re-creation of state or policy	Annihilation of the state, or people
Willingness to use WMDs	Limited use of chemical	Biological or nuclear
Value of human life	Low	Nonexistent

The following tourism and terrorism principles also apply to the world of the sports, and its participants, fans, and its players.

- Tourism and sporting events are interconnected with transportation centers. People travel using various forms of transportation, and the more "important" the event, the longer the distance that people will travel to it.
- Tourism and sports are big business, with millions of dollars or Euros at stake.
- The world of sports is interrelated with multiple other industries, and the world of sports depends on everything from uncontaminated food to the lodging industry.
- Tourism and sports are highly media-oriented. In order to attract ticket sales and advertising, the sporting industry must have a great deal of media coverage. One only has to note the number of pages devoted to sports in any newspaper to see interconnection between the media and sports.
- In reality, no one knows who enters a sports stadium, and like other forms of tourism, the sports industry must deal with people who have no record of dealing with law enforcement, so there is often no database.
- Major sporting events become national events, and many nations connect the success of their team to their national prestige.
- Sports, as both a spectacle and pastime, is a point where business intersects with leisure.
- Tourism and sports centers are often seen as national symbols, so there is a sense of nationalism, from the flying of flags to the playing of national anthems, that interconnects sports with patriotism.

- Terrorism chooses soft targets including the following:
  - Airlines
  - Cruise ships
  - Buses, trains, and transportation terminals
  - Restaurants and outdoor cafés
  - Major events, whether sporting or festivals
  - Places where people congregate
  - Sports stadiums and arenas
  - Wherever people are carefree and happy.

TYPES OF TERRORISM: A TYPOLOGY

Listed below, in alphabetical order, are just a few of the many new strains of terrorism. It should be noted that this typology, like all typologies, is an academic oversimplification of the problem. It was created to allow an easy understanding of the intricacies within terrorism. In real life, there is an overlapping of many of the forms listed below.

- **Art theft terrorism**. This may refer to people who object to specific forms of art, finding them offensive for ideological reasons, or the sale (or theft) of art for the purpose of funding a terrorist organization.
- **Terrorism in the form of crimes against cultural institutions**. Many terrorist organizations cannot tolerate either the freedom of expression found within cultural organizations or may object to a specific expression of culture. From their perspective, such organizations are subversive and run counter to the organization's purported morality, and for this reason must be destroyed, even if the destruction involves murder.
- **Hate crimes terrorism**. We can argue that hate crimes are midway on the scale between crime and terrorism. They are aimed at a specific person or group due to that person's or group's nationality, religion, or race. Acts of terrorism that fall into this category include the bombing of a church because its congregants are of the "wrong" race, or an attack on someone wearing clothing that marks that person as a member of a particular religious or cultural group.
- **Left-wing terrorism**. Most left-wing terrorists find their inspiration in some form of Marxism. They see the established government as having rigged the economic system against them and often portray themselves as modern-day Robin Hoods. Most have as a set goal the destruction of capitalist societies and the replacement of these societies with their particular form of socialism or Marxism. Left-wing terrorism groups can be found in numerous European nations, and in the Americas, ranging from the United States through Central America and on to South America.

- **Narco terrorism**. This term might refer to cooperation between narcotic groups and terrorist groups in both Latin America and the Middle East. It also relates to the sale of narcotics for the purpose of financing terrorist groups. Often, this latter role fits more within the criminal element than the terrorism side of the equation. However, the world of narcotics often is built around "gangs," often called "cartels," and gang warfare, and there is an overlap between the criminal and the terrorist side of the narcotic trafficker.

- **Pathological terrorism**. This less-common form of terrorism borders on mental illness. It refers to the committing of an act of terrorism for the sheer purpose of the "joy of harming others." It is killing for its own sake or to express personal anger. Some of the recent school shootings in both the United States and Europe are examples of pathological acts of terrorism. The murder/terrorist has no other apparent motive than death for the sake of death.

- **Religious terrorism**. This term can refer either to terrorism sponsored by a religious sect or as an outgrowth of a particular ideology (or against people of a different faith). Religious terrorism is not new. In the European theater, it was practiced under the guise of the Spanish and Portuguese Inquisitions, and in the Americas, multiple, native pre-Colombian nations employed religious terrorism as a means of social and political control, especially in the southern parts of Mexico, and also in Peru and Bolivia. In the latter years of the 20th century and in the beginning decades of the 21st century, religiously motivated terrorists seeking martyrdom have employed such tactics as suicide bombings as a means not only of creating havoc, but also (for some) the realization of the belief that such martyrdom will ensure them a place in heaven. Religious terrorism has been prevalent in Europe, the Middle East, and the Indian subcontinent.

- **Right-wing terrorism**. This term is often used to describe anything from some form of fascism to hate groups that attack an individual or group due to religious beliefs, skin color, or ethnic background. Often, those involved claim to be fighting against a change in the social or demographic order. Right-wing terrorists are not known to work alone, but rather as part of a gang or even a self-proclaimed militia. They tend to be dismissive of members of law enforcement, government officials, and people who are not part of the perceived majority.

- **Separatist terrorism**. In a sense, these at least purport to represent single-issue groups, with the cause being separation from an occupying nation. The goal is the establishment of a new state that would turn a current minority into a majority within a smaller state. Separatist movements exist, or have existed, in places such as Canada, China, France, multiple parts of Africa, Spain, Turkey, the United Kingdom, and the United States. In each case, the separatist movement sees its members as under occupation and its fighters not as terrorists, but as freedom fighters.

- **Single-issue terrorism**. The motivation behind this form of terrorism is one, single issue, anything from animal rights to extreme environmentalism. The key to understanding them is that their members are so sure of the righteousness of their cause that they are capable of committing murder in its furtherance. Examples include murderous attacks on abortion providers, or on furriers by members of proanimal-rights groups.
- **State terrorism**. These are actions taken directly by the state as a means to maintain power or for political reasons. Often, a state tortures its opponents as a means of frightening other opposition groups.
- **State-sponsored terrorism**. When governments provide funding or military aid to an independent terrorist group, this form of terrorism is often called "state supported." Nations such as Iran are famous for their acts of state-sponsored terrorism. The use of state-sponsored terrorism is a way for a political state to hurt its opposition without being directly involved. A famous case is the attack on the AMEIA in Buenos Aires by Iranian operatives.

HISTORIC INCIDENTS OF TERRORISM AT MAJOR SPORTING EVENTS

Some sporting events are major news stories, and as such, acts of terrorism—although relatively rare— can also become major news stories. By using the term *relatively rare*, we are comparing the statistical odds of a member of the public and/or a sports figure being injured or killed in a terrorist attack against the odds of the same though another form of violence, including nonaggressive acts such as an inadvertent car crash. From a purely statistical perspective, terrorism has hurt relatively few athletes. As of the writing of this book, in American sports there have been two major incidents. The first was the 1996 bombing just outside the venue of the Atlanta Olympic Games, which killed one or two people (depending on how one counts), and injured 111 people. The second is the 2013 Boston Marathon, at which some 264 people were injured and three people were directly murdered, as well as one police officer, who was murdered in the aftermath. These two events are separated by 16 years, thus making direct terrorist attacks on US sports a rarity. This statistical fact does not, however, take into account the untold damage of negative publicity, damage to the economy, and, of course, damage caused not only to its direct victims, but also to the victims' friends and families.

As noted—as in all cases of terrorism—these attacks, although a relatively rare form of violence, cause major shockwaves throughout the political system. Below is a list of some of the major terrorist attacks since the end of World

War II. This list does not include state-sponsored terrorism or prejudicial actions such as those taken by Germany prior to the Second World War.

As the following 10 examples illustrate, terrorism and sport have a difficult interaction. Often, what in other realities would be considered a failure, in the world of terrorism turns out to be a success. *Time* magazine noted this in the following:

> Security has been beefed up at major sporting events following the events of 9/11. Indeed, there's a case to be made that the threat of terror has almost been as pronounced as the actual attacks themselves. Shortly after the attacks, the United States Ryder Cup team pulled out of the bi-annual fixture due to be held in Britain. In general, most of soccer's major tournaments have seen an "intensive exchange of ideas" on counterterrorism efforts.

> And both post-9/11 Olympic Games have been prime examples of increased security at sporting events. Ahead of the Beijing Games, for example, China deployed a massive security presence, saying it had foiled a terrorist hijacking plot, yet warning it faced further threats in its Muslim-majority northwest. Just five days before the flame was lit, there was an attack by Muslim separatists in the city of Kashgar in China's far western Xinjiang region that left 16 policemen dead and an equal number badly wounded.[6]

The following examples are meant to indicate the variety of terrorist attacks at world sporting events against the sportsmen and women, sport venues, and the event's host location.

1. **Attacks on Olympic athletes at the Munich Olympics on September 5, 1972.** Palestinian terrorists invaded and held hostage members of the Israeli Olympic team. Owing to a poorly coordinated negotiation and a botched rescue attempt by the German police and military the kidnappings resulted in the deaths of the 11-man team, a German police officer, and five Palestinian terrorists. Four other Palestinian terrorists were captured. The results of this attack were multiple. Eleven Israeli families were left bereaved, and their children became orphans. Germany, which had hoped that the 1972 Olympics would not only be a way to cleanse the stain of the Nazi Berlin Olympics in 1933, had a new stain on its history, and numerous people noted the tragic irony that this major attack occurred, in all places, on German soil. There are still questions as to the actions of the International Olympic Committee. It is only at the 2016 games in Rio de Janeiro that a moment of silence finally occurred to commemorate the tragedy.

---

[6] Time. Top 10 worst sport terrorism attacks. http://content.time.com/time/specials/packages/article/0,28804,1882967_1882966_1882959,00.html; 2016 [accessed 08.02.16].

2. **1996 Manchester bombing on June 15, 1996.** This attack did not take place directly in a sports stadium, but was inspired by a sporting event. The Irish Republican army took "credit" for exploding a 3,300-pound bomb in Manchester, injuring some 200 people. The explosion took place on the day prior to the German–Russian football (soccer) match for the 1996 European Football match. The Manchester bombing serves as an example of how terrorists use sporting events to gain publicity and use a theatrical backdrop for their actions.

3. **Atlanta Olympics bombing on July 27, 1996.** As previously noted, the 1996 tragedy outside the Atlanta Olympic Games venue was the first attack on a sporting event in the United States. The explosion occurred in the earliest morning hours (1:22 am) on July 27, killing two people and injuring 111. A security guard, Richard Jewell, was falsely accused of setting the explosion. Although eventually cleared of all wrongdoing, Jewell never fully recovered psychologically from the false accusation, and some have connected his early death to the false accusation. A *New York Times* headline from August 30, 2007, puts the tragedy into perspective: "Richard A. Jewell, whose transformation from heroic security guard to Olympic bombing suspect and back again came to symbolize the excesses of law enforcement and the news media, died Wednesday at his home in Woodbury, Ga. He was 44."[7] The actual bomber was Eric Rudolph, who serves as an example of domestic terrorism, stating that "he targeted the event because it promoted socialism and that he wanted to embarrass the US government. He also said that the plan was to force the games to cancel and in doing so, ensure that the money spent on arranging the event were spent on something else."[8] Hess saw himself as a Robin Hood or freedom fighter figure. It appears that he actually called in the bomb to the Atlanta police, but due to lack of coordination, they did not arrive at the scene in time to clear the park of the bomb. Hess saw the Olympic Games as a misuse of public funding and hoped to use them as a backdrop to make his case to the general public.

4. **Madrid Soccer Bombing on May 1, 2002.** Once again, this is an incident that took place near rather than in, a sports stadium. On May 1, 2002, the Basque terrorist separatist group ETA set off a car bomb near Santiago's Bernabeu stadium in Madrid. A second bomb exploded about one mile from the stadium. The bombings injured 17 people. The bombs were timed to go off shortly before one of Spain's most important football (soccer) teams, Real Madrid, was to

---

[7] *New York Times.* Richard Jewell, 44, hero of Atlanta attack, dies; http://www.nytimes.com/2007/08/30/us/30jewell.html; 2007 [accessed 08.02.16].
[8] Wikia. Eric Rudolph, http://criminalminds.wikia.com/wiki/Eric_Rudolph; 2016 [accessed 08.02.16].

play its Barcelona rival in the European Champions League final. This is an example of terrorism using a sporting event to seek a particular goal, in this case, Basque independence. The Basque's separatists were not necessarily trying to kill people, but rather, used the act of terrorism as a methodology toward gaining publicity and making a point.

5. **Sri Lanka Marathon on April 6, 2008.** In this case, the "Liberation Tigers of Tamil Eelam" dispatched a suicide bomber to kill and maim citizens at the Sri Lanka marathon. The terrorists succeeded in murdering some 14 people (including the nation's highway minister at the time, Jeyaraj Fernandopulle) and injuring close to 100. Like the Basque ETA, this group had one political goal in mind. The sporting event was an attractive option to sow chaos in the country and cause people to lose faith in the government's ability to protect the populace.

6. **Dakar Rally, 2008.** Danger and the Dakar Rally have long been bedfellows, as dozens of participants have perished while racing across some of the world's most inhospitable terrain. But last year, organizers deemed the threat of al-Qaeda too risky, and the rally was cancelled for the first time in its 30-year history. Organizers cited safety warnings from the French government after the al-Qaeda-linked slaying of a family of French tourists in Mauritania—where 8 of the competition's 15 stages were to be held—and "threats launched directly against the race by terrorist organizations." This appeared to be a one-off, as the rally returned earlier this year, albeit in South America. Sport's bright light will remain undimmed.

7. **Sri Lankan Cricket Team Ambush on March 3, 2009.** Terrorism struck Sri Lanka's sporting industry on this date, this time on the bus of the Sri Lankan cricket team, who were headed to Qaddafi Stadium in Lahore, Pakistan. The bus was ambushed in close proximity to the stadium by 12 gunmen. The ambush cost the lives of six police officers guarding the team, and two bystanders. Eight cricket players were injured.

   The Associated Press reported that the gunmen were armed with submachine guns, rocket-propelled grenades, pistols, 25 hand grenades, and plastic explosives. Some of the gunmen fled the scene in motorized rickshaws. The attack added to the fear among international teams playing there, and not only hurt Pakistan's image and economy, but reinforced the idea that foreigners should stay away from Pakistan.

8. **Attack on World Cup Fans in Uganda on July 11, 2010.** Uganda has had its share of tragedy. Tragedy touched Uganda once more on July 11, 2010, when terrorist(s), most likely belonging to the militant Somali group al-Shabab, which is linked to the international terrorist organization al-Qaeda, claimed responsibility for at least three bombs near an outdoor venue and Ethiopian restaurant where fans were watching a World Cup soccer match between Spain and the Netherlands

on television. The bomber might have been a suicide bomber. First reports indicated that the bombs killed about 50 innocent civilians, but that number was later revised upward and the final death toll was rose to 74, Ugandan officials said. The attack was allegedly retaliation for Ugandan involvement in Somalia. The World Cup provided an easy soft target at which the terrorists could make their point.

9. **Commonwealth Games, 2010**. This is an example of terrorists doing nothing and still "winning" by default. In 2010, India hosted the Commonwealth Games amidst widespread fear that an attack, like the Mumbai massacres of 2008, might occur. Numerous athletes withdrew from the games after being warned, or being of the opinion, that there was a "high threat of terrorism throughout India." Furthermore, news media reported that Indian security was not prepared to properly handle security. In reality, the games were held without incident. However, this example serves as a reminder that terrorism operates both through actions and psychological warfare, and that at times, the media plays into the hands of terrorists.

10. **Boston Marathon Bombing on April 15, 2013**. The Boston Marathon was one of two major sports terrorism incidents in the United States, the other being the 1996 Atlanta bombings near the Olympic stadium. This terrorist attack killed 3 people at the event and 1 police officer after the event, and injured more than 170 people. It was a major news story not only in the classical media, but also in social media. Many people also found it shocking that immigrants to the country, who became US citizens, carried out the attack. The attack dominated the news media for many days.

11. **Paris attacks on the Stade de France on November 16, 2015**. From an operational standpoint, these attacks were not successful. The terrorists had intended to detonate several bombs as the President of France watched an international soccer match between the French and German national teams. The terrorists were not successful in entering the stadium, but did manage to explode three bombs outside the stadium. The British Broadcasting Company reported that:

A man wearing a suicide belt was reportedly prevented from entering the stadium after a routine security check detected the explosives. A second man detonated his suicide vest outside a different stadium entrance at 21:30.

A third suicide bomber blew himself at a fast-food outlet near the stadium at 21:53. The attackers all wore identical explosive vests.[9]

---

[9] BBC. Paris attacks: What happened in Stade de France? http://www.bbc.com/news/world-europe-34839080; 2015 [accessed 08.02.16].

Although the terrorists did not succeed in entering the stadium, France and much of Europe is still feeling the aftermath and aftershocks from these and the other coordinated terrorist attacks on that day.[10]

Despite the fact that the terrorists were unable to explode their bombs inside the stadium, they were successful in a number of other ways. These include the following:

1. They garnered a great deal of international publicity.
2. They were able to harm the French economy.
3. When seen as part of a series of intercoordinated and almost simultaneous attacks, they demonstrated to the world a new, higher level of sophistication.
4. They succeeded in creating an atmosphere of fear.

This list highlights some of the attacks against sports or athletic centers over the last two decades and is not meant to be complete, but rather representative of the different forms of terrorism that have plagued the world of sports.

It should be noted that these different types of terrorism have certain commonalities. Among these are the following:

1. Terrorists seek soft targets or places where security is lax. The one possible exception to this is the Munich Olympic attacks, and in that case, questions have been raised about the commitment of German security to the protection of Israeli (Jewish) athletes less than 30 years after the end of Nazi Germany.
2. Often, the attacks did not occur at the sports venue, but nearby. In all cases, the terrorists sought to create fear among members of an unarmed public. In fact, a commonality is that no one at any of these events could have confronted a terrorist before the police arrived.
3. Law enforcement and security personnel were able to interdict the terrorists when they were on the scene. Nevertheless, the advantage lies with the attacker (terrorist), as law enforcement must be both omnipresent and ever vigilant. Law enforcement and security personnel must be successful all of the time in the prevention of attacks, while the perpetrators can fail to carry out an attack and still succeed in creating fear, even if only occasionally.

TYPES OF SECURITY TECHNIQUES

The section above provides, in at least one way, ample evidence that despite our best efforts, security failures have occurred. On the other hand, it is

---

[10] BBC. Paris attacks: What happened in Stade de France? http://www.bbc.com/news/world-europe-34839080; 2015 [accessed 08.02.16].

essential to take into account that there is no perfect security situation and to live at all involves risk. Also we hear about the security failures but tend not to know about the security successes. Security successes are rarely publicized as (1) they often do not attract the public's eye and (2) publicizing successes often means providing terrorists with the notoriety they crave. When we consider, however, the number of potential attacks and the fact that groups such as Al Qaeda, the Islamic State, and the Taliban are competing with each other to harm the Western world and democracies, then it is clear that many of the tourism security techniques now in place are working. Statistically, we might expect many more terrorism "successes" than those that have occurred at the time this book was written.

Once again, we must divide our study of security techniques with the following components that need protection:

1. The locale (athletic venue).
2. The athletes and those dealing with the athletes themselves.
3. The viewing public (spectators).
4. The location at which the event occurs.

In the examples given above, all four of these subsets were either victims or intended victims of at least one terrorist attack. It should be stated that each case is special, and that no professional security agency, whether public or private, is going to make public all of its security protocols. What the reader will find below is an overall draft outline of some of the principal techniques used and known to the public. Each agency will fill in the missing lacunae as needed and adapt them to a particular situation. Finally, no matter how good the agency's professionals might be, they are well aware of the fact that there is no single person, thing, place, or reputation that cannot be harmed, stolen or destroyed. The goal, then, is to create a realistic expectation of what is doable with the realization that risk is ubiquitous.

SOME GENERAL PRINCIPLES

First, it is essential to remember that security is a form of risk management. As such, the first principle that can never be overlooked is that there will never be sufficient manpower, resources, or time to eliminate all risk. Instead, good risk managers and security professionals must set logical and achievable priorities, understanding that there will always be some missing elements or flaws in even the best security plan.

Second, one must recognize that the media and general public tend to reject the first principle. That is, despite reality, both the public (often driven by the media) and other members of the "chattering classes," often concentrate on the single error out of a hundred actions, rather than the 99 successes. A *USA*

Today story published on May 2, 2013,[11] titled "Holes in Stadium Security," noted, problems at the Kentucky Derby.

Regarding the security guards, *USA Today* stated:

> But who are the private security guards protecting the nation's stadiums? Are they more often tasked with subduing an inebriated fan than defusing a terrorist plot in the making? How good are they?
>
> It depends. Stadiums and entertainment venues across the nation routinely rely on low-paid, part-time security guards with spotty training and even criminal convictions, an investigation by *USA TODAY* Sports has found.

The article went on to list the following problems:

1. Some security guards had criminal backgrounds.
2. Gaps in guard training and licensing.
3. Low pay due to cost cutting and, therefore, lesser security.
4. Loose definitions of who is responsible for doing what job.

The article also noted that two students showed how easy it was to enter into the Super Bowl on February 3, 2013, without being checked or stopped. The article ended with a statement from David Scott, president of the Stadium Managers Association: "Each facility might have a different answer for this … But as a general statement, there are long-standing relationships with the companies that provide that staffing."

Although the charges made in the article should be taken seriously, it also should be noted that the article does not address the many successes that security has achieved. Of course, as has been stated numerous times, security professionals cannot afford to err even once, while terrorists need to succeed only once.

It must also be recognized that all security has an element of luck and successful timing. Even the best equipment used by the best-trained and best-paid personnel cannot be everywhere at all times. Although good training can lower the probability of a successful terrorist attack, it can never guarantee total security. Furthermore, in a world of constant, 24/7 news coverage, even a failed attack has some success if it generates widespread publicity.

---

[11] *USA Today*. Schrotenboer B. USA TODAY sports investigation: Holes in stadium security, http://www. usatoday.com/story/sports/2013/05/02/stadium-security-boston-marathon-kentucky-derby/2130875/; 2013 [accessed 08.02.16].

RISK MANAGEMENT PRINCIPLES

As noted, security on some level is an issue of implementation of risk management principles. As the world becomes a more dangerous place, there is an ever-greater need for sports tourism professionals to identify and manage risk. As seen by media coverage, people working to maintain safety for the players, stadiums, crowds, and local communities need to ask themselves questions such as: How much risk is acceptable? Can we afford insurance to cover the costs of the risk? What risk can never be covered by insurance? What are my risk priorities? When considering the challenges posed by terrorism, sports tourism security professionals, whether law enforcement or private security, need to divide the risks into the following categories:

- Physical/security risks to the client (spectator, athlete, stadium, and so on).
- Physical/security risks to the staff.
- Risks due to issues of health such as food and water safety, for staff and clients.
- Risks to the environment. For example, will the event or tour damage the local ecology?
- Risks to the local community in the event of a terrorist attack.
- Risks to the business reputation of the sport or team.

The first thing to consider is that the best way to prevent a terrorist crisis is to have good risk management. Crises develop when risk management fails. To avoid failure, one should consider the following:

Be aware of how intertwined safety and security are when dealing with terrorism. Terrorism is so expansive that there is little or no difference between safety (personal injury) risk and security risk. Terrorists can poison food or set off a bomb; both are risks. Either, if poorly managed, will destroy a tourism industry, a sport or a community. Instead of dividing these risks into two types, consider placing them under the heading of "surety risk management." Then, try to determine where the interactions are between all of the surety risks that touch every aspect of the sport. For example, security begins with good customer service, in the sense of interacting with people at the venue. If your personnel do not provide good customer service, they might put forth a major security flaw and expose the entire sporting event to unneeded risk.

Take the time to look at how you will fund losses should a risk materialize. Many sports entities assume that insurance will pay all recovery costs. Terrorism, however, might be declared an act of war and thus void an insurance policy. Since sporting events are always in the public eye, the assumption that insurance is enough may not be true. Also factor in the cost of a negative headline about your sporting event. What is the public relations cost of having the press expose the fact that your company did not adequately train employees? How long will it take you to overcome negative, word-of-mouth publicity, and can you afford this risk? The following steps can help guard against these risks.

- Do a full risk assessment. Where are you most exposed to loss? What techniques are you using to minimize this (these) loss(es)? How often do you actually implement these techniques, and can you demonstrate that you have monitored and compared these results with previous results?
- List and rank every peril to which your side of the tourism industry is exposed. Risk management is only as good as the assumptions on which you base your decisions. There is no way to eliminate every risk; thus, there is a need to rank risks. First, rank which risks are most likely, then those that would be most devastating to your office, business, or community. You might divide these risks into the following four categories:
  - Low probability of occurring and low impact should the risk occur.
  - Low probability of occurring and high impact should the risk occur.
  - High probability of occurring and low impact should the risk occur.
  - High probability of occurring and high impact should the risk occur.

Then consider the issue of time. Is the impact of a particular negative event short- or long-lived? How much would it cost you to counteract any negative impact?

Deal first with risks that have a high probability of occurring and a high-risk impact. Those with a low probability of occurring and low impact should be dealt with last. Rank each risk mentioned in the introduction found above. Then, ask yourself what the exposure to loss is for each of these risks. Will they result in a lawsuit, loss of personnel, reduced morale, property damage, business interruption or loss of reputation, or some combination of these factors? How well could your community's convention and visitors' bureau or business withstand your worst-case scenario?

When evaluating risk, determine not only your recovery strategies, but also your avoidance strategies. First, develop a list of whom you should speak with in order to identify risks. How well trained are your police in risk assessment? Often, in tourism, police departments' lack of knowledge might lead to a false sense of security. We often forget that the best way to recover from a risk is to prevent the risk. Evaluations always should include how much you can afford to self-insure, a listing of what software and hardware you need, what technical support is needed, what political preparations are needed, and how your budget would withstand the risk. For example, if you had to lay off employees, would you be able to rehire them? What is the cost of seeking out new employees, addressing low employee morale, and retraining?

Monitor what you have done and where you need to go. Never fail to monitor and evaluate the results of your risk assessment and maintain a timeline of where you have been in the past, where you have corrected past mistakes and how changes in the political, economic, social, and cultural environment have necessitated changes on your part. Consider what proactive measures, what human resource measures, and managerial techniques you might need to implement or fine tune.

Risk management in the world of sports travel, then, is an ongoing process that touches every aspect of the business, from its accounting practices to the public's satisfaction with a company, and from managing costs to dealing with issues of fraud. Risk is part of every aspect of the travel and visitor industry, and cannot be avoided. To fail to recognize risk, then, is perhaps the greatest risk of all.

In dealing with the four major groupings listed below, it is essential to utilize good risk management techniques such as those discussed in *Event Risk Management and Safety*, by Peter Tarlow. Then, using these techniques, consider each of the four units mentioned above. Below are several suggestions for each of these four units.

Protecting the locale (athletic venue). When we think of sports security, people often immediately think of stadium/venue protection. Most people (and most governments), assume that the harder the target, the safer it is. This assumption is based on the premise that terrorists tend to seek out soft targets, so a hard target displaces the terrorist. Hardening a target is usually a combination of technical equipment, such as metal detectors and Closed Circuit Television (CCTV) cameras, a large and highly visible security presence, and information sharing. It should be emphasized that all are necessary. Questions have been raised, however, regarding whether a venue or location can become "too hard." For example, in writing about the Sochi 2014 Olympic Games, Sulastri Osman and Joseph Franco from the Centre of Excellence for National Security, a constituent unit of the S. Rajaratnam School of International Studies at Nanyang Technological University, noted that:

> A growing body of research, as exemplified by a study from the University of Sydney, has revealed how in some cases hardening public venues can paradoxically lead to more insecurity. On one hand, defending conspicuous targets can result in potential attackers seeking more accessible and possibly numerous other targets. On the other hand, a hardened target can also prompt attackers to seek deadlier attack methods. A separate research

has shed light on a correlation between increased hardness of targets and the likelihood of suicide bomb attacks. Simply put, signalling (sic) that a target is worth defending makes it more attractive to attackers.[12]

The authors point to the need for up-to-date data sharing practices. The Homeland Security University Center of Excellence program at Rutgers University, called Command, Control, and Interoperability Center for Advanced Data Analysis, also noted the importance of data collecting and sharing, emphasizing as part of its best practices the following principles for sports venue safety and security:

1. Do basic and baseline risk assessments.
2. Incorporate into the security program, the right people, the proper use of technology, and good and clear protocols (procedures) for detecting a threat, for deterring the threat, for defending against the threat's realization and for mitigation should the threat occur. It should be emphasized that people are number one on this list. Good technology is essential to helping the human element, but unless there are the right people doing the right job at the right time, nothing else will really matter.
3. Hire and train the best workforce possible. Part of a functioning workforce is professionalization, the realization that no one knows everything and that personal feelings have to be subordinated to the professional task at hand.
4. Develop and manage good communications. These communications need to be multidirectional, that is, between members of the staff, between the staff and the media, between the staff and the spectators and vice versa. It is essential that the public also become the eyes and ears of the security team.
5. Train, train, and train. Training should be from training in classroom to training on site, from tabletop exercises to full-scale cooperation exercises.[13]

The second area to be protected concerns the athletes and the staff members that accompany the traveling athletes. Owing to the many types of athletes, and issues of notoriety and stardom, this area is perhaps the most difficult. Previous chapters have examined many of the challenges in the welfare and security of traveling athletes. First and foremost is that all athletes are human beings, and therefore open and vulnerable to all of the risks and dangers facing any other human being, only to an even greater degree because of the

[12] RSIS. Osman S, Franco J. Security of sports venues: Protecting events from terrorism; https://www.rsis.edu.sg/rsis-publication/cens/2308-security-of-sports-venues-pro/#.VoQfTBFEzHg; 2014 [accessed 08.02.16].
[13] [http://www.nxtbook.com/nxtbooks/kmd/hst_20151201/index.php#/42 (accessed 08-07-16]

athlete's potential notoriety and strains on his or her body. Often, a good way to start is to think of the athlete as another person needing/deserving of executive protection. It is, therefore, a good idea to review many of the articles that deal with executive protection. The American Society for Industrial Security is a good place to seek guidance on executive protection. A number of key points run through the vast literature on the topic, including the following:

1. Security personnel should be well informed about whom you are protecting, the person (persons') needs, and what information the security professional should have that is not being provided. The more the security professional knows about the *who's*, *what's*, *where's*, and *when's* of the situation, the better the protection is going to be.

2. Dress as part of the team or blend in. In most cases, the idea is not to draw attention to the security professional. The security professional, when creating safe zones for the traveling athlete, is going to want to blend in with the crowd rather than risk exposure. After all, security professionals are people who could also be harmed.

3. In the world of protection, boring is good. The last thing a team or athlete wants is for the security professional to be in the middle of a fight or, even worse, become the subject of a news story. Good security work means doing the necessary research and taking the necessary precautions so that trouble is avoided. Not having a crisis is far better than solving a crisis.

4. Be polite, but firm. Often, athletes believe that they are invincible and enter a form of "group think." This is especially true with younger teams that travel together. The security professional is just that—the security professional. Security is not open to democratic, group decisions. Even if the team wants to do X, this does not mean that its members have the right to override something the security professional is doing for the team's (or athlete's) protection. Just as medical personnel do not allow their decisions to be open to a vote, the same must hold true for sports security professionals.

5. The more people the security professional can call upon, the more effective he or she will be. Tourism security professionals cannot take care of a team by themselves. Developing close professional ties with law enforcement, the stadium or athletic venue's security teams, and the hotel's security team makes the professional's job a lot more efficient. Make a list of what can go wrong, and then find people who would be important to know in order to resolve any problem. Establish these relationships before the crisis, not after one has occurred.

6. Protecting the viewing public (spectators) is in an age of terrorism a never-ending job. Stadiums draw huge numbers of people. As noted in

previous chapters, sports fans tend to be sociologically similar to many tourists. They are interested in the spectacle, in seeing and being seen, and often pay very little attention to their own personal safety. The security professional needs to be an expert not only in building security, but also in issues of crowd control. Often, spectator security is defined by what a spectator cannot bring into a stadium. For example, the National Football League website states that:

Prohibited items include, but are not limited to: purses larger than a clutch bag, coolers, briefcases, backpacks, fanny packs, cinch bags, non-approved seat cushions*, luggage of any kind, computer bags and camera bags or any bag larger than the permissible size. … As the season approaches, we encourage fans to visit individual NFL team websites for specific stadium information. *Non-approved seat cushions include large traditional seat cushions that have pockets, zippers, compartments, or covers. Please see your club guest services office to have your seat cushion examined.[14]

Security professionals, however, have to be more than guards telling people what they cannot bring into a stadium. Many cite the Israelis as the gold standard of security. The Israelis start with a simple question: "What is the cost of human life? If you want to have a bomb in a stadium and 20 or 30 people are killed and 170 wounded, and that's not worth a half-million dollars in security, then human life is less favored than human life in Israel. … At the end of the day, it's about how much you value a human life."[15] Israeli security experts note that a key difference is that in Israel, security personnel do not watch the event, they watch the crowd. Israel does not permit unattended bags, and the public is trained to ask questions. This public participation helps makes the difference. Israelis look around, and if they see something, they are not afraid to say something to well-trained security personnel. Unlike in many other Western nations, Israeli security professional have a high level of prestige, are highly trained, and they see themselves and are viewed by the public as highly trained specialists.

It is essential to have policies for crowd control and evacuation; assuring that loudspeakers are not only audible, but understandable; issues of health; attacks from the air; purity of foods and drinks; clarity as to the concessionaires' personal backgrounds; and how concessionaires might react under moments of high stress.

---

[14] NFL. NFL teams to enhance public safety and improve stadium access for fans, http://www.nfl.com/qs/allclear/index.jsp; 2016 [accessed 08.02.16].

[15] *USA Today*. Schrotenboer B. USA TODAY sports investigation: Holes in stadium security, http://www.usatoday.com/story/sports/2013/05/02/stadium-security-boston-marathon-kentucky-derby/2130875/; 2013 [accessed 08.02.16].

7. Protecting the location in which the event occurs. Since athletes are not necessarily restricted to the safe zones of the hotel or stadium, it is essential to work with law enforcement on a broader scope. In an age of terrorism, perpetrators realize that during major events, there might be entertainment zones filled with fans, higher levels of both liquid and other forms of substance abuse, and the ever-present risk that violence may occur due to hooliganism or other causes, such as spectator fanaticism or simply loss of common sense. In theory, the team's security officers ought to be able to restrict athletes from entering areas where trouble might occur. Even if athletes are not present, however, there is no way that after-game violence will not impact the viability of the game and the reputation of the sport. For example, the *New York Daily News* reported on October 15, 2015, that Los Angeles police had to don New York Mets uniforms to deal with potential fan violence:

> Undercover Mets. That's how far L.A. cops say they will go Thursday to prevent any violence like the kind that broke out after Game 1 in Dodger Stadium, where a brutal beatdown (sic) left a fan in critical condition. ...A post-game parking lot fight left a man in critical condition Friday after a Bakersfield man banged his head on the concrete ground and lost a piece of his skull, police and witnesses said. Officials said police were looking for a mother and son—a 40- to 50-year-old woman and a man in his 20s — in connection with the attack.[16]

Although this altercation took place close to the stadium, the article's key point is that some fans become so involved in the game that they lose all measures of proportionality regarding the game's importance to reality. Perhaps what makes Israeli security so good is that their security personnel have taught the public that the only real game is that of life and death, and in that game there are no second chances.

---

[16] *New York Daily News.* Greene L. LAPD officers to don Mets jerseys at Dodger Stadium as "hundreds" of undercover cops patrol crowd to prevent another brutal playoff beating, http://www.nydailynews.com/news/national/lapd-cops-undercover-mets-fans-game-5-article-1.2398725; 2015 [accessed 08.02.16].

CHAPTER 6

Athletes at Home and on the Road

Sports teams and athletes do not live in a vacuum. When on the road, players not only visit new locales, but also, during the time of their visit, they become a part of these locales. They eat at local restaurants, use local facilities, and expect the same public services, such as police and fire protection as does everyone else. This chapter will look at both university athletes and professional athletes when they are on the road. Perhaps the question that must always be held in the background is: Is travel as hard as it is purported to be and if so, then (1) why do players subject themselves to these trials and tribulations, and (2) how do players overcome these trials and tribulations?

THE UNIVERSITY STUDENT-ATHLETE

University teams are composed of players who attend specific universities as students. This basic fact means that when off the field, athletes are part of the university community and are as liable to any of physical, academic, or security challenges as is any other student. Athletes, just as would any other student, attend classes, go to university activities, socialize with both teammates and classmates, and—just as also happens to other students—unfortunately, at times get into trouble. Often, both their fellow students and the media forget that college athletes are first and foremost college students and as such, for most student-athletes, their athletic endeavors are part of their overall university experience.

THE PROFESSIONAL ATHLETE

The world of professional athletes is similar, but also different, to that of the university student. Professional athletes are in reality businesspeople. The media often portray athletes as something other than businesspeople or entertainers. Often, the media create illusions around the athlete's persona, creating differences between reality and the media's portrayal of reality. In

131

Sports Travel Security. DOI: http://dx.doi.org/10.1016/B978-0-12-805099-6.00006-3

truth, professional athletes are sociologically similar to entertainers traveling on a business trip. Even in the case of university athletes, we may see them as unpaid (or paid in-kind through scholarship packages) businesspeople.

In the case of professional athletes, these men and women are sociologically similar to other individual entertainers or entertainment troupes. Either as part of a team or as independent athletes (such as golfers or tennis players), the professional athlete's salary depends on his or her sports success, along with his or her media image. Many athletes are good enough "to play the circuit" or be part of a team, but are not necessarily celebrities. Often, the public forgets that professional athletes, just like other people, have private lives, and that they share many of the same problems and challenges that impact other people. Just as in the case of other traveling entertainers, professional athletes may have families to support and are part of the fabric of their local communities.

This chapter examines these athletes from four unique perspectives.

1. The university athlete who on some level is a visitor on his or her own campus.
2. The university athlete when she or he travels to a location, both as a private citizen and as an athlete, and who has free time in a "business" location away from home.
3. The professional athlete when he or she travels for a nonbusiness trip, and with or without other family members.
4. The professional athlete, who despite being from that location is at some level really a guest in his or her own community.

All four of these subsets require the person interested in sports travel security and safety to examine both the individual athlete and the athlete who is a member of a team. To understand issues of security, we must also understand the personality or social profile of the people we are protecting. Our task is to understand the challenges that they face and the social services that exist to help the athlete deal with the trials of travel, whether on the road or even at "home." There is also the interplay between the athlete and the media.

For example, some athletes might be media favorites whom the media protect. There are also other athletes whom the media attack no matter what they do, or under what circumstances. Those who fall into the second category must be "on" at all times without regard to place, or if they are on "free time" or on "business time." Athletes while traveling must be mindful that their reputation accompanies them wherever they might be. Smart athletes know that one mistake and a hostile media can destroy a reputation that took years to build.

TRAVEL AIDS FOR ATHLETES

Whether athletes are male or female, or university or professional (as will be shown in this chapter), they have certain things in common. One of the universal problems faced by all traveling athletes is the need to stay healthy and well. The traveling athlete is such a common phenomenon that whole industries have grown up around the athlete's needs. Travel, as is seen throughout this book, is hard on the body and especially hard on an athlete's body for a number of reasons. Among the challenges faced are:

1. Athletes are often bigger in physical size than other people. A famous travel refrain is that "airplanes are the revenge of little people." It is not easy, especially for a big man, to fit into a little seat, and in the case of commercial airlines, as people grow larger, the seats seem to be growing smaller!
2. Meals are often eaten at irregular times and on the run. All too often, fast food replaces proper nutrition.
3. Athletes, especially professional athletes, may change climates a number of times during a single week. When we add personal climate changes to airplane's recirculated air and germs that live everywhere from public toilets to public locker room showers, athletes are subjected to continual hygiene challenges.
4. Athletes change time zones; they often take late-night trips to between one city and another, and at times lack sleep, all of which is hard on the body.
5. Athletes, especially well-known personalities, are public figures and live in a world of stress. Stress is an important factor in breaking down the body's resistance to disease and illness.

One industry that has grown up around these challenges is the food supplement industry. Unfortunately, there is both fact and fiction surrounding this industry. As the Federal Drug Administration (FDA) does not regulate most supplements, athletes often are confused as to what is the right supplement(s), (if any) to take.

> A word of caution! No matter what the advice is or who it is from, athletes should always check first with their physician and never take anything without their physician's expressed approval. It is strongly recommended that the information below be brought to the attention of a personal physician and discussed on a one-by-one basis with the athlete's physician.

The Academy of Nutrition and Dietetics has published an article titled "Supplements and Ergogenic Aids for Athletes." Among the article's recommendations are the following.

To determine if a supplement is safe and useful, well-planned and controlled research is required. But, there are some red flags of junk science to look out for. To help protect your body and your wallet, be wary of any supplement that:

- Boasts that it is quick and easy.
- Uses testimonials from "real users" to promote its benefits.
- Claims it's right for everyone.
- States it has been used for millions of years.
- Belittles the medical or scientific community.
- Has a secret formulation.[1]

The article then goes on to give an overview of several commonly used supplements. Once again, all athletes are cautioned to do nothing without first speaking to their doctor and making sure that the particular supplement is correct for their specific personal needs. With this caveat, here are several supplements often used by athletes.

BETA-ALANINE: ACTS AS A BUFFER IN THE MUSCLE

- *Claim:* Improves high-intensity exercise performance.
- *Evidence:* Insufficient evidence to rate effectiveness.

BRANCHED-CHAIN AMINO ACIDS: LEUCINE, ISOLEUCINE, AND VALINE

- *Claim:* Delays fatigue; boosts the immune system.
- *Evidence:* Branched-chain amino acids (BCAA) can provide fuel for endurance activity, but has not been shown to delay fatigue as a result. Growing research suggests that it may play a role in supporting immune function.

CAFFEINE: MILD CENTRAL NERVOUS SYSTEM STIMULANT

- *Claim:* Helps you burn fat and protect carbohydrate stores; makes you feel energized.
- *Evidence:* Caffeine increases alertness and acts as a central nervous system stimulant. Although caffeine promotes fatty acids release, fat

---

[1] Eat Right: Academy of Nutrition and Dietetics. Denny, S. Supplements and ergogenic aids for athletes, http://www.eatright.org/resource/food/vitamins-and-supplements/dietary-supplements/supplements-and-ergogenic-aids-for-athletes; 2014 [accessed 08.04.16].

burning does not appear to increase during exercise and carbohydrate stores are not protected. It also helps with mental sharpness and decreases perceived exertion. Caffeine is considered a banned substance by the National Collegiate Athletic Association (NCAA) if too high an amount is found in urine. It also helps with mental sharpness and decreases perceived exertion.

CARNITINE: FOUND IN MUSCLES AND USED FOR ENERGY PRODUCTION

- *Claim:* Helps you burn fat.
- *Evidence:* Does not increase fat burning when taken as a supplement.

CHROMIUM PICOLINATE: A MINERAL, FOUND IN FOODS, THAT PLAYS A ROLE IN GLUCOSE UTILIZATION

- *Claim:* Weight loss aid; body composition changes.
- *Evidence:* Insufficient support for use in weight loss and body composition changes. May cause oxidative damage; therefore, not recommended.

CREATINE: FOUND IN MUSCLES AND USED FOR ENERGY PRODUCTION

- *Claim:* Increases lean body mass, increases strength and improves exercise performance, especially for high-intensity workouts.
- *Evidence:* Positive results have been found for increasing total body mass and lean mass, but some athletes have found to be nonresponders. Improves short-term intense exercise performance; aids with recovery; increases strength gains with exercise; and appears to be safe but not effective in some individuals.

MEDIUM-CHAIN TRIGLYCERIDES: FATTY ACIDS

- *Claim:* Increases endurance; promotes fat burning in long-duration exercise.
- *Evidence:* Medium-chain triglycerides (MCT) do not enhance endurance performance. May increase blood lipid levels; therefore, not recommended.

PYRUVATE: END PRODUCT OF CARBOHYDRATE METABOLISM

- *Claim:* Increases endurance and decreases body fat; promotes weight loss.
- *Evidence:* Does not enhance endurance performance and insufficient evidence for weight or fat loss. Side effects may include adverse gastrointestinal effects, such as gas and nausea.

Below is a listing of resources, which may provide additional information, although there is no resource as good as the athlete's personal physician.

- Food and Nutrition Information Center
- HFL Sport Science
- Informed-Choice
- International Olympic Committee
- National Center for Complementary and Alternative Medicine
- The National Center for Drug Free Sport, Inc.
- National Collegiate Athletic Association
- Office of Dietary Supplements
- The Academy's Sports, Cardiovascular, and Wellness Nutrition Dietetic Practice Group
- The Academy's Nutrition in Complementary Care Dietetic Practice Group[2]

UNIVERSITY ATHLETES ON TRAVEL

University athletes on travel not only have a responsibility to their team members and themselves, but also to their school and its reputation. In some ways, travel for student-athletes is harder than on many professional athletes. Student-athletes might be under 21 years of age, which means that they might find themselves, at times, in socially awkward situations. These athletes, especially if they are not part of a team, might also discover that, being under 25 years of age, they cannot rent a car and might feel themselves to be at the mercy of others. In reality, university athletes, like all students, have adult bodies, but when traveling, might find that they lack adult rights and privileges. Student-athletes, as noted in Chapter 4, are considered by their schools to be first and foremost students. The public and media, however, often do not view them as students first and athletes second. This conflict of interest

---

[2] Eat Right: Academy of Nutrition and Dietetics. Denny, S. Supplements and ergogenic aids for athletes, http://www.eatright.org/resource/food/vitamins-and-supplements/dietary-supplements/supplements-and-ergogenic-aids-for-athletes; 2014 [accessed 08.04.16].

creates a number of problems for student-athletes, not only when they are at their home universities, but especially when they travel.

Student-Athletes on Campus

To understand the problems of the student-athlete when he or she is on travel, we must first begin to understand how athletes see themselves on their home turf—that is to say, on their campus. In 2014, the NCAA under the direction of Dr. Lydia Bell, Dr. Thomas Paskus, and Christopher Radford, presented at its San Diego convention a profile of the way that student-athletes see themselves. The study, titled "NCAA Study of Student-Athlete Environments," presented an insightful sociological look into the way that student-athletes see themselves and how they perceive that those with whom they interact see them. The NCAA states that it is "...a membership-driven organization dedicated to safeguarding the well-being of student-athletes and equipping them with the skills to succeed on the playing field, in the classroom and throughout life."[3] The organization states that among its core values are the following:

- The collegiate model of athletics in which students participate as an avocation, balancing their academic, social, and athletics experiences.
- The highest levels of integrity and sportsmanship.
- The pursuit of excellence in both academics and athletics.
- The supporting role that intercollegiate athletics plays in the higher education mission and in enhancing the sense of community and strengthening the identity of member institutions.
- An inclusive culture that fosters equitable participation for student-athletes and career opportunities for coaches and administrators from diverse backgrounds.
- Respect for institutional autonomy and philosophical differences.[4]

This large and stratified sampled NCAA study[5] was a blind study (people were not specifically selected) and was administered across all three divisions to give a representative sample of different sports and different divisions. The information given below represents athletes in general and not any one particular sport or type of academic institution. Some of the major research areas included:

- How athletes perceived that professors, administrators, and other students saw them.
- Were the athletes trusting of others?

---

[3] NCAA. About the NCAA, http://www.ncaa.org/about; 2016 [accessed 08.04.16].

[4] NCAA. NCAA core values, http://www.ncaa.org/about/ncaa-core-values; 2016 [accessed 08.04.16].

[5] Bell, L., Paskus, T., Radford, D. NCAA study of student-athlete social environments, https://www.ncaa.org/sites/default/files/social_environments_draft_convention2014_0.pdf; 2014 [accessed 08.04.16].

- What was the athletes' level of engagement with fans?
- Do athletes have a sense of entitlement?
- Did they manifest off- and on-field aggression?
- Did athletic departments offer guidance vis-à-vis character and moral issues?

It should be noted that a basic rule of tourism science, taken from sociology and called the Thomas Theorem,[6] carries over into the world of athletics. Adapted to our purposes, the theorem states that although perceptions may not be true, these perceptions are always true in their consequences. How athletes feel about their role at the university tells us a great deal about who they are. Travel is not easy. Business travel, especially, can exacerbate the negative. Despite the common refrain that we can get away from our problems, in reality, we not only take our problems with us, but they often become worse when we are away from home. Thus, if we understand on-campus needs, we can do a better job of predicting athletes' needs when away from their campus environment.

It should not come as a surprise that most student-athletes reported that their closest friends tend to be, first, their teammates and coaches, and then other student-athletes and athletic personnel. Athletes spend a great amount of time at practice sessions and most human beings tend to develop bonds with people who have similar likes and interests. The English word *like* expresses this sociological phenomenon as we tend "to like" people who are "like/resemble" us. As the student-athlete merges into the greater college or university environment, she or he tends to interact first with other students, faculty, and university staff, and then locals (townies), fans, and alumni, and finally, members of the media. It should be noted that this image does not take into account family members or nonuniversity acquaintances. Understanding this friendship pattern also provides a good understanding and indication of athletes' comfort zones during travel. Thus, 93% of the male athletes and 92% of the female athletes in the study reported feeling most comfortable with their teammates. The levels of comfort with nonathlete, nonuniversity community levels drop to 63% (male) and 62% female. It is of note that male and female comfort levels parallel each other to the point that in reality, there are no statistical differences between the sexes. The high level of comfort clashes, however, with issues of trust. Athletes tend to trust their coaches (63% male and 68% female) but when asked if they trust most people, the numbers drop to 29% male and 28% female. These numbers would seem to indicate that if this lack of trust is the case on the university campus, then it is essential during travel that security professionals, such as hotel security professionals

---

[6] Thomas, W. I., Thomas, D. S. The child in America: Behavior problems and programs. New York: Knopf; 1928, p. 571–572.

or risk management professionals, gain the trust and support of the coaches and other people whom the athletes trust. If the security professional does not gain these people's trust, then she or he may have a more difficult time convincing an athlete that security decisions are made in the athlete's best interest.

In regards to feeling comfortable with other students, no student cohort (male vs. female, divided by division I, II, or III) felt that others perceived him or her to be a poor student due to the athlete's participation in a sport. The group that reported this "prejudice" the most were male Division I athletes (40%) and the group that reported the least stereotyping in this regard was women athletes at Division 3 schools. On the other hand, a majority of athletes in all categories wanted their fellow students to know that they were student-athletes, with the fewest falling into the group of male athletes from Division I schools, and the most being women athletes from Division II and III schools (66% vs. 65%). The data supported the statements in Chapter 4 that some student-athletes have a hard time with their professors. Only 21% of the men and 30% of the women believed that their professors viewed them, as student-athletes, favorably. This statistic bears out the fact that student-athletes often feel additional stress when traveling, especially when they have multiple taskmasters, coaches, and professors. Yet, in all categories, student-athletes wanted their professors to know that they participate in athletics, and in no category did they indicate strong feelings of prejudice against them due to their athletic participation. Most student-athletes feel comfortable both at their institutions of higher learning and in the local community. Few reported having to deal with negative stereotypes (20% is the highest number, those being male and from a Division 1 institution, with a low of only 7% for females at a Division III institution). However, they feel the least amount of negative stereotyping when they are with other teammates. This datum would suggest that when traveling and in new locations, athletes are more likely to travel in groups, rather than as solitary individuals.

The media do not fare poorly as far as student-athletes are concerned. Both men and women athletes believe that the media are not out to get them. Assuming that the athletes understood the questions correctly, students reported a rather positive view of the media.

Since tourism and travel are both frustrating and at times can produce a sense of "self-centeredness," how athletes see themselves regarding their sense of entitlement is a revealing measure. Most athletes, both male and female, do not see themselves as "special human beings" but rather, see themselves as needing to take their turn and undeserving of special treatment.

These self-analytical statements somewhat contradict a common statement by others that when student-athletes travel, they tend to be noisy and exhibit a sense of entitlement. It also contradicts the reports of others regarding how professional athletes see themselves and are seen by others. Much to the contrary, both men and women athletes report that they do not have trouble controlling their tempers; few believe that their friends see them as anger prone; and under 20% of the men (and only 8% of the women) report having been so angry that they wanted to break objects or smash walls. It should be noted that most student-athletes have other student-athletes as their principal friends, and that the information collected was self-reported.

Since the data indicate that student-athletes have a grouping tendency (they prefer to be with other athletes and feel safer with their friends), their willingness to intervene in another person's problems provides a great many clues as to what they will and will not do on travel. From the perspective of travel, the fact that student-athletes are community minded and willing to intervene if it means keeping people safe is an important point in understanding the student-athlete when he or she is on the road. Although student-athletes (just as in the case of most tourists) will not have to face actual violence, the fact that a majority of student-athletes would intervene so that a colleague would not do something that might prove harmful is a major plus.

Student-Athletes on Travel

In previous chapters, we have discussed some of the physical and health problems of student-athletes when traveling. These included issues of food, housing, time zone changes (jet lag), deep vein thrombosis and space limitations on airplanes, and quality of water. We also have discussed issues of transportation safety, especially when it comes to smaller or less-wealthy teams that must use vehicles with questionable safety records, such as 15-seat passenger vans.

In this chapter we look at the other side of the coin. The athlete is now at the location where the competition is to take place. Clearly, his or her first obligation is to the sport or team. Not all student-athletes, however, intend (or have the ability) to become professional. For many of these athletes, these out-of-town excursions might be their only chance to see or experience different places and cultures. These students are caught between their personal desires and their responsibilities to their team or sport. From the surveys of student-athletes on their home campuses, we have learned a great deal about their social psychology. It should not be forgotten that surveys provide us with nothing more than composite pictures. As will be seen in Chapter 10, individuals are unique, and it is impossible to fit all people into all norms. In some sense, we are all exceptions to the rule. To a great extent, safety and security concerns are less about the person who chooses to live in the norm and more about the outliers, the person who is the anomaly or the exception to the rule.

For example, the University of Indiana published the following health guidelines for athletes who travel. What is important here is less about the actual health tips and more about the fact that the university felt compelled to remind students of basic health procedures. The university notice published in 2015 reminds students to do the following:

- Prior to competition, wash your hands thoroughly and often. Keep your distance from relatives or friends when colds or flu have made a recent appearance.
- Whether you travel by air or use ground transportation, you're exposed to a lot of germs when you're away from home. Carry hand sanitizer and use it often.
- Dry air and dehydration can irritate the lining of your nose and prime you for respiratory infections. Carry saline nose sprays to cleanse and soothe irritated tissue.
- Assign an adult chaperone or a team assistant to be the keeper of an assortment of over-the-counter medications, including aspirin, acetaminophen, nonsteroidal antiinflammatories, decongestants, antacids, and antidiarrhea and cold medicines.
- When you travel internationally, check the website for Centers for Disease Control to determine what vaccines are needed before you go. Stay informed about ordinary illnesses that may be present in the area at the time of your visit.
- If you're traveling across time zones, adjust your body's internal clock a few days ahead of the trip, so you can show up rested for competition. Consult your team physician for problems with sleep. A properly timed dose of antihistamine can often help you fall into your normal sleep routine.
- Carry an adequate supply of snacks, water, and personal items such as plastic spoons.
- Keep hygiene in the forefront of everything you do. Don't share water bottles or eating utensils. Wash coolers thoroughly with warm soapy water. Clean equipment with sterile wipes. Wash athletic clothes immediately after use. If you don't have access to a washer and dryer, hand wash clothes in your hotel room. Carry a portable clothesline and hang them to dry overnight.
- Dehydration can be a huge problem for athletes, especially during air travel. A good measure of adequate hydration: you should need to go to the bathroom at least once every hour or two. Get a drink immediately after you pass through security and keep it with you on the flight. You can't always depend on flight attendants to keep liquids flowing.

- Be aware of differences in food preparation that might upset your digestive system. Keep your diet as similar to the food you eat at home to avoid stomach or intestinal issues. Pack a few snacks or energy bars to supplement meals when your preferred foods aren't available or travel delays your meals.

The memo to traveling student-athletes then goes on to remind them that:

> Even at its best, travel is yet another stress to the body. You can minimize the toll it may take on your athletic performance with a little common sense and few preventative steps. Visit IU Health Orthopedics & Sports Medicine for expert, compassionate care of all your sports medicine and healthcare needs.[7]

Numerous universities have issued policies and procedures for traveling student-athletes. These policies cover such issues as travel conduct, what to wear (attire), that the team is not to divulge its travel routes, and rules of accommodation and eating. It is assumed that in most cases, students will have (1) no free time, (2) if there is free time, they will stay with the group, and (3) that room and board will be provided for the athlete.

Often, universities default to NCAA rules and regulations. It is also clear that universities are afraid of potential lawsuits. For example, the Louisiana State University online handbook reads:

> In general, all team members must travel to and from an away event with their teammates and must stay with them at assigned lodgings. However, exceptions may be made at the discretion of the Head Coach, with the approval of the Associate Athletic Director of Compliance, the Assistant Athletic Director for Student Services and the administrator who manages the sport.
>
> If approval is granted to a team member to travel separately, the student-athlete must sign a letter of release, which is co-signed by the Head Coach and the student-athletes parent or guardian. The letter releases the Department of Athletics and the University, from any liability or risk involved in the alternate travel plans.[8]

The issues that student-athletes have while on campus do not disappear when on the road. Much to the contrary, we could argue that away games or periods of travel tend to deal with many of the same concerns, but at a more profound or intense level. For example, female athletes have often have to deal with issues of unwanted physical touching or sexual innuendos, and

---

[7] IU News Hub. 10 healthy travel hints for student athletes, http://iuhealth.org/news-hub/detail/10-healthy-travel-hints-for-student-athletes/#.V6NXyixIiUm; 2015 [accessed 08.04.16].
[8] LSU Sportsnet. Travel: teams, http://www.lsusports.net/src/data/lsu/assets/docs/ad/policymanual/pdf/601B.pdf?DB_OEM_ID=5200; 2010 [accessed 08.04.16].

at times, exploitative behavior or unwanted tension. When the athlete is on home turf, she has the added protection of her own space and knowing to whom to turn. Once she is on the road, the situation might change dramatically and become much more complicated. When a student is away from her (or potentially his) location, there is much less privacy; students tend to be housed together, often in the same location as coaches and other staff members; and independence is subsumed into "group togetherness."

Thus, student-athletes spend a great deal of time together, and, especially during travel, the potential for sexual problems becomes magnified. Problems may arise between students, between coaches and students, or between staff and students.

ISSUES OF COACHES AND STUDENTS

Perhaps part of the social problems that arise from time to time have their basis in the simple fact that it is a coach's job to physically be there for the athletes.[9] When we add that often a female athlete is coached by a male coach, the potential for new problems arises. In a report titled "Staying in Bounds,"[10] prepared for the NCAA by Deborah L. Blake and Maria Burton Nelson, the authors noted that:

> During this time, the coach scrutinizes the student-athlete's body: the shape of it, the speed of it, the skill of it. If, as a swimmer, she wears a new suit, he notices its cut, calculating its drag in the water. If, as a gymnast, she starts to fall, he catches her. If, as a runner, she develops a cramp, he may massage her foot, calf, or thigh. If her weight goes from 123 to 126, he will notice, and may ask her to lose three pounds.[11]

The report then added that:

> The nature of competitive sport provides many opportunities for escalating intimacy between a coach and an athlete. Coaching may properly involve hands-on touching. For the student-athlete who is accustomed to some physical contact with a coach, it can be difficult to discern when physical contact moves from proper sport-related touching and into a sexual realm—and even more difficult to say no.[12]

---

[9] It must be noted that in the great majority of cases, any social problem is the exception and not the rule. Most coaches conduct themselves in a highly professional manner.

[10] Brake, D., Burton Nelson, M. Staying in bounds: An NCAA model policy to prevent inappropriate relationships between student-athletes and athletics department, http://www.ncaa.org/sites/default/files/Staying+in+Bounds+Final.pdf; personnel; 2016 [accessed 08.04.16].

[11] NCAA: *Staying in Bounds*, p. 12.

[12] Ibid.

If this situation can cause sexual conflict when both the athlete and coach are on home ground, the situation may become more problematic when they are at an away event. Once again, as seen in the on-campus study, athletes tend to hold their coaches in high regard and athletes have a preference to travel in a pack. This means that they spend a great deal of time together, allowing for a potentially (sexually) explosive situation to occur. The authors then noted that especially when athletes-coaches are on the road, "The introduction of sexuality into the relationship is typically gradual, making it less likely to trigger resistance or even be noticed as a progression."[13]

There is much less literature dealing with male athletes being sexually assaulted either by females or other males. This paucity of literature could be in part because these assaults happen less often, and when some form of male assault does occur, the victim may be ashamed to report it. Male athletes might feel that they would not be taken seriously, would be publically humiliated, or that their lives might be threatened. Furthermore, few academics or writers are willing to touch the subject. Male athletes being assaulted might be considered too much of a taboo, or it might be extremely difficult to get men who are seen as "macho" to be willing to admit that they were victims of assault. For this reason, it might be impossible to determine if, or at what rate, males are assaulted. It is also possible that this phenomenon occurs so infrequently that, for the most part, it is ignored or there is a conspiracy of silence.

One author who has studied the issue seriously is Michael Scarce, whose book *Male on Male Rape: The Hidden Toll of Stigma and Shame* begins to address the problem. Although the book is not exclusively about male athletes being assaulted, it does touch on the subject and provides specific examples. It is also conceivable that the added problems that women athletes face when away from home are also the same problems that male athletes face although the scale of the problem may be less.

ISSUES OF STUDENT-ON-STUDENT PERSONAL VIOLENCE

Not all athletic competitions are single-sex competitions. There may be occasions when both sexes compete in the same event or what is more common, multiple events taking place at concurrent times. For example, men's and women's volleyball matches may be composed of two separate teams, but as the events are occurring at the same location and within close (or parallel)

---

[13] Ibid.

time proximities, the teams may travel together and even stay at the same location. There is a considerable body of literature that tends to argue that male athletes have a greater propensity to commit sexual assault (against women) than the general male population. For example, Judith Siers-Poisson on Wisconsin Public Radio has spoken about the academic work of Laura Finely, an assistant professor of sociology at Barry University (Florida) stating that "American society has made great strides in many areas in the past two decades, but unfortunately, the prevalence of rape and sexual assault perpetrated by student-athletes is one area in need of dramatic improvement."[14] In fact, Finely argues that the situation has not only improved but has worsened. She goes on to state that: "American society has made great strides in many areas in the past two decades, but unfortunately, the prevalence of rape and sexual assault perpetrated by student-athletes is one area in need of dramatic improvement."[15] Furthermore, she argues that there is a spillover effect into other forms of mistreatment of women including domestic violence. She notes that: "Sports where athletes don't seem to commit rape and sexual assault disproportionately are more individualized sports, according to Finley. These include swimming, tennis and running."[16] Finley does not specifically address the issue of travel, although she stated that not all athletic travel may be for the purposes of the sporting event. Often mixed groups of athletes travel together for reasons of team recruitment and there is no reason to believe that the same sociological principles are not at work during recruitment travel just as in athletic competition travel. The National Sexual Assault Hotline also supports these propositions. For example, its webpage states that: "Over the past 20 years it has become evident that a disproportionate number of sexual assaults on campus are committed by college athletes, often in situations involving gang rape (2 or more assailants)."[17] The reasons given for this phenomenon include:

- A sense of celebrity entitlement.
- Values placed on aggression.
- Academic leniency leading to the (false) belief that the same rules do not apply to athletes.
- Team mentality leading to group think.

The author then concludes that sports culture values, encourages, and rewards aggression. When athletes transfer this aggression to the social arena, it can

---

[14] Wisconsin Public Radio. Student-athletes commit rape, sexual assaults more often than peers, http://www.wpr.org/student-athletes-commit-rape-sexual-assaults-more-often-peers; 2014 [accessed 08.04.16].
[15] Ibid.
[16] Ibid.
[17] http://pact5.org/resources/prevention-and-readiness/athletes-and-sexual-assault/ [accessed 08.08.16].

lead to sexual conquest that exhibits the same kind of "just do it" mentality that gains them accolades on the playing field. Rutgers researcher Sarah McMahon suggests that athletes need to be coached to understand how to take "the pressure to be aggressive and dominant within the context of sports and then to turn it off—that is, how to manage the privilege and sense of entitlement that often accompany the male athlete status."[18]

On the other side of the argument is the research conducted by Ronald B. Woods. Woods noted that the relationship between higher levels of male aggression toward women and athletics is not yet settled science. He writes that:

- A three-year study showed that while male student-athletes make up 3% of the population on college campuses, they account for 19% of sexual assaults and 35% of domestic assaults on college campuses.
- Athletes commit one in three college sexual assaults.

  The general population has a conviction rate of 80% for sexual assaults, while the rate for athletes is only 38%.[19]

He, however, then goes on to state that:

Yet it is not clear that athletes are any more involved in serious crime than the general population is. In a follow-up study, Blumstein and Benedict (1999) showed that 23% of the males in cities with a population of 250,000 or more are arrested for a serious crime at some point in their life. That compares with the 21.4% of NFL football players who had been arrested for something more serious than a minor crime as reported in Benedict's earlier study (Benedict and Yaeger 1998). In fact, when Blumstein and Benedict compared NFL players with young men from similar racial backgrounds, they discovered that the arrest rates for NFL players were less than half that of the other group for crimes of domestic violence and nondomestic assaults. Is it difficult or nearly impossible to turn the violence off as soon as practice or the game is over? The majority of athletes who display violent on-field behavior don't continue their aggression off the field.[20]

---

[18] Ibid.

[19] Human Kinetics. Does on-field violent behavior lead to off-field violence? http://www.humankinetics.com/excerpts/excerpts/does-on-field-violent-behavior-lead-to-off-field-violence; 2014 [accessed 08.04.16].

[20] Ibid.

Finally, Woods questions if there may be a racist component to these statistics, noting that there are large numbers of African-American men who play football and basketball and wondering if there may be a proclivity among members of the media and academia to emphasize supposedly violent traits in these particular racial groups.

LEGAL ISSUES

There is little doubt that the United States is a litigious society; some may even argue that it is the national sport! Not only does travel involve potential felonious crimes, but also institutions that promote travel, such as universities, must always be aware of potential lawsuits. For example, the *Seattle Times* on April 14, 2014 reported that two former Boise State University students are suing the school because they say athletic officials ignored their reports of sexual assault and harassment by a star athlete.[21] The article goes on to note that: "The women contend that the male athlete openly spanked the female athletes during practices, and made sexual comments and sexual facial expressions at them, including suggestively biting his lip."[22] Lawsuits regarding sexual abuse of women athletes have blossomed around the nation. For example, in Nyack, New York, it was reported that: "Three female student-athletes on the Nyack College women's softball team are suing the school for claims stemming from multiple instances of sexual assault and sexual harassment committed by the college's former head softball coach …"[23] These types of lawsuits demonstrate that women athletes are beginning to take legal action as a means of self-protection. A study conducted by the National Coalition Against Violent Athletes (NCAVA) indicated the extent of the problem with the following statistics:

- A 3-year study shows that while male student-athletes comprise 3.3% of the population, they represent 19% of sexual assault perpetrators and 35% of domestic violence perpetrators. (Benedict/Crosset Study)
- Athletes commit one in three college sexual assaults. (Benedict/Crosset Study)
- In the 3 years before 1998, an average of 1000 charges were brought against athletes each year. (Benedict/Crosset Study)

---

[21] The Seattle Times. 2 women sue Boise State over sexual-assault response; http://www.seattletimes.com/seattle-news/2-women-sue-boise-state-over-sexual-assault-response/; 2014 [accessed 08.04.16].
[22] Ibid.
[23] Nyack Patch. 3 Nyack college athletes sue over softball coach abuse, http://patch.com/new-york/nyack/3-nyack-college-athletes-sue-over-softball-coach-abuse; 2015 [accessed 08.04.16].

- In 1995, while only 8.5% of the general population was charged with assault, 36.8% of athletes were charged with assault. (Benedict/Crosset Study)
- The general population has a conviction rate of 80%. The conviction rate of an athlete is 38%. (Benedict/Crosset Study)
- A new incident of athlete crime emerges once every two days—that does NOT include crimes that were unreported in the media. (NCAVA)
- Around 84% of the public believes that colleges should revoke the scholarship of a player convicted of a crime. (ESPN SportsZone Poll)
- Around 20% of college football recruits in the Top 25 Division I teams have criminal records.
- A college rapist will have raped seven times before being caught.[24]

Assuming that these statistics are accurate, it is extremely troubling that a rapist will have attacked on average seven times before being brought to justice.

The reader is cautioned not to see these statistics as demonstrations of causality. There may be many reasons for a particular statistic and research bias in either direction must always be considered.

MENTAL HEALTH ISSUES

As we shall see below, student-athletes, like professional athletes, also live in a world in which others often confuse physical strength with mental strength. It is not uncommon for everyone from professors to media specialists to take the position, especially true in the case of male athletes, that big/strong people do not feel emotions at the same level as other people do. All too often these people suffer from the mistaken notion that they are better capable of coping with these emotions.

Of course, such an assumption is simply not true, but the projected stereotype makes the athlete's seeking of help or displaying of emotions all the more difficult. To paraphrase a famous song by the singing quartet, *Jersey Boys*, "Big men do cry!" To add to difficulties in their seeking counseling and expressing his or her feelings in a safe environment, many athletes must face a number of cultural issues. Thus, there is not only the issue of the general campus environment and the specific subcampus culture of the student-athlete, but athletes may hail from numerous cultural backgrounds and each of these subcultures has its own set of norms, values, stereotypes, and prejudices. Mary Jo Loughran of Chatham University and Edward F. Etzel of West Virginia University writing about counseling concerns for the student-athlete have noted that:

---

[24] NCAVA. Statistics, http://www.ncava.org/statistics.html; 2016 [accessed 08.04.16].

Collegiate athletics is a world in which participants hail from every conceivable ethnic and demographic background. Student-athletes may represent the most diverse student group on campus, at least in terms of racial composition. For example, African-American students comprise 12.7 percent of the national student body (*Journal of Blacks in Higher Education*, 2007), but make up 20.6 percent, 18.1 percent, and 7.3 percent of Division I, II, and III athletes, respectively (Lapchick, 2006). Consequently, effective ethical intervention with collegiate athlete clients requires a thorough understanding of the potential interplay between cultural background and psychological variables.[25]

The authors also speak about what they call "gender oppression," a phenomenon that is different for men and women. Women athletes suffer from gender oppression when they have to deal with the role conflict inherent in femininity and sports. Many of these women suffer from the inherent conflict between these two worlds. Men, on the other hand, may be overly hesitant to admit a problem or to seek psychological assistance. This reluctance is further exacerbated by the fact that:

> For most students, seeking help is largely an anonymous act. This is not so, however, for the highly recognized student-athlete (Etzel et al., 1991). Many college student-athletes enjoy a sense of 'celebrity status' on campus and may not want to be seen at a counseling center for fear it may jeopardize their image as 'heroes' by revealing a perceived need for help (Etzel et al., 1991).

In a study of students' attitudes and expectations about sport psychology (Linder, Pillow & Reno, 1989), male and female undergraduate students rated case study athletes lower in terms of prestige if they were said to be seeking counseling services. Therefore, student-athletes may rationalize that potential benefits of seeking help are less than negative consequences of a tarnished image and, subsequently, do not seek counseling services.[26] The above quotes refer principally to student-athletes at their home campus.

Once we refer to the traveling athlete the situation becomes worse. For example, when traveling, the student-athlete most likely will share a room with his or her teammate(s). This simple fact means that she or he may be forced to hide emotions from people with whom the athlete not only shares a room but with whom the athlete may socialize and with a person who is a "business" colleague. The athlete may have no place to turn either physically or psychologically during something as simple as a lovers' quarrel to a being in

---

[25] Athletic Insight: The Online Journal of Sport Psychology. Ethical practice in a diverse world: The challenges of working with differences in the psychologicaltreatment of college student-athletes, http://www.athleticinsight.com/Vol10Iss4/Ethical.htm; 2008 [accessed 08.04.16].

[26] https://www.counseling.org/resources/library/ERIC%20Digests/2003-01.pdf [accessed 08.08.16].

a state of depression. Furthermore, the traveling student must deal with the possibility of gossip and social stigmas. Should the problem be one of sexual identity, the problem may be much more severe.

The above issues are issues for the athlete on his or her home campus. Away from home there may also be issues of trust. The athlete on travel does not know if his or her roommate(s) may not "share" the athlete's personal information with others, or even if there is a place where she or he can go to hold a private conversation. Room sharing means that, just as in any other relationship, a personal issue may become a point of contention between the players, especially if the players are not friends or are merely tolerating each other.

THE WORLD OF THE PROFESSIONAL ATHLETE

In many respects, professional athletes share the same problems as university athletes. Just as in the case of university athletes, professional athletes either travel as "single or small group" of businesspeople or as part of a larger team. Just as in the case of the student-athlete, those who are part of richer organizations have a greater number of people caring for them and are able to seek better modes of transportation and housing. Additionally, just as in the case of college athletes, there are the same accusations made, especially in regard to sexual harassment and many of the same emotional problems. On the other hand, there are differences. Professional athletes are in some ways less beholden to others who see their athletic skills as interference rather than as a job. Professional athletes do not have to worry about homework assignments or missing a test or class. Although the public may become excited about a team's wins or losses, from the athlete's perspective, she or he is at work.

This simple fact means that athletes on travel must deal with everything from how taxes are paid to issues of gun control, and from combining business with family travel to seeking to mix business with culture or relaxation. Professional athletes are first and foremost businesspeople. A CNN news article emphasized this fact, stating that:

> You might not consider baseball or basketball players to be your typical business travelers. But the realities of life for professional athletes, whose job requires them to spend months on the road each year, means they become every bit as travel hardened as the most experienced sales executive.
>
> Golf legend Gary Player claims to have racked up about 15 million miles during his career, while Major League Baseball teams play 162-games a season, traveling across the United States in the process.[27]

---

[27] CNN. Riddel, D. Ex-wives and king-size beds: On the road with sports stars, http://www.cnn.com/2012/08/11/business/sports-stars-hotels/index.html; 2012 [accessed 08.04.16].

Randy Newson, a former professional baseball player, perhaps summed up the pain–pleasure aspects of professional athletic travel by stating that:

> All in all, my experience was that road trips are actually the hardest and sometimes the most fun part of the job. Traveling with a group of guys with a common goal is an experience that not a lot of people get to have. Some of my best friends and best stories came out of road trips. Whether it be drinking in a Durham bar with three guys I used to watch playing in the World Series when I was in HS, or hanging out with a random college girl's soccer team you meet in a college town in A ball, the experiences were varied and typically a lot of fun. That said, you can't leave a road trip or take a day off. If your best friend is getting married during the season, you're typically out of luck. And no matter how nice the spread is and what level you are at, sleeping in a hotel, eating the same types of meals day in and day out, can be a grind.[28]

Here are some of the other issues that professional athletes face while on the road. Professional athletes, like any businessperson, will have mixed emotions about being in a new city. On one side of the ledger, there are new places to see and explore (assuming they have the time to see the locale); on the other side of the equation, many athletes must leave behind families and undergo stress by being absent from their spouse's or children's lives. This dilemma means that professional athletes have to find ways to balance their work and their personal lives. There is also a major difference between the professional athlete who controls his or her schedule and the team athlete for whom travel arrangements are made. The public does not always understand this need to balance work and personal live. Many in the public do not completely understand that when an athlete is "playing," he or she is "performing." In the world of professional athletes, we may call it play, but the reality is that we are dealing with work. "This realization that athletes are more than merely playing," but that their "play" is their work may be one of the reasons behind the concept of "sports psychology." Bob Tewksbury, director of player development for the Major League Baseball Players Association and former pitcher for the St. Louis Cardinals, said that "most of the 30 major-league teams have a full-time staff person or consultant available to work with players, and he's an additional resource for them."[29] Tewksbury notes the growth of the field of sports psychology and Rebecca Voelker of the American Psychological Association supports his ideas, noting that:

---

[28] Quora. What are some interesting details about team road trips as a professional athlete? https://www.quora.com/What-are-some-interesting-details-about-team-road-trips-as-a-professional-athlete; 2013 [accessed 08.04.16].

[29] Fast Company. How pro athletes strike a work-life balance, and you can, too, http://www.fastcompany.com/3032506/work-smart/how-pro-athletes-strike-a-work-life-balance-and-you-can-too; 2014 [accessed 08.04.16].

We live in a sport-loving society. Industry analyst Plunkett Research Ltd. estimates that the U.S. sports market—everything from ticket sales for major league games to equipment sold in sporting goods stores—generates $400 billion in revenue in a typical year. Our passion for sports, however, means that the athletes we cheer for face increasing pressures to achieve consistent peak performance. 'Everyone is trying to figure out how to maximize talent,' says Scott Goldman, Ph.D., director of clinical and sport psychology at the University of Arizona.[30]

This need to maximize talent means that a great deal of stress and pressure is put on players. For the professional athlete, not performing at the level demanded of him or her by both bosses and the public may mean being fired or transferred, and the transfer may create additional stress not only at work, but also within the family.

Experts in the field no longer think of peak performance as a natural by-product of practice and physical conditioning, says Brown. Now they take a broader view. Instead of focusing on playing-field victories, they recognize that athletes need the same sharp mental skills used to compete successfully in business, the arts and in the operating room.[31]

Bradley Busch, a British sports psychologist, noted the importance of the field (sports psychology) both on and off the field. When asked how top football (soccer) players maintain a clear mind and concentrate on the game, Busch notes that:

'Research proves that how you talk to yourself affects the chemistry in your brain and your hormones,' says Busch. 'Negativity and criticism is associated with the stress hormone cortisol, which reduces the ability of the frontal lobe to function effectively. Positive, energised language releases dopamine, which is linked to certainty and confidence, as well as noradrenaline and DHEA which enable your prefrontal lobe to fire more effectively. As a nutritionist advises you not to eat rubbish before matches, we advise players not to fire the wrong chemicals and hormones through their brains. In training, we ask them to practise capturing negative thoughts and converting them into positive ones. We call this 'squashing ANTs' (Automatic Negative Thoughts).'[32]

---

[30] American Psychological Association. Hot careers: Sport psychology, http://www.apa.org/gradpsych/2012/11/sport-psychology.aspx; 2012 [accessed 08.04.16].
[31] Ibid.
[32] The Telegraph. Baily, M. Mind games: how footballers use sports psychology, http://www.telegraph.co.uk/men/active/10568730/Mind-games-how-footballers-use-sports-psychology.html; 2014 [accessed 08.04.16].

Professional players may have a different set of problems in new cities from college athletes. At the university level, most games are within a conference and many students (and student teams) are fairly controlled and chaperoned. Furthermore, the potential against a university is always present, and therefore, university lawyers will do everything possible to protect the university's reputation and economic resources. The same is not true of professional athletes. Professional athletes are most likely over 21 years of age and are from both a legal and sociological perspective closer to the profile of traveling businesspeople than to that of student-athletes.

At times, teams have an extra night in a new city and team members can do as they please. It is not impossible that some "fun" activities may include sexual and libation diversions. At times these two forms of diversion may go together and although they may not be illegal (depending on what option is chosen and when and where), they also can produce the potential for a publicity nightmare. A perfect example of what ought not to happen occurred at the National Basketball Association's (NBA) 2007 all-star game where the *Las Vegas Sun* reported that:

> For the record, 403 people were arrested from Thursday to Monday night, more than half in relation to prostitution. Also for the record, there were many unconfirmed shootings. That body that fell off a Strip hotel parking ramp? Neither the Metro nor the county coroner's office had a record of that.[33]

The fact that players often spend much time in other cities, and often these are cities that promote good times means that the potential for personal disaster is ubiquitous. When temptation is combined with homesickness, the potential for crises looms large. Furthermore, new players are not used to the often-brutal professional travel schedule, or to the fact that they are expected to perform personal supervision without a "protector" watching over them.

If we add to this unhappy mixture, ingredients such as long periods away from home combined with a life based on living out of a suitcase, being to some degree constantly in the public's eyes, and irregular sleeping and eating habits, it is clear that this is a recipe that may well wear down the athlete's psyche. We must also add to this mixture problems and frustrations due to airlines delays and increasingly uncomfortable seats, and jet lag. Additionally, during the athlete's season she or he may have few personal breaks. When we combined with off-season training, and a constant battle between "what one ought" to do and what "one wants" to do, It then becomes clear that

---

[33] Las Vegas Sun. Schoenmann J. NBA weekend: When cultures clashed, http://lasvegassun.com/news/2007/feb/25/nba-weekend-when-cultures-clashed/; 2007 [accessed 08.04.16].

professional athletes have a less-romantic job experience than what many in the public believe to be true. Travel may involve periods of loneliness or frustration, and the feeling that one can never get away or be oneself. To add to this problem of "isolation with company" there is often the stereotypical belief that athletes should be as mentally strong as they are physically strong. Thus, Robert Firestone spoke of what he called the "critical inner voice," stating that:

> This internal enemy preys on any vulnerability or perceived weakness, telling us that we are nothing, that we are different, that we are less than, undeserving, or alone. When athletes start to feel separated from the world, they may start to listen to and increasingly believe the commentary of this cruel inner critic. This process may exacerbate their feelings of seclusion, depression, or grief. When a person experiences these symptoms and fails to seek the help they need, tragedy can result.[34]

This process means that it is at times hard for athletes to talk about their personal problems. If it is hard to chat about these problems at home when an athlete is in a more diverse population, it is even more difficult when the athlete is on travel and lacks nonathletic confidants with whom he or she can share problems. A *New York Times* article from October 2012, titled "With No One Looking, a Hurt Stays Hidden," noted that the larger problem is the deep-seated sports ethos that embraces a tradition of mental toughness, emotional fortitude and inner resourcefulness that makes it difficult, if not impossible, to say, "Help." The article goes on to note that in a world where strength is prized and often physical strength is confused with mental strength, athletes are placed in a very difficult position when it comes to seeking help. Once again, and despite the fact that the public in its rational moments knows that athletes, just as other famous celebrities, are merely human beings with a special talent, the rational becomes irrational and athletes are expected to be supermen and superwomen who do not share the fears and foibles of other human beings. Do we place our athletes in untenable situations when it comes to mental health? The article goes on to note that:

> 'Professional athletes are used to seeing themselves as warriors able to withstand multiple physical challenges, and have battled to get to the next level because of their mental and physical toughness,' Taylor said. 'Now they may be sidelined by an enemy they can't even see: their mind.'[35]

[34] The Huffington Post. Firestone L. The Price of Being Strong: Risks to the Mental Health of Athletes, http://www.huffingtonpost.com/lisa-firestone/athletes-mental-health_b_1647866.html; 2012 [accessed 08.04.16].

[35] The New York Times. Rhoden W. With no one looking, a hurt stays hidden, http://www.nytimes.com/2012/10/30/sports/with-no-one-looking-mental-illness-in-athletes-can-stay-hidden.html?_r=1; 2012 [accessed 08.04.16].

Loneliness and depression, jet lag, and health problems are not the only problems faced by traveling athletes. It is often forgotten that athletes are businesspeople and, as such, are subject to multiple layers of taxes. In the United States, where there may be city, state, and federal taxes, paying one's taxes to multiple tax authorities can become a daunting task. Michael Lankford of the Tax Institute addressed the problem of multiple taxing authorities, stating that:

> Possibly the biggest tax obstacle of the professional athlete is the potential requirement to file a separate state tax return for each state the taxpayer earns income. Each state has its own tax system and tax laws which may or may not require the taxpayer to file a tax return and pay that state's income tax on the income earned while in the state. On the other hand, some states do not have an income tax (Texas and Florida, for example). Each player must generally pay tax in the state the income is earned. For example, if a Missouri resident plays a game in Wisconsin and receives game day pay, the player will owe income tax to Wisconsin on the earnings from that game—while all other income is not taxed in Wisconsin.[36]

From the perspective of taxes, players are merely taxable businesspeople from whom the state can exact what it considers to be its fair share. The fact that taxes must be paid to various jurisdictions can become an accounting nightmare. Not only are there different amounts of taxes that must be paid in different states, but also there is no rational level of consistency when it comes to what can or cannot be deducted. To add to issues of deductions, there are additional problems, such as playing in a charity game. Is such an action a tax-deductible gift, a form of self-promotion, or does it fall into some other category? Since professional athletes travel to such a great extent and tax laws are often unique to each state, financial choices must be made. For example, should the professional athlete legally reside in the same state as his or her team? In large states, that decision may be more difficult but in smaller states, such as those along the northeast coast of the United States, there is a real possibility that an athlete could commute to work across state lines. Steve Piascik, a tax specialist, has noted that: "Whether they are rookies or veteran players, having a tax minimization strategy is critical for athletes. A trusted tax adviser who understands the unique financial needs of professional athletes can help them to manage and understand what expenses they can deduct, so they can take full and proper advantage of the tax code."[37] Piascik encourages

---

[36] H&R Block. Lankford M. Paying taxes in every state!? taxes & the pro-athlete, http://blogs.hrblock.com/2013/09/05/paying-taxes-in-every-state-taxes-the-pro-athlete/; 2013 [accessed 08.04.16].
[37] Sports Business Daily. Piascik S. Income tax deductions no professional athlete should overlook, http://www.sportsbusinessdaily.com/Journal/Issues/2012/04/09/Opinion/From-the-Field.aspx; 2012 [accessed 08.04.16].

athletes who travel a great deal to seek professional tax advice and advocates that these athletes discuss questions such as the following:

1. What are the best state residency options for a particular athlete?
2. Can a sports agent's fees be claimed as a tax deduction?
3. Are messages a legitimate medical business necessity?
4. Are an athlete's fines contributed to charities and if so, are they then tax deductible?
5. What personal athletic equipment is a legitimate business expense?
6. Does temporary housing make financial sense for an athlete, and is this housing then a business expense?
7. Are "rookie" expenses, such as taking teammates out to eat, a legitimate business expense?

Piasick then noted that: "To the average American taxpayer, these deductions may seem unusual. But for a professional athlete, these tax deductions are critical. Regardless of an athlete's annual salary—from millions to several thousand—deductions can lower their tax bracket and can save them plenty."[38]

OTHER MONEY ISSUES

With all the difficulties of travel, it is not unfair to ask, Why do it? Clearly, once reason has nothing to do with fame or fortune, but rather, love of the game. However, professional sports is big business, and although few will admit it, the same can be said for college sports, especially football. Coaches are paid enormous salaries, certainly much more than academics, or even university administrators. Some see sports as a parallel universe within the American university model. Others see it as an essential part of the student's character development, and still others see it as merely the "curse of edutainment." In reality, all three statements have kernels of truth, and yet none is completely accurate. Despite the protestations, the cold fact is that university athletes are willing to put up with a great deal of travel stress because they hope to get a job in professional athletics. According to Jake New, in an article published on January 27, 2015, in *Inside Higher Ed*: "According to NCAA surveys, most students will never fulfill their dream of going pro…"

He continues, writing that:

according to NCAA surveys, more than 60 percent of Division I college men's ice hockey players think it's likely they'll play professionally, but less than 1 percent ever go on to the National Hockey League. About 45 percent of Division I women's basketball players think they have a chance to play

---

[38] Ibid.

professional basketball, but only 0.9 percent of players are drafted by a Women's National Basketball Association team. (The NCAA said that it is currently procuring data on a player's chances of joining other professional leagues, such as those in Europe, but the information is not yet available.)[39]

New then goes on to show just how unrealistic most players are, writing that:

Men's hoops players are the most unrealistic. More than three-quarters of men's basketball players in Division I say they believe it is at least 'somewhat likely' they will play professionally. More than half of Division II players say the same, as do 21 percent of Division III players. Only 1.2 percent of college basketball players will be drafted by a National Basketball Association team.[40]

Yet, despite the low possibilities of realizing their dream, the lure of becoming a professional athlete, of being seen and having at least some fortune and fame, is often enough to encourage people to pay less attention to their studies, practice long hours and suffer through the travails of travel.

Student-athletes dream of making it big in the professional leagues; those who have made it, now tend to desire to reach goals of both fame and fortune. Yet, ironically, many athletes have earned a great deal of money, only to lose their winnings. This pattern is not only true in the professional team sports world, but perhaps as true, or even more likely, when it comes to the nonteam sports, such as boxing or tennis. According to Robert Pagliarini of Money Watch and quoting a *Sports Illustrated* article. "A *Sports Illustrated* article reports the grim statistics—78 percent of NFL players face bankruptcy or serious financial stress within just two years of leaving the game and 60 percent of NBA players face the same dire results in five years."[41] The author gives numerous reasons, from the "dumb jock" hypothesis to being in an anomic state. Among the reasons that he cites are the following:

1. Issues of trust.
2. Psychological profiles that are different from the average person.
3. Too focused on the here and now.
4. Pressure from friends and family to spend.
5. Crave excitement.
6. Being in another world when it comes to money.[42]

---

[39] Inside Higher Ed. New J. A long shot, https://www.insidehighered.com/news/2015/01/27/college-athletes-greatly-overestimate-their-chances-playing-professionally; 2015 [accessed 08.04.16].
[40] https://www.insidehighered.com/news/2015/01/27/college-athletes-greatly-overestimate-their-chances-playing-professionally [accessed: 08.08.16].
[41] CBS Money Watch. Pagliarini R. Why athletes go broke: The myth of the dumb jock, http://www.cbsnews.com/news/why-athletes-go-broke-the-myth-of-the-dumb-jock/; 2013 [accessed 08.04.16].
[42] http://www.cbsnews.com/news/why-athletes-go-broke-the-myth-of-the-dumb-jock/ [accessed 08.08.16].

In Linda Holmes's review of ESPN's *Broke,* she noted that:

> And then there's the extravagant spending. Cars, houses, jewelry, tailored suits ... the culture of active professional athletes, at least in the NFL and the NBA, is one that encourages excess, and because it attracts such competitive and driven people, some describe becoming competitively profligate, which is sort of a disaster, as you can imagine. Remembering a fox coat he bought and wore only a couple of times, NFL linebacker Bart Scott speaks not with mild regret but with ... well, this: 'It almost makes me look like a silverback.'[43]

It is interesting that neither author identified the strains placed on athletes who must travel for a living and connected that factor to many athletes' inability to hold onto their money, but when we consider the physical, psychological, and even spiritual strains of constantly being on the road, of potentially having a life in which loneliness is filled with both legal and illegal substances, and the search for increasing sexual gratification, it is an hypothesis that ought to be considered.

---

[43] NPR. Holmes, L. ESPN's "broke" looks at the many ways athletes lose their money, http://www.npr.org/sections/monkeysee/2012/10/02/162162226/espns-broke-looks-at-the-many-ways-athletes-lose-their-money; 2012 [accessed 08.04.16].

CHAPTER 7

Security for the Fans and Athletes with Special Needs

FAN ASSOCIATION WITH ATHLETES OR ATHLETIC TEAMS

This chapter deals with the interaction between athletes and the public at large. It then examines the issues of spectator security at stadiums and legal issues when a problem arises, with sporting event violence, and the special needs of athletes who have physical challenges and disabilities, and how these challenges impact travel.

ATHLETES AND SPECTATOR INTERACTIONS

Many athletes are public figures. This notoriety means that at least some members of the public will identify with particular athletes. As in any other cases of psychological projection, one-way, love–hate relationships are not uncommon for anyone who is in the public spotlight. The players might not know their fans by name, but the reverse is not true. Often, sports fans not only know the players' names, but also follow their professional and private lives. For example, Kirk Wakefield, in his book *Team Sports Marketing*, noted that:

> Within the realm of sports, association is when an individual reacts to events that occur to the team or player as if the events happened to him or her. ... Highly identified fans will internalize or adopt the team or player's attitudes and behaviors as their own. If you are highly identified with a team, you feel good when the team wins and bad when the team loses. You believe the team is a representation of who you are to yourself and to others. You practically feel as though you are part of the team.[1]

Wakefield continued to explore this deep, one-way fan relationship with star athletes, noting that:

> Fan passion is the degree to which one devotes one's heart, soul, mind, and time to the object of the passion. ...The team and player's performance is

---

[1] Wakeland, K. Team sports marketing. 1st ed. New York: Routledge; 2007.

Sports Travel Security. DOI: http://dx.doi.org/10.1016/B978-0-12-805099-6.00007-5

frequently on your *mind*—that is, you devote free time to thinking about how they are doing (e.g., analyzing why they are currently playing well or are in a slump). By prioritizing your *time* so that you can follow the team (attending, watching on TV, listening on the radio, checking the team website, reading the newspaper, receiving team emails, etc.), you are offering evidence that they occupy a portion of the deepest part of your soul. You feel as though you cannot live without them.[2]

The *New York Times*, in an article written about sports psychology by James C. McKinley, Jr. (August 11, 2000), also noted that:

Some researchers have found that fervent fans become so tied to their teams that they experience hormonal surges and other physiological changes while watching games, much as the athletes do. The self-esteem of some male and female fans also rises and falls with a game's outcome, with losses affecting their optimism about everything from getting a date to winning at darts, one study showed.[3]

The article goes on to quote Dr. Robert Cialdini, stating that "His [Cialdini's] later research showed that sports fans tend to claim credit for a team's success, saying 'we won' to describe a victory, but tend to distance themselves from a team's failure, saying 'they lost' when describing a defeat."[4]

In many cases, fan association might be a positive marketing tool and a harmless basis for conversation. Association with a sports team, under the proper circumstances, assures the team of a ready pool of "customers" and permits an easy entrance into marketing. Not only does this association with a particular team assure team loyalty, but it also will have a potentially positive impact for the products, brands, and services connected with the team. A team's (or an athlete's) positive association with a particular product is so powerful that producers of a wide variety of products seek out these product endorsements as an important part of their advertising campaigns. Some extremely well-known athletes might even earn more money from product endorsements than from their (already large) salaries. For example, the website *Live Sports Reviews* reports that among Ronaldo's 2015 earnings are contracts from Nike worth some £14.1 million a year, from Armani worth £1 million a year, and from KFC worth US$2 million a year.[5]

---

[2] Ibid.

[3] McKinley J. *New York Times*. Sports psychology; it isn't just a game: clues to avid rooting, http://www.nytimes.com/2000/08/11/sports/sports-psychology-it-isn-t-just-a-game-clues-to-avid-rooting.html?pagewanted=all; 2000 [accessed 08.10.16].

[4] Ibid.

[5] Live Sports Reviews. Cristiano Ronaldo endorsement contracts & earnings, http://www.livesportsreviews.com/cristiano-ronaldo-endorsement-contracts-earnings/; 2015 [accessed 08.10.16].

The carry-over from team association to a specific team hotel is obvious and, under the assumption that there will be no violence, highly positive.

Not all mental associations, however, are necessarily positive and peaceful. Sports and sports fans also have a violent side. George Orwell captured this side of sports best when he noted in his essay, "The Sporting Spirit" (1941), the following:

> Nearly all the sports practised (sic) nowadays are competitive. You play to win, and the game has little meaning unless you do your utmost to win. On the village green, where you pick up sides and no feeling of local patriotism is involved. It (sic) is possible to play simply for the fun and exercise: but as soon as the question of prestige arises, as soon as you feel that you and some larger unit will be disgraced if you lose, the most savage combative instincts are aroused. Anyone who has played even in a school football match knows this. At the international level sport is frankly mimic warfare.[6]

Later in the essay, Orwell turns to the spectators and states:

> But the significant thing is not the behaviour (sic) of the players but the attitude of the spectators: and, behind the spectators, of the nations who work themselves into furies over these absurd contests, and seriously believe—at any rate for short periods—that running, jumping and kicking a ball are tests of national virtue.[7]

Orwell then goes onto write that: "Serious sport has nothing to do with fair play. It is bound up with hatred, jealousy, boastfulness, disregard of all rules, and sadistic pleasure in violence. In other words, it is war without shooting."[8] Few people will argue that there is a violent nature to sports, although many might argue that Orwell has overstated his case.

Marketers long ago appear to have answered the question: Does team association spill over into fans relationships with products such as a hotel or hotel brand? In a study titled "The Impact of Team Association on The Hostile and Instrumental Verbal Aggression of Sport Spectators," by Daniel Wann et al., and published in the *Journal of Social Behavior & Personality*, 0886–1641, June 1, 1999, Vol. 14, Issue 2, the authors state the following:

> Highly identified fans should be particularly likely to display hostile aggression for two reasons. First, because the role of team follower is a central component of the social identity of highly identified fans (Tajfel, 1981; Tajfel &

---

[6] Orwell. G. The sporting spirit; http://www.orwell.ru/library/articles/spirit/english/e_spirit; 1945 [accessed 08.10.16].

[7] Ibid.

[8] Ibid.

Turner, 1979; Wann, Royalty, & Roberts, 1999), the team's performances are highly relevant to the fans' sense of self-worth. Consequently, the fans can become hostile when their team performs poorly because such performances have negative implications for their self- image. Second, research has revealed that highly identified fans often become aroused and anxious when watching their team in competition (Branscombe & Wann, 1992a; Wann, Schrader, & Adamson, 1998). Because arousal and anxiety are related to hostile aggression (Berkowitz, 1993; Geen, 1990), highly identified fans should be particularly likely to act in a hostile fashion.[9]

The authors reported that there is a positive correlation between a fan's team association and one's willingness to consider violence against the opposition. It should be emphasized that not all team associations lead to violence, in fact, often they do not. The issue is not team association per se, but rather the fact that the spill over effect of team association might lead to both positive marketing results for a hotel or, if handled incorrectly, to negative and potentially violent results. Thus, hotels that house well-publicized teams, or teams with high level of fan association, will need to consider how this association impacts both hotel security and the security of the team that the hotel houses.

The fact that sports produces a great deal of passion means that hotel and sports security officials must develop highly cooperative relationships to be able to protect sports figures, many of whom are idolized by their fans and demonized by others.

SOME INTERACTIONS BETWEEN FANS AND ATHLETES

Professional or university athletic events attract large crowds, and these fans are an essential element in sports tourism security. Athletics is more than the mere expenditure of energy in a competitive setting. It is also the "spectacle" of the event. We see this spectacle element in such athletic-related events as half-time performances during (American) football games, the idea of cheerleading, fan demonstrations in favor of a team, and even in parades that take place, such as Pasadena's (California) Rose Bowl parade, or a New York ticker-tape parade to celebrate a championship by a New York hometown team.

As noted, some spectator sporting events attract huge crowds, and these crowds are many times greater if we take into account the millions of fans who are "remote spectators," that is, people watching or hearing the game not in person, but via an electronic devices such as radio, television, or the

---

[9] Wann, D., Carlson, J., Schrader, M. The impact of team identification on the hostile and instrumental verbal aggression of sport spectators. *J Social Behavior & Personality* 1999; 14:2, http://web.csulb.edu/~djorgens/Wann.pdf; [accessed 08.10.16].

internet. The June 14 edition of the British journal *The Economist* provided an estimate of the number of spectators that attend major sporting events around the world. *The Economist* noted that although the most-viewed (on television or online) sporting event is soccer's (European Football) World Cup:

> It turns out that a sport which Americans call "football" is considerably larger on a per game and per season basis. The sport with the greatest number of fans, in terms of overall popularity, is North American baseball, wooing 74 m Cracker Jack eaters to the stands each year, four times more than American football.[10]

The Economist provides the following figures:

Sport and Organization	Country	Avg. Attendance Per Game	Total Spectators Per Season (in millions)	% of Total Population
US Football/NFL	US	68,401	17.3	5.5
Soccer/ Bundesliga	Germany	41,914	13.0	15.9
Soccer/Premier league	UK	35,903	13.7	24.4
Australian football/AFL	Australia	32,163	6.9	30.1
Baseball	US/ Canada	30,514	74.0	21.1
Basketball/ NBA	US/ Canada	17,721	21.3	6.1

These figures are for professional sports only. It should be noted that although more people attend a professional football game than a professional baseball game, there are many more baseball games played, so the combined total for baseball is considerably higher.[11]

Since we often manipulate statistics to say what we desire them to say, caution is always advisable. For example, a 2014 *Forbes* study argued that professional car racing attracts even more people than baseball. The *Forbes* study stated that:

> one in three adults in the United States consider themselves NASCAR fans. This totals up to about 75 million people, not including children who enjoy watching the sport. Seventeen of the top 20 most-attended sporting events in the United States are NASCAR events. The sport is popular outside the United States and North America. NASCAR events are broadcast in more than 150 countries around the world.[12]

---

[10] *The Economist*. Daily chart: The spectacle of sports, http://www.economist.com/blogs/graphicdetail/2014/06/daily-chart-2; 2014 [accessed 08.10.16].

[11] Ibid.

[12] Reference. What is the most popular spectator sport in America? https://www.reference.com/sports-active-lifestyle/popular-spectator-sport-america-f31b8e48cad5dea8; 2014 [accessed 08.10.16].

From this book's perspective, the type of sport or the sports' ranking regarding number of fans, is less important than is the fact that sports attract millions of fans. These fans are both paying customers and liabilities in need of protection. Large crowds of fans mean that athletes play in front of thousands of emotionally charged people who are both apart from the spectacle of the game and at the same time, part of the spectacle. This level of behavior is not the same across all sports or in all countries. For example, anyone who has ever attended a university or professional US football game, or a European soccer match, knows that the crowd energy level is higher than at a more subdued US baseball game. The fans' enthusiasm creates a cybernetic loop in which the greater the fan psychological participation, the greater the energy, which tends to attract more fans.

This cybernetic loop is noted when Vijay Parthasarathy wrote, in *Open Magazine*, the following: "Now it's all very well to appreciate a sport for its qualities, but fans are not unbiased creatures. They need something to root for, colorful (sic) characters to valourise (sic) and pillory; they want war without the consequences of bullets." He goes on to cite a German study that indicated that:

> There is a biological correlation between a viewer's investment in the spectacle and the quality of performance of a favourite (sic) player or team. A German study conducted during the 1994 Soccer World Cup indicated an increase of 28 per cent in testosterone levels in Brazilian fans whose side was winning, and a 27 per cent decrease in Italian fans whose side was losing. According to the study, levels of testosterone in fans rise in an anticipatory manner prior to competition. 'Winning' can further elevate levels, while "losing" can result in a decrease.[13]

When spectators are part of the event and apart from the event, athletes might interact with spectators both physically and psychologically. In a like manner, spectators interact not only with the athletes, but also with themselves. At major sporting events, there is what Urry and Larsen[14] called the "tourist gaze." Spectators come both to see and be seen, to experience the event and to be part of the event. Owing to this interplay between the gaze, the game, the spectator, and the athlete, there is often no way (or few ways) to separate spectator safety and security from athlete safety and security.

For example, in the case of baseball, part of the goal is to hit the ball "out of the park." Hitting a ball out of the park, however, means hitting it into the

[13] Parthasarathy, V. Open: The magazine. Sport as spectacle, http://www.openthemagazine.com/article/sports/sport-as-spectacle; 2011 [accessed 08.10.16].

[14] Urry, J., Larsen, J. The tourist gaze. London: SAGE; 2011.

stands. The question then becomes, is an athlete, or his or her team, responsible for a spectator who is hurt by a stray ball? Clearly, it is not the intention of the athlete to hurt his or her customer, but being at a stadium involves risk, and in a litigious society risk can easily transform into lawsuits.

There are a great many articles within the legal literature regarding fan and athlete liability. The fact that this is a topic of legal concern tells us that this is more than a mere theoretical issue. For example, Michelle Fabio, Esq. noted in an article titled "Spectator Injuries at Sporting Events"[15] that baseball teams have taken a great deal of care to protect fans. Among these protections are the following:

- The use of nets to shield the most susceptible seats from an inadvertent stray ball.
- The use of Plexiglas along first and third base lines.

Fabio also noted that baseball is not alone in fan injuries, stating that:

> Although fan injuries are most common in baseball, it isn't the only sport to deal with spectator liability. Hockey poses the danger of wild pucks flying into the stands. Injuries occur less frequently, though, because of the rink's protective glass. Even so, tragedy can occur, as when a young girl died from being hit by a puck a few years ago. Football has no obvious peril of objects sailing into the crowd. The National Football League intends to keep it that way by fining players who throw souvenir pigskins into the stands.[16]

Spectators might be subject to criminal acts, and in the case of a terrorist attack, and acts of violence, such as terrorism or a mass shooting, they are also potential victims of intentional (or more likely) unintentional harm by the athletes, and finally, with the large numbers of spectators at stadiums, from spectator-on-spectator violence. This spectator-on-spectator violence might be the result of uncontrolled enthusiasm by people rooting for the same team or because of animosity against other spectators who are fans of the opposite team. Although there is always the potential of (uncontrolled) violence between athletes, the chances of uncontrolled fan-on-fan violence are much greater. This differential is due in part to the fact that athletes are monitored and are, in the end, "businesspeople" subject to loss of work or being fined, while on the other hand, other than being arrested or even sued, most fans have much less to lose.

---

[15] Fabio, M. Legalzoom. Spectator injuries at sporting events, https://www.legalzoom.com/authors/michelle-fabio; 2009 [accessed 08.10.16].

[16] Ibid.

SPECTATOR SAFETY AT THE STADIUM

The sports industry, as any business, needs customers (called in sports "fans"). It may be due to the seeking of fans that baseball is developing ballparks, there are more parks than stadiums. The older form of stadiums might be emotionally colder, but they did protect the spectator from inadvertent harm, such in the case of baseball, of a ball landing in the stands or even the bleachers, and hurting a fan. Some of the newer ballparks are more intimate and charming, and at the same time, more dangerous. A ball can enter a stand at speeds of 120 miles an hour or more. This inadvertent interaction between players and spectators made Michelle Fabio, Esq., pose the question: "Is going to a baseball game really this dangerous?" Her answer was mixed:

> Yes and no. Make no mistake, (sic) the chance of being hit by flying baseball equipment is real. The few Major League clubs that have released statistics on spectator injuries see around 35 to 50 bumps and bruises annually. Considering there are about 80 home games each season and tens of thousands of fans per game, these numbers aren't so bad. Indeed, Major League Baseball has seen just one death from a foul ball. The death total for the history of professional baseball only reaches five.[17]

LEGAL LIABILITIES TOWARD FANS

This book is not meant to be a law book, and the reader is advised not to take the material included in this, or any section of this book, as legal advice. Readers should obtain legal advice only from qualified lawyers or legal experts. The lawyer or legal expert must be qualified law expert in the reader's specific jurisdiction and/or in the jurisdiction in which the case is to be settled. The material found below is presented to the reader in the most general of terms and is meant to provoke questions and allow the reader to interact in an intelligent manner with a certified lawyer or legal expert. Since we live in a litigious society, and often legal issues form the basis between the consumer (in this case, the fan) and the service provider (stadium or arena owner and/or player) a part of this section is dedicated to these issues. The material in this book, however, should under no circumstances be construed to be legal advice.

There is a vast body of international literature on athletic, stadium, or athletic sites, and fans' legal rights and liabilities. Multiple legal authorities have addressed the issue of the rights of spectators attending (professional) sporting events. Much of the legal literature, but not all of it, deals with issues of personal injury.

---

[17] Ibid.

We can divide this literature into at least three broad sections. First, there are those issues that deal with standard premises liability. Examples of such liability issues might be when a spectator falls due to poor maintenance, or slips on a wet surface that lacked proper attention or warning signs. In these cases, the issue concerns whether the person fell or slipped due to the fact that the surface was known to be wet and could have been better marked or isolated, or if the wetness occurred beyond the control and knowledge of the stadium's management. A second broad legal category is when someone is hurt due to a flying object, such as a ball or hockey puck, that has gone awry and hit an unintended victim. In this case, the issue is more philosophical in nature, asking the question: Does attending a sporting event imply risk, and when is the risk reasonable, or not? The third section addresses the question of violence perpetuated either by or among fans (against each other), between fans and athletes, and between athletes. The issue has been addressed as follows:

> In the first case, that of the "slip and fall," the law seems to indicate that a fan's statement that there was, in our hypothetical case, a wet bathroom floor would not be sufficient to held an owner liable. In this case, the accuser would have had to prove that the stadium or arena owner knew that the floor was wet and slippery and chose not to do anything about it. David Goguen has stated this concept succinctly when he wrote, Often, the key liability questions in slip and fall cases are: (1) Who are the potentially liable parties? and (2) Were those parties actually negligent, i.e. by causing or failing to prevent the slip and fall accident? From the perspective of the injured person, in a slip and fall insurance claim or lawsuit, another critical element is anticipating and defending against a claim that the injured person's own carelessness somehow caused or contributed to the accident.[18]

Lawsuits are not always about a fan suing a stadium, arena owner, or manager. For example, in the legal literature, we find the case of the Washington Redskins suing season ticket holders who had not paid in full due to personal financial hardship. *The Washington Post* interviewed a number of the sued fans and reported that:

> 125 season ticket holders who asked to be released from multiyear contracts and were sued by the Redskins in the past five years. *The Washington Post* interviewed about two dozen of them. Most said that they were victims of the economic downturn, having lost a job or experiencing some other financial hardship.[19]

---

[18] Goguen, D. AllLaw. What you must prove to win a slip and fall injury claim, http://www.alllaw.com/articles/nolo/personal-injury/prove-win-slip-fall-claim.html; 2015 [accessed 08.10.16].

[19] Grimaldi, J. *The Washington Post*. Washington redskins react to fans' tough luck with tough love, http://www.washingtonpost.com/wp-dyn/content/article/2009/09/02/AR2009090203887.html; 2009 [accessed 08.10.16].

LEGAL ISSUES OF SPECTATOR RISK

Numerous legal experts have written about the role of risk in litigations. For example, David F. Tavella, in his article in the *Florida Law Review*, noted that:

> Millions of people attend sporting events as spectators every year, whether professional, college, high school, little league or even pick-up games at a local park. While most of the spectators are aware that there is some risk of injury in attending these events for example, being hit by a foul ball at a baseball game—few, if any, consciously analyze all the potential risks associated with viewing a particular sporting event. However, the courts have long recognized that certain risks are inherent in sporting events, including injuries to spectators, and have often imposed limited duties on the owners of the facilities and organizers of the sporting events.[20]

When it comes to spectator injuries, a good deal of legal precedent comes from Canada. For example, Tomlinson, Nicolini, Mutcheson, Bagheri, and Nassereddine, writing from a Canadian perspective, stated that:

> When a spectator plaintiff is harmed while watching a sporting event, they will generally commence an action against the occupier of the facility where the sporting event was held. Occasionally, the action will include individual athletes, teams, or others that might be appropriate in the circumstances. The owner/operator of the facility, as "occupier," has a legislated duty to ensure that the venue where the sporting event is being held is reasonably safe. It is important to note that the standard of care is based on foreseeable risk, which is to be distinguished from an absolute guarantee of maintaining a completely risk-free environment.[21]

The authors above noted that, although these types of lawsuits are not uncommon, the courts have upheld in most cases what is called the Volenti defense. This term or defense comes from the Latin phrase: *volenti non fit injuria* (which means, *to a willing person, injury is not done*). The doctrine of Volenti is essential in the protection of sports arenas and stadiums. The basis for this doctrine is that if a person willingly chooses to place himself or herself in a position where harm might occur, then that person cannot

---

[20] Tavella, D. Florida A&M University Law Review. Duty of care to spectators at sporting events: A unified theory, http://commons.law.famu.edu/cgi/viewcontent.cgi?article=1031&context=famulawrevie w&sei-redir=1&referer=http%3A%2F%2Fwww.google.com%2Fsearch%3Fq%3D%22protecting%2Bspe ctators%2Bat%2Bbaseball%2Bgames%22%26hl%3Den%26gbv%3D2%26revid%3D915308463%26o q%3D%22; p. 181, 2010 [accessed 08.10.16].

[21] Tomlinson, J., Nicolini, A., Mutcheson, M., Bagheri, F., Nassereddine, M. McCague Borlack LLP. Occupier liability and sports fans: Legal implications and risk management strategies for sports and entertainment facilities operators, http://mccagueborlack.com/uploads/articles/118/occupiers_liability_ sports_fans.pdf?1348848736; p. 1, 2012 [accessed 08.10.16].

claim negligence. What is true in Canada is also true in the United States. The authors noted that: "Appellate Courts in the United States have held that under a Volenti defense, a person is deemed to have assumed 'those commonly appreciated risks which are inherent and arise out of the nature of the sport generally and flow from such participation.'"[22]

We might assume that the Volenti defense would stop most lawsuits of this type. This assumption, however, has not proved to be valid. Despite the fact that it is extremely hard to win such lawsuits, people still pursue them. The reasons might be because many people believe that the sports industry has large pools of resources. There is the mistaken belief that a victory in court will lead to a large settlement. There might also be some form of subliminal anger involved, especially if a member of an opposing team causes the injury. Despite warnings to the contrary, the public often does not recognize the fact that attendance at a sporting event, such as baseball or ice hockey, involves elements of risk. For example, Leigh Augustine, Esq., has written an article titled "Who Is Responsible When Spectators Are Injured While Attending Professional Sporting Events?" He noted that:

> More than 15 million Americans attend professional sporting events each year, and injuries to spectators as a result of objects leaving the field (or rink) are commonplace. One study found that during 127 National Hockey League ("NHL") games, pucks injured 122 people, 90 of which (sic) required stitches, and 57 required transport to a hospital emergency room. Another study found that injuries to Major League Baseball ("MLB") fans from foul balls occur at a rate of 35.1 injuries per million spectator visits. Contrast this with the incidence of injuries on passenger planes, defined as having 10 or more seats. In 2006 there were only four serious injuries of the total 750 million passenger enplanements and going to a professional sporting event is comparatively much more risky than air travel.[23]

Agustin agreed, stating that:

> In sum, when spectators attend professional sporting events, they assume the risks of the inherent dangers of the event, including pucks, balls, bats or tires and other objects inherent to the game which might come off the playing field and cause bodily injury of even death, unless the venue owner/operator severely deviates from their duty of care.[24]

---

[22] Ibid., p. 5.

[23] Augustine, L. University of Denver Law Review. Who is responsible when spectators are injured while attending professional sporting events? https://www.law.du.edu/documents/sports-and-entertainment-law-journal/issues/05/05-Augustine.pdf; p. 12, 2015 [accessed 08.10.16].

[24] Ibid.

In fact, there are those who believe that violence in professional sports has not only become a major problem, but also a *de rigueur* part of many athletic events. The website USLegal.com notes that:

> Violence in sports has become so prevalent that professional sports leagues and other governing bodies have had to police such activity themselves and provide punishment (i.e., penalties). In some sports, a stick or ball could conceivably be used as a deadly weapon to seriously hurt an opponent. Most spectators and prosecutors believe that such activity is just part of the game. Some scuffles and plays are so violent, however, that professional and amateur sports leagues have had to form rules that penalize players with fines and suspensions.[25]

In most cases, this violence concerns athletes attacking other athletes. It is less common for athletes to attack fans. The articles above dealt with these issues under the assumption that the fan is inadvertently hurt. In the cases above, there is no suggestion that there was any intentional desire on the part of the athlete to hurt the fan. Unfortunately, this is not always the case. Often, we tend to forget that athletes are people with a full range of emotions who work under stressful conditions and with a great deal of passion. These emotionally charged situations can result in times when athletes also lose their tempers and act in ways that are unprofessional and might even be on the borderline of legality.

Although a great deal less common than inadvertent accidental incidents involving a spectator and an athlete, there are cases when a professional athlete has lost his temper and attacked a "fan." For example, as far back as 1991, *The New York Times* reported on the case of Albert Belle, who, according to *Times*, reacted in what might be best called an unprofessional manner when he specifically attacked a heckler. The *Times* stated that "Indians outfielder Albert Belle threw a baseball at a heckler in the left-field stands at Cleveland Stadium today, hitting the man in the chest."[26] Incidents of professional athletes attacking spectators are not confined to the last century. In 2004, the National Football League (NFL) fined defensive tackle Shaun Ellis $10,000 for throwing packed snow on a Seattle Seahawks fan. Another example of an athlete losing his temper is the case of Frank Francisco, of the Texas Rangers. Francisco grew tired of being heckled and threw a chair at the heckler. To make matters worse, the chair did not hit the heckler, but accidently struck a

---

[25] US Legal. Sports violence, http://sportslaw.uslegal.com/sports-violence/; 2016 [accessed 08.10.16].

[26] The *New York Times*. Baseball; Belle hits fan with a ball, http://www.nytimes.com/1991/05/12/sports/baseball-belle-hits-fan-with-a-ball.html; 1991 [accessed 08.10.16].

woman sitting close to the heckler. In this case, the police charged Francisco with a felony and the league suspended him for 16 games.[27]

It should be noted that attacks are not a one-way street. Just as in the case of athletes attacking fans, sports security specialists must also face the problem of fans attacking athletes and other fans. For example, the Columbia Broadcasting System (CBS) news department produced an exposé on fan-on-fan violence (September 23, 2014). The study shows that:

> The NFL is trying to stop us (fans) from hurting each other. It's trying hard, and it's trying to keep it mostly a secret, because going public with this sort of thing is no way to grow your business. They are not going to say to the public: Please come to our games; we'll try to make sure you don't get beat up!

> And the NFL is trying. The NFL is failing, if only because failure is unavoidable. Put 70,000 people in a confined space, add alcohol and testosterone—estrogen, too—and multiply that by the surge of adrenaline that comes from being emotionally invested in the game, and violence is going to happen.[28]

It would be a mistake to believe that fan-on-fan violence is only an American phenomenon. This form of violence occurs throughout the world, and in multiple sports. The British Broadcasting Company (BBC) reported in its May 28, 2015, news edition that:

> The Council of Europe has urged its 47 members to step up efforts to combat spectator violence on the 30th anniversary of the Heysel disaster. The human rights body is revising a European Convention on how to deal with the problem, including safety at venues and improving cross-border policing.[29]

In 2016, the independent research center called the Social Issues Research Centre (SIRC; Oxford, England) released a study of fan-on-fan violence (often called hooliganism) at soccer games (called, in this study, "football"). The study noted that hooliganism was a pan-European problem, although the quantity and reasons for fan-on-fan violence varied across nations and cultures. The study stated that:

> Apart from Britain, the nations currently experiencing the most significant problems of football-related violence are: Italy, Germany, the Netherlands and Belgium. The available data indicate that levels of football-related violence in

---

[27] Ibid.

[28] http://www.cbssports.com/general/writer/gregg-doyel/24722022/serious-fan-violence-taking-on-life-of-its-own-can-it-be-stopped [accessed 08.11.16].

[29] BBC. Council of Europe wants more done to tackle fan violence, http://www.bbc.com/sport/football/32921120; 2015 [accessed 08.10.16].

these countries are roughly similar, with incidents occurring at around 10% of matches (or around 10% of supporters classifiable as "violent").

Austria, Sweden and Denmark also experience some problems with football-related violence, although these appear to be on a smaller scale. In Denmark, a new style of non-violent, carnivalesque fan-culture, promoted by the "*Roligans*" (a pun on "hooligans," from "rolig" meaning "peaceful"), is gaining popularity.[30]

Violence is also a part of the football (soccer) "culture" in many Latin American nations.

Returning to the United States, the same CBS report as noted above stated that:

In college football this past Saturday (September 2014), law enforcement officials had to clear out roughly 3,000 people and arrest about 15 when a common tailgating spot for Nebraska fans in Lincoln turned ugly. Violence is also known in sports such as baseball where in 2014 a Dodger fan was stabbed to death.[31]

To add to this problem, due to media competition for viewers or readers, violence is now reported more frequently and with more rapidity. Thus, the smart phone has created a situation in which:

"Incidents [that] used to happen within a venue and no one would really ever know outside of that venue, but because of smartphones and other technology, we're seeing these incidents being more publicized," says Tamara Madensen, associate professor of criminal justice at the University of Nevada Las Vegas and director of the university's crowd management resource council. "Not only can that hurt the venue, but the sports league in terms of its reputation."[32]

There are numerous reasons given for this fan-on-fan violence. For example, the SIRC noted that football (soccer) has been associated with violence since the 13th century. In fact, the game evolved from what might be considered a controlled mob scene into a more sophisticated manner for the expenditure or energy and pent-up frustrations and anger. The center noted that:

Medieval football matches involved hundreds of players, and were essentially pitched battles between the young men of rival villages and towns—often

---

[30] Social Issues Research Centre. Executive summary, http://www.sirc.org/publik/fvexec.html; 2016 [accessed 08.10.16].

[31] http://www.cbssports.com/general/writer/gregg-doyel/24722022/serious-fan-violence-taking-on-life-of-its-own-can-it-be-stopped; 2014 [accessed 08.11.16].

[32] Athletic Business. How to prevent fan violence at sporting events, http://www.athleticbusiness.com/stadium-arena-security/how-to-prevent-fan-violence-at-sporting-events.html; 2015 [accessed 08.10.16].

used as opportunities to settle old feuds, personal arguments and land disputes. Forms of "folk-football" existed in other European countries (such as the German *Knappen* and Florentine *calcio in costume*), but the roots of modern football are in these violent English rituals.[33]

From this perspective, it not only is surprising that some form of fan-on-fan violence would occur, but given the history of soccer, it might be almost expected.

The historical perspective provides insights into hooliganism (fan-on-fan violence) but does not explain the whole picture. Modern sports serve not only as an outlet for potential pent-up frustrations and even anger, but also might be ways to cover up classical racial and religious hatreds. Perhaps nowhere is this form of religious intolerance better demonstrated than in the Netherlands, where fans of the Dutch team Ajax are regularly taunted with both Nazi and other anti-Semitic taunts.

Peter McVitie's special report on Dutch anti-Semitism in football included information such as:

> An outsider can say 'you sing songs about Hamas and burning Jews, this is anti-Semitism, this has nothing to do with football.' If they want to sing something, they should at least sing about Ajax, but they don't, they only sing about the Jewish aspect, they never sing about Ajax. To hide behind the vacuum of a footballing (sic) context is flawed and naïve. It is quite easy for the tribalism in the stands to spread out into society.[34]

The Netherlands is not the only society where sports are used as a cover for the undercurrent of religious and racial bigotry. For example, the SICR report also noted that:

> Elsewhere in Europe—particularly in Germany and Austria—there are some indications that the problem might be more persistent. In one survey, 20% of German fans reported sympathies with the neo-Nazi movement. In many cases, however, Nazi symbols and slogans might be used purely to shock and provoke, without any underlying political conviction.

> The problem is certainly being taken seriously across Europe, and a number of initiatives have been launched, including the 'When Racism Wins, The Sport Loses' campaign in the Netherlands, 'No al Razzismo' in Italy, and the Europe-wide initiative, 'All Different—All Equal.'

---

[33] Social Issues Research Centre. Executive summary, http://www.sirc.org/publik/fvexec.html; 2016 [accessed 08.10.16].

[34] Goal. Special report: A video of PSV supporters singing about Jews in Manchester highlighted to foreign fans a dark but intensely debated aspect of football culture in Netherlands, http://www.goal.com/en/news/1716/champions-league/2015/12/07/18047052/if-you-dont-jump-youre-a-jew-does-dutch-football-have-an; 2015 [accessed 08.10.16].

Since both anti-Semitism and racism are first and foremost European social problems, it does not come as a surprise that these social ills will appear in situations of high stress and high emotion. Europeans tend to identify with their sports teams, and a team's success or failure might subconsciously symbolize the fan's success or failure. Furthermore, in a society in which many people live lives of anonymity, the fact that these sports "fights" or acts of violence often are televised might be a way in which people seek notoriety, even if it is negative.

DEALING WITH SPORTING EVENT VIOLENCE

Unfortunately, throughout the world, both athletes and fans are subjected to acts of nonsports-related violence. These nonsports-related acts of violence are not only prevalent in some professional sports, but also in university sports settings. It should be emphasized that most sporting events occur without violence. Violence at sporting events is often random and, with the exception of certain sports, hard to predict. Furthermore, although certain sports seem to attract the most media attention, this violent side of spectator participation might occur even at those sporting events where one might least expect it. Anyone who has ever participated or observed a children's Little League (baseball) game in the United States is often shocked, not by the children's behavior, but rather, by the behavior of their parents. Although it would be wrong to exaggerate the number of violent acts, at least some violence seems to be intertwined with some sporting events. In a 2015 article in *Gameday Security*, the journal makes the following observation:

> Violent fan behavior is a gameday tradition all sports security professionals are trying to limit or eliminate. Ray DiNunzio, the NFL's director of strategic security, has taken a variety of steps during his tenure to ensure the safest environment for the 60,000 to 80,000 fans in attendance at the nearly 300 regular and postseason football games each year. 'Any fan misbehavior is unacceptable,' DiNunzio says. 'We're doing a number of things to respond immediately when troubling things occur, while also taking proactive measures to make sure there are consequences for violations of our fan code of conduct.'[35]

There is also the psychological side of fan violence. *National Geographic*, quoting Christian End, an expert in sport fan behavior at Xavier University in Cincinnati, Ohio, stated that the environment at major sporting events allows, and even encourages, many behaviors well outside the norm: "Face

---

[35] Athletic Business. How to prevent fan violence at sporting events, http://www.athleticbusiness.com/stadium-arena-security/how-to-prevent-fan-violence-at-sporting-events.html; 2015 [accessed 08.10.16].

painting, at the stadium, is socially acceptable," the psychologist said. "People yell things that they definitely wouldn't be yelling in the boardroom or if their name and home phone number were available." [36] Furthermore:

> Many sports fans are subject to "bracket morality," noted Rick Grieve, a psychology professor at Western Kentucky University in Bowling Green. The phrase describes the idea that during a game, athletes will do things to win that they wouldn't necessarily do outside of the game.[37]

> "I think it's a shared experience or phenomena, because we can look not only at aggressive behaviors but superstitious behaviors, rituals, the things people say and chant, all those things that are supposed to help the team win."[38]

The Center for Problem-Oriented Policing (CPOP) at the University of Albany (New York) stated that stadium misbehavior is a form of violence about which police officials need to be aware:

> The spectator violence in stadiums is part of a larger set of problems related to misbehavior in sport and concert arenas. It is also related to issues of crowd control at other types of locations. However, this guide addresses only the particular harms that result from spectator-related conflicts occurring within and directly outside stadiums. Related problems not directly addressed in this guide include:

- Public intoxication;
- Ticket scalping;
- Underage drinking;
- Crowd control in open fields and along public thoroughfares;
- Student party riots;
- Littering;
- Terrorism acts;
- Loitering; and
- Traffic congestion.[39]

> The center advises looking at the characteristics of the stadium's layout, the event's characteristics, and the staff's characteristics. For example, how big is the stadium, how are seats arranged, how much noise does the stadium carry, how important (or emotionally charged) is that particular game, are there particular characteristics with the crowd's demographics that police

---

[36] Handwerk B. *National Geographic*. Sports riots: The psychology of fan mayhem, http://news.nationalgeographic.com/news/2005/06/0620_050620_sportsriots.html; 2005 [accessed 08.10.16].

[37] Ibid.

[38] Ibid.

[39] Madensen, T., Eck J. Center for Problem-Oriented Policing. The problem of spectator violence in stadiums, http://www.popcenter.org/problems/spectator_violence/; 2008 [accessed 08.10.16].

should note, is the game part of a larger series or a single match, what are the stadium's alcohol policies, how well are security personnel trained, and how well do they interact with local police? The center notes that not all law enforcement or crowd control needs to be carried out, or should be carried out, by professionals. There are a number of other people who can also maintain spectator control including the following:

- Friends or relatives at the event might have a calming effect or directly intervene to pacify the spectator if he or she gets aggressive;
- Police or private-contract security who are directly tasked with monitoring and controlling spectator behavior can respond to the incident;
- Stadium staff assigned to nonsecurity (*sic*) functions (e.g., ushers, ticket-takers, vendors) can directly intervene or call for security; and
- Other spectators can act as peacemakers or alert security if violence occurs.[40]

One of the areas that stadiums and arenas need to explore is the greater use of technology. It is important that crowd control be thought-through, not by using technologies of the past, but rather, those of the future. Once a technology is widely used, methods for undercutting that technology will soon appear. Technology, if not used wisely, can be a very expensive and useless tool. Thus, the first step in deciding on technology is to do a full evaluation of the sporting site. What are the challenges that the particular site faces? These challenges can range from evacuations due to an act of terrorism to an evacuation due to hostile weather conditions. Technology also needs data. What type of background checks can sports security specialists perform? Do they have checklists and background names, and if not, what can be done to compensate for these lacunae in the data? Crowd control also means thinking out of the box. For example, many stadiums, especially university stadiums, forbid the sale of alcoholic products. However, there is growing body of literature that argues that the sale of alcoholic products in a stadium might lower its abuse and facilitate crowd control, especially if in-stadium alcohol sales serve to reduce the number of pregame parties.

It should be emphasized that even the best and most up-to-date technology is worthless if there are not the right people supporting and using the technology. This simple fact means that there must not only be a physical presence, but a well-trained physical presence. Physical presence is more than the mere presence of guards. It also is the total team, from those selling food and drinks to those who are part of the medical or rapid response team. It might well be the person who is overlooked who will be the most important during

---

[40] Ibid.

a crisis. Sporting events, then, can be dangerous both to the players and to the spectators. There is risk in sport. This risk can never be totally eliminated, but it can be controlled.

THE NEEDS OF THE CHALLENGED ATHLETE

When most people think about sports and athletes, their assumption is that we are dealing with people who are both physically fit and possess close to perfect bodies. This model of "human beauty" was perhaps established at the first Olympic Games, held in Greece around 776 BCE. The notion of the ideal body might have preceded the original Olympics, but the connection between athlete and body has existed in the Western world for nearly 3,000 years. People who were not "whole"—who had lost a body part, or were in some way incapacitated, were "lesser" human beings. The prejudice against them is reflected in the word *invalid*, meaning "someone who is worth less." It took many millennia for the idea that a person's worth was in some manner not determined by the perfection of his or her body to change. In reality, many of the early ideas still exist in our culture. Billions of dollars are spent on all forms of body treatments and techniques to change one's body. From cosmetics, to programs to thin down or shape up, to cosmetic plastic surgery, there is a deep connection in the Western psyche between a perfect body and the ideal person.

Perhaps another aspect of the ancient Athenian ideal of the perfect body comes to us from another part of ancient Greece: Sparta. The Spartans were a war-oriented society and as such, focused on the able-bodied. This fixation on the able-bodied was so great that children who were born "less than perfect" were left to die. Catherine Shafer has noted that:

> Ancient Spartan society (around 800 BCE) involved rule of the state in deciding whether weak children were to be reared or left to die. In Sparta, children were the property of the state and not the property of the parents. The abandonment of babies who appeared disabled was a legal requirement. The community elders inspected each child immediately after birth. The child was brought before a council of the elders and, through Apgar-style tests, the council determined whether the child would live or die. If the child looked robust and healthy, it was allowed to live. If the child was "ill-born" or "ill-formed," the father was ordered to expose it. The law was aimed at developing a master race: only the strongest and brightest were to have children.[41]

---

[41] Catherine Shafer. History of how we treated people with disabilities, http://www.catherineshafer.com/history.html; 2012 [accessed 08.10.16].

Does the combination of the Athenian ideal of beauty, mixed with the Spartan idea of rejection of the weak or disabled, still dominate Western culture? Perhaps the historical analysis is less important than the realization that not all people fit into these ideals. Although, in today's culture, we do not murder people with disabilities, some of the ancient ideals regarding the ideal body continue to exist. Fortunately, humanity seems to have progressed, although all too slowly.[42] For the most part, Western civilization has come to the realization that human beings who either have been born "not whole" or who have suffered bodily injury are valid and often valuable members of society who deserve our respect.

There are disabled people in our society and, unlike Sparta or Nazi Germany, they are very much part of society. These disabilities might be due to a birth "defect" or due to an injury caused either by an accident or as a result of violence, such as during combat. No matter what the reason, it took millennia for society to begin to understand that a person does not lose his or her validity simply because of an injury. It is, again, against this background that over 2,000 years later, the Paralympics were born.

THE PARALYMPICS

There is no doubt that the world's premier athletic games are the summer and winter Olympic Games. Participating in these games are athletes who have trained for years and are at the height of their physical and mental abilities. Ever since the ancient Olympic Games, people have connected the idea of sport to the athlete who has perfected his or her body. We might call this mental image the classical Olympic ideal, and as we have noted, this ideal has penetrated into almost every aspect of much of world culture.

Life, however, does not always reflect artistic ideals. In real life, there are people born with a disability, or who have had the misfortune to have suffered a personal injury, either due to an accident or to a human-caused injury. For many people, this injury or disability created great difficulties. For some, this new status in life meant that they suffered through life; for others, life barely seemed to be worth living; and for others, the challenges simply seemed too great a burden to shoulder and suicide became a viable option. It was only in the 19th century that the first ideas that despite one's personal handicaps, life had both purpose and meaning began to take hold. This change of attitude resulted in what would become the Paralympics.

---

[42] There have been, however, moments of backtracking. For example, Germany under the Nazis was focused on what it considered to be perfect bodies and the elimination of those classified as worthless.

HISTORY OF THE PARALYMPICS

Soon after the Olympic Games end, another set of Olympians take the stage. These are the athletes who compete in the Paralympics. The history of the Paralympics perhaps reflects a new stage in human development and an appreciation of the fact that all people have value. The games are a reflection of the period of time toward the end of the 19th century that is often called, in Western history, the *fin de siècle*. It was a time of optimism and a belief in progress. Set five decades before the death camps of Hitler's Europe, this was a time when people believed not only in what was then called "progress," but also a time in which humans on the macro level might be taught to respect each other on the micro level. The realization that sport belonged not only to the full-bodied, but also to those who had suffered an injury or were born with a physical challenge, then, is typical of the ideals of this *fin de siècle* period.

The year 1888 is a red-letter year in the history of modern sports. This is the first recorded year when people began to understand that a person did not need a perfect body to gain the benefits of sporting activities. In that year, people began to see the world not through Spartan eyes, but rather through the realization that there were people with both athletic skills and physical impairments. The struggle for the physically impaired to also participate in competitive athletics, however, was not a simple process. While Berlin established sports clubs for those with hearing impairments in 1888, it would not be until 1948 that Dr. Ludwig Guttmann opened a center (in England) for those with spinal injuries, using rehabilitation sports as a healing technique. Thus, to some extent, competitive athletics for the physically impaired did not truly commence until the middle of the 20th century. Rehabilitation sports soon morphed into recreational and competitive sporting competitions. What caused this change? Although historians do not necessarily speak of the connection between World War II and competitive athletic events such as the Paralympics, it is not hard to imagine that there were thousands of young (mainly) men who had fought and were wounded in World War II. These wounded warriors now returned home. They were heroes; they were veterans, and many were not willing to be placed on society's sidelines. This new postwar period was a time of awakenings. Former colonies became independent, economies boomed, the first buds of equality movements were beginning to form, and veterans who had fought and bled for their nation wanted more than a free visit to a veterans' hospital.

The sporting world was also part of this new awakening. Sports culture became more sensitive to the needs not only of physically fit athletes, but also those with physical impairments. Owing to the World Wars, it was now almost impossible not to recognize that there was a major group of people who had been overlooked. The impaired were not lesser beings, but often heroes, and for these people, sporting activities were not only a leisure activity, but also a form of physical and psychological therapy. The physically impaired reminded the world that this resulted from their self-sacrifice; that freedom had been saved from the grips of Nazi German tyranny.

It was against this historic background that the first (summer) Paralympics were held in Rome, in 1960. The games were both needed and successful, and became the seeds from which International Organizations of Sports for the Disabled (IOSD) sprouted. This new form of sports competition was perhaps more revolutionary than most people realized decades later. Not only did the games change the way the public would view the disabled, but it meant that whole new forms of travel had to be developed to accommodate these "new" athletes.

These new games adopted the name Paralympics, derived from the Greek preposition *para*, meaning *beside or alongside*, and the word *Olympic*. Those coining the phrase hoped that the word would see these games as parallel games to the Olympics, and that the physically impaired were not less worthy than those who were not impaired. The organizers also wished to convey the idea that those who were physically impaired were no less athletes than those who had never suffered any impairment due to a birth defect or injury. As noted, the first (summer) Paralympics were held in Rome 1960. Some 400 athletes representing 23 nations participated that year, and the games were declared a success. Sweden hosted the first winter Paralympics in 1976.

The Paralympics were more than simply a revolution in competitive sports. They were also, perhaps, a revolution in travel. Anyone who travels knows that travel creates multiple challenges. As seen in earlier chapters, athletes often have more travel challenges than does the average traveler. Anyone who has ever seen a large-bodied athlete trying to place himself or herself into an airplane seat understands the saying that "travel is the revenge of little people." If travel is difficult, and even more difficult for the well-bodied athlete, then we can be certain that it offers still greater challenges to the athlete who suffers from physical handicaps.

The last 40 years, however, have not all been smooth. In fact, despite the good done by the Paralympics, the handicapped community is not totally convinced that a separate Paralympics is a good or bad thing. The debate over the value of the Paralympics more or less breaks down along the following lines.

The Positives

Those who argue for the Paralympics state that athletic participation is especially positive for those with disabilities. Such a position not only is held by many private citizens, but also by most governments and the United Nations.

For example, the United Nations' Division for Social Policy and Development Disability has a special section on its website dedicated to sports. It states that:

> Persons with disabilities often face societal barriers and disability evokes negative perceptions and discrimination in many societies. As a result of the stigma associated with disability, persons with disabilities are generally excluded from education, employment and community life which (sic) deprives them of opportunities essential to their social development, health and well-being. In some societies persons with disabilities are considered dependent and seen as incapable, thus fostering inactivity which often causes individuals with physical disabilities to experience restricted mobility beyond the cause of their disability.[43]

Those in favor argue that sports can help reduce the stigma and discrimination associated with disabilities. They note that sports can also transform community attitudes about persons with disabilities by highlighting their skills and reducing the tendency to see the disability instead of the person. They also note that these events tend to bring people together. Thus, by means of athletic participation, persons without disabilities have an opportunity to interact with persons with disabilities. This interaction creates new ways of seeing the disabled. From this perspective, sports participation forces the able-bodied to reshape "old" prejudices and assumptions about what persons with disabilities can and cannot do. These are not the only arguments for games such as the Paralympics. Others have noted that these games demonstrate to the world, and in a public forum, that the disabled can overcome their disabilities though hard work and determination. They see these games as creating inspirational education and role models for other disabled people. From their perspective, the Paralympics are more than mere competitive sport. These games, and others like them, stand as a human monument to humanity's ability to overcome obstacles and to achieve great (physical) results no matter how hard the task might be.

Others argue that the Paralympics serve dual roles. They challenge the stereotypes and at the same time, force governments, businesses such as airlines, and the general public to realize how challenging it can be to move around locations that simply do not accommodate special needs travelers. Those who favor the Paralympics have noted that:

> for individuals with a disability, the physical and societal barriers to participating in physical activity and sport are often difficult to overcome. One recent survey showed that 56% of people with a disability reported participating in no daily exercise, versus 36% of people without a disability

---

[43] United Nations. Division for Social Policy and Development Disability, https://www.un.org/development/desa/disabilities/issues/disability-and-sports.html; 2016 [accessed 08.10.16].

(Rimmer, 2004). Discrimination and lack of access in several key areas have been shown to discourage individuals with a disability from participating in physical activity and sport.[44]

Those in favor of these events tend to see the Paralympics as fostering athletic activity. They note that increased athletic activity not only tends to help to decrease the risk of obesity-related diseases, but also permits athletes, especially those who were injured as adults, to regain greater amounts of functional use of their bodies. Paralympics supporters, furthermore, point to the psychological benefits of these competitive athletic competitions, including renewed self-confidence and the augmentation of self-esteem. Furthermore, disabled people who participate in some form of athletic activity tend to be more productive members of society, earn more money, and thus add to the overall economic well-being of their locale.

The Negatives

As noted above, there also are those who argue that although the Paralympics served a worthwhile purpose in the mid-20th century, they have now outlived their *raison d'être*. Those who hold the contrary position have noted that:

> For individuals with a disability, the physical and societal barriers to participating in physical activity and sport are often difficult to overcome. One recent survey showed that 56% of people with a disability reported participating in no daily exercise, versus 36% of people without a disability (Rimmer, 2004). Discrimination and lack of access in several key areas have been shown to discourage individuals with a disability from participating in physical activity and sport.[45]

Critics of the Paralympics argue that these games are no longer good for disabled people. They state these games tend to place people in either one of two categories: the "superman" or hero category, or the "loser" category. From the perspective of the contrarians, these games do not uplift the great majority of disabled people, but rather unconsciously point to them as losers. They argue that most disabled people are neither heroes nor losers, but rather, people just like everyone else. The disabled are simply people who live a wide range of emotions, successes, and failures in a way no different from those who are able-bodied. They stress that just as most able-bodied people are not Olympic athletes, the same can be said for the disabled. The

---

[44] http://assets.sportanddev.org/downloads/62__the_paralympics___promoting_health_and_human_rights_through_sport.pdf [accessed 08.11.16].

[45] Evenbreak. The Paralympics—good or bad for disabled people? http://www.evenbreak.co.uk/blog/paralympics-good-or-bad-for-disabled-people/; 2012 [accessed 08.10.16].

"detractors" argue that everyone has some problem or handicap, that everyone is not good in something, and these games, rather than focusing on the average person who struggles day in and day out with his or her handicap, create a make-believe world in which society measures the many by the few. Detractors argue that rather than create positive role models, these games create a false narrative and serve more to cover up the real daily problems that the handicapped face. Those opposed to the Paralympics note that although the games do help the "lucky" few who participate, they also create a two-tier world for the disabled, a world composed of those few who have beaten the odds, and of the many who struggle daily, and in most cases, will be unable to beat their handicap.

The detractors also object to the fact that the Paralympics are held at a separate time from the Olympics. The fact that the games are not held in parallel with the Olympic Games, but after the Olympic Games, tends to reinforce the notion of being of lesser importance and separate from society in general. These people see this "segregation" as a subtle form of "separate but equal" in which the disabled are in the second class.

For example, in referring to the London Paralympics, Hannah Thompson wrote:

> I am faced with a problem. I love the idea of the Paralympics: there is no doubt that it promotes disability awareness and gives athletes who could not otherwise the opportunity to compete in an elite sporting environment. But is the rigid segregation between able-bodied and disabled helpful here? I am worried that having an overtly separate sporting event encourages the general public to see the Paralympics (and thus its athletes and then disabled people generally) as second-best sportspeople and second-class citizens. The first incarnation of the Paralympic Games was the International Wheelchair Games which (sic) took place at Stoke Manderville in 1948 to coincide with the 1948 London Olympics. Now that the Paralympics has become an established part of the Olympic calendar, perhaps it is time, in this year when the Olympics and the Paralympics return to Britain, to rethink their relationship with each other.[46]

Another argument against the Paralympics is that throughout the world, most sports facilities are far from inclusive when it comes to providing physical access to the handicapped. Contrarians note that most facilities do not meet the needs of the disabled. Thus, most people cannot become "athletes" even if they wanted to. For example, they point to the fact that in the real world there is a lack of specially equipped bathroom facilities, much of the

---

[46] Thompson, H. Blind Sport. The Paralympic problem, http://hannah-thompson.blogspot.com/2012/03/paralympic-problem.html; 2013 [accessed 08.10.16].

equipment is useless for people who have disabilities, and that many people cannot afford the cost of training or participating in athletics.

There is also the problem of what might best be called "thoughtlessness." For example, during India's preparation for National Paralympics international cricket matches in 2015, it was reported that:

> The athletes were put up in shabby places for the National Paralympics Games, in Ghaziabad. Many of these athletes have been put up in absolutely unhygienic conditions, with unappetizing food, and dysfunctional toilets. Many of these facilities do not even have wheel-chair ramps. Some of the athletes, who need to use walking sticks, have been put up in the second floor, or higher.[47]

Are the Paralympics, and to some extent the Olympics, a mere "talent" show that is less about capability than economics? Contrarians also point to the fact that many people who work in athletic facilities have a less-than-positive attitude toward those with handicaps. From this perspective, for every disabled athlete who gains self-confidence through sports, there are others who are psychologically injured by acts of intolerance.

It should be noted that neither those who favor these games nor those who oppose them see the games as in any way sinister or manipulative. Instead, they look at the games from different perspectives. The arguments presented by those who favor the games tend to emphasize the benefits of the games on the micro, or individual, level. Their arguments look at each person's story and see the games as helping these people reintegrate into life. On the other hand, there are those who take the opposite view, questioning the usefulness of the Paralympics from the sociomacro level. Their arguments have little to do with the individual benefits of athletic competition but rather, with the societal messages given to the greater public. We might argue that those favoring the games tend to see them from the perspective of the individual athlete. For those who take a contrary position, the message to the outside world is of greater importance.

The issues surrounding the Paralympics are far from hypothetical for the millions of handicapped or physically challenged people around the world. They also serve to underscore many of the problems faced by handicapped travelers, among whom we find handicapped athletes. As we have noted in previous chapters, travel is never easy, and in an age of violence and terrorism, seems to get harder by the day. Travel can be stressful and challenging even for the able-bodied and frequent traveler. Almost all travelers have had to face, at one time or another, flights that are canceled, and travel staffs

---

[47] Latha, M.S. Saddahaq. Disabled sports problems go deeper than what we saw in Paralympics National, https://www.saddahaq.com/disabled-sports-problems-go-deeper-that-what-we-saw-in-paralympics-nationals-says-medalwinning-swimmer-madhavi-latha; 2015 [accessed 08.10.16].

who are rushed, stressed, or overworked. Travel problems are not necessarily related to staff members. Often, members of the traveling public panic or become rude. Outbound travelers must face issues of crime, scheduling difficulties, poor or nonexistent signage, and transportation hubs that are overloaded and often highly inefficient. Inbound travelers also must deal with lost or delayed luggage, and long lines at immigration and customs. Flight delays, airport tie-ups or weather-related problems can cause people to undergo personality changes. To add to this mixture, terrorism is a constant fear reinforced by the media and, at times, government agencies.

For those who have disabilities, the difficulties of travel become even more pronounced. The disabled traveler must deal with all of the problems listed above, plus the added challenges presented due to the athlete's physical condition. The challenges the athlete shall have to face, of course, depend on the person's disability, capabilities to overcome this disability, and the location (and environment) that is the athlete's destination. For example, travel in the United States has been made easier due to the American Disabilities Act (ADA) of 1990. However, what is true for the United States or Western Europe is not necessarily true for all parts of the world. Before we turn to the disabled traveling athlete, it first behooves us to examine some of the travel problems of the disabled within the general population.

TRAVEL DIFFICULTIES FOR THE DISABLED

Disabled travelers traveling within the United States have several laws that work not only to accommodate them, but also to protect their rights. In fact, due to the aforementioned 1990 ADA, we might argue that for much of the world, the United States provides the "gold standard" of care and facilitation for the disabled traveler.

The United States takes the travel rights of the disabled so seriously that the US State Department provides a special section called the National Clearinghouse on Disability and Exchange (NCDE) to help travelers. The NCDE is also known by the acronym MIUSA (for Mobility International USA). The NCDE provides numerous free services and information. Its purpose is to provide free travel services to the disabled and to ensure that they travel with both respect and dignity. According to Cerise Roth-Vision of the US State Department, in referring to disabled travelers, "You have a right to go anywhere in the world, and there's a concept of challenge by choice, which is how much challenge are you up to."[48] It should be emphasized that

---

[48] Krystal B. *The Washington Post*. Disability travel: Resources and tips, https://www.washingtonpost.com/lifestyle/travel/disability-travel-resources-and-tips/2013/07/25/7e14d0aa-cd54-11e2-9f1a-1a7cdee20287_story.html; 2013 [accessed 08.10.16].

rights do not necessarily translate into compliance, and compliance might not be equal throughout the world, or even within the United States. Thus, it behooves the disabled traveler to remember that just because he or she has the right to travel, does not mean that all locations are equal in accommodating or respecting that right. Many nations, such as those in Western Europe, and Israel, provide disabled travelers with conditions that would meet the demands of the ADA. There are other locations in some of the less-developed or less-affluent parts of the world that provide a disabled traveler with a much more rigorous and (unfortunately) challenging experience.

The United Nations also has a division meant to help meet the travel needs of the physical challenged. The United Nations' Division for Social Policy and Development Disability (UNDSPDD) is a good resource to learn about levels of travel (and other types of) aid for those who are disabled, on a country-by-country basis.

Not all travelers have the same level of disability or need the same level of help or special services when traveling. All travelers with disabilities, however, have extra challenges. How serious these challenges are depends on numerous factors. To assess these factors, we must create a priorities scale that deals with the individual traveler's specific situation, including the following:

- The type of disability.
- The severity of the disability.
- The location from which the traveler is departing.
- The location to which the traveler is going.
- Specific local conditions, such as language issues, weather-related issues, and political or social issues.

These five broad categories encapsulate many of the problems faced by all disabled travelers. As there is no one definition of who constitutes a handicapped traveler, much of "who needs what" is left to the discretion of the traveler and service provider. Part of the reason for the lack of precision is the fact that not only are there multiple degrees of disabilities, but disabilities also come in many shapes and forms. To add to the difficulties, some disabilities are permanent, and others are merely temporary. How the disability impacts the traveler might depend on numerous factors, from the traveler's location to the weather conditions on a specific day.

The type of travel aids needed will also depend on the form and severity of the disability. For example, a seeing-eye dog might eliminate many travel difficulties for a blind person, but not all difficulties, such as posted signs. If we continue with the example of a blind traveler, we note that there is a difference between a person who is totally blind and one who is minimally sighted, yet declared legally blind. People in wheelchairs have other forms of difficulties. In some cases, where transportation terminals force travelers to go long distances between gates, or between check-in centers and gates, a person in a wheelchair might need additional personnel to help him or her navigate. In other cases, the use of ramps and easy-access doors might be sufficient to eliminate the problem. Travelers' physical impairments might range from the lack of one of the five senses (sight, hearing, taste, smell, and even, in some cases, touch) to mobility issues. Disabilities might also be due to a medical problem, a psychiatric issue, a mental challenge, or problems with speech. Since the concept of "disabilities" covers such a wide range of possibilities, it is a wise idea for a traveler to make contact with the location of departure, the transportation company, and the location of arrival prior to travel. This prenotice will allow each component to prepare for the traveler's needs or, in the case of foreign travel, permit the traveler to know what services will or will not be provided.

We should never compare the severity of a physical disability with the frustration felt by most able-bodied traveler. In the world of travel, almost all travelers to foreign lands suffer from what we might call an "anomic disability." We can define *anomie* in this context as meaning the disability that comes from being out of one's element, from being in a place where the norms are different from what the traveler knows. For example, not knowing the local language might create a momentary disability. The reason that this concept is important is that if all travelers have at least some anomic disabilities, the truly disabled traveler also finds himself or herself in an anomic state, and at the same time suffers from the additional difficulty of having to deal with this anomic state from a less than advantageous position. As shall be seen later, travel for the athletic disabled becomes even more challenging.

Below is a partial listing of travel situations and types of challenges that they provide to the disabled.

Type of Disability	Some Travel Nodules Locales	Some of the Key Issues
Mobility issues	Transportation terminals, such as airports or bus stations, lodging establishments, stairwells, restaurants, and stadiums	▪ Limited access ▪ Might not be wheelchair-friendly ▪ Issues of restroom access ▪ Inability to evacuate quickly
Sight issues	Transportation hubs, places of lodging, stairwells, restaurants, sidewalks, and corridors	▪ Inability to read signage ▪ Need for aid to arrive at location ▪ Dependency on others for transportation needs

Type of Disability	Some Travel Nodules Locales	Some of the Key Issues
Hearing disability	Transportation centers, places of lodging, telephone and communication centers	■ Might need special care in case of emergency ■ Cannot hear alarms
Intellectual disabilities	Transportation centers, places of lodging, wherever there is signage	Might need special explanations (need for information to be presented in an appropriate manner)
Speech difficulties	Foreign lands and wherever personal communication is necessary	Inability to speak might result in errors, vulnerability to crime, frustration, end even medical issues

Although some nations, or cities within nations, such as the United States, the European Union, and Israel, are more sensitive to the needs of the disabled than other nations, in reality, almost all travelers to a lesser extent have felt disabled.

INTERNATIONAL ISSUES FOR THE DISABLED TRAVELER

Nations that have suffered from political acts of violence, whether terrorism, conventional war, or internal crime wars, might have a higher percentage of the population that needs extra care. Owing to a higher percentage of the disabled in their own populations, these nations might already have the need to create physical and social situations that serve the disabled. The disabled traveler, then, will benefit from that particular nation's historic reality.

Just as the word *disabled* has a variety of meanings, so does the word *accessible* or *accessibility*. Accessibility means different things in different countries. The wise traveler, especially the disabled traveler, asks for the definition of what is considered accessible. Does the word refer to the way a building is constructed, or that there is someone there to help the disabled person?

Part of this semantic problem might also be due to language issues when traveling to foreign lands. Even when translated literally from one language to another, cultural differences might invalidate the accuracy of the translation.

In much of the world, the travel industry has not paid enough attention to travelers with special needs. Furthermore, many transportation nodules or hubs, such as airports, bus stations, train stations, and seaports, have simply not been built to accommodate travelers with special needs or disabilities, and often are nearly incapable of handling the extra stress placed on them by added security and larger ships, aircraft, or even buses. Often these are older edifices or terminals that are hard to adapt to the changing patterns of tourism.

IDEAS TO MAKE THE TRIP A BIT EASIER

There is often no way to change the geography of a locale or modify a building's architecture. For this reason, it behooves the special needs or handicapped traveler to understand the challenges before he or she begins a journey. For example, some European and Middle Eastern cities are many centuries, or even millennia, old. Their narrow alleys or cobblestones streets are quaint and picturesque, but they were not constructed to be wheelchair-accessible. Other, older, cities were built up the side of a mountain; once again, these highly photogenic locations are beautiful, but almost impossible to navigate for the disabled person.

Cobblestone streets are not only wheelchair-unfriendly, but they also pose multiple challenges for those with sensory problems, such as vision or hearing issues. Below, the reader will find a list of some of the basic considerations that any disabled traveler should consider when traveling.

1. When going to a new location, take the time to preplan routes and know where not to go. Route planning means more than knowing how to get from Point A to Point B. This also means knowing which routes present the disabled traveler with nonviable obstacles. Disabled travelers need to know if there is only one way to get from Point A to Point B, or if there are alternative routes, especially in case of an emergency.
2. Be sure to choose locations with workable accessibility that accommodate your particular handicap. For example, try to stay in the locale's most accessible areas and plan ahead should someone need to come to provide aid or in the case of any other potential evacuation.
3. If you will need a wheelchair, think not only about the potential transportation issue, but about what type of wheelchair will be needed upon arrival. Speak with hotel and attraction management prior to arrival, especially in nations that do not easily accommodate the disabled traveler. Before staying at a particular locale, the special needs traveler should always have an exit strategy prepared.
4. Always notify a place of lodging of a traveler's special needs as far in advance as possible. For example, if a traveler will need special bathroom facilities at a hotel, make sure that you review what the hotel can offer and find out as early as possible about availability. The same also holds true for people who might have dietary restrictions or special needs due to allergies. In all cases, the sooner a travel notifies a hotel, stadium, attraction, or transportation center about the situation, the easier it will be to accommodate the traveler's special needs.
5. Make sure that there is a backup plan. For example, if a flight is canceled, be sure to have a listing of places of lodging that have the

capability of dealing with your special needs. If you are using a guide or tour operator, then be sure to investigate how much experience the guide or operator has in working with people who have special needs.

INFORMATION LOCATIONS FOR HANDICAPPED TRAVELERS

Many governments and NGOs (nongovernment organizations) provide additional help for the special needs traveler. For example, in the United States, the US State Department has dedicated part of its website to traveling with disabilities. Information can be found at: <https://travel.state.gov/content/passports/en/go/disabilities.html>.

The State Department's information tends to be bland and of a common-sense variety. Its big advantage is that it centralizes many of these guiding principles in one place. The State Department's website serves as a good reminder of basic issues, and it also lists other resources that the disabled traveler might find useful. Among the more unique and valuable points that the State Department's website raises are the following:

1. The importance of being prepared when one flies. It notes that the Air Carrier Access Act and its amendments have resulted in the Department of Transportation (DOT) instituting regulations to ensure that persons with disabilities are treated without discrimination in ways consistent with the safe carriage of all passengers, domestically and internationally. Carriers are prohibited from imposing charges for providing required facilities, equipment, or services to an individual with a disability that is covered by DOT's Air Carrier Access regulations.[49]

2. The website also emphasizes the need to research medical care and costs. The State Department advises that disabled travelers carry medical alert information and a letter from their health care provider describing their medical condition, medications, potential complications, and other pertinent medical information. Note that environmental conditions at their overseas destination may contribute to specific health concerns, particularly if they are sensitive to altitude, air pollution, humidity, or other conditions.[50]

3. The State Department's site also addresses the issue of service dogs and other assistance equipment. Service dogs are an increasingly popular phenomenon, but different countries have different admittance

---

[49] US State Department, Bureau of Consular Affairs. Traveling with disabilities, https://travel.state.gov/content/passports/en/go/disabilities.html; 2016 [accessed 08.10.16].

[50] Ibid.

standards and also have different regulations as to what these dogs are, or are not, allowed to do. For this reason, it is wise, prior to arrival, to have exact written information on the arriving nation's policy regarding service dogs.

4. The website encourages disabled travelers to know national and hotel policies regarding service dogs, wheelchairs, and other machines.
5. Finally, the website reminds US travelers to know what type of electrical outlets are used in a particular location or locations, and if the voltage is 110 or 220. Having an electrical device, from a phone to an electric wheelchair, that cannot be recharged might make the device unusable.

Another valuable website for the disabled traveler belongs to the Centers for Disease Control and Prevention (CDC). This website also provides additional information and the website can be located at: <http://wwwnc.cdc.gov/travel/page/disability>.

This site is not meant to be all-inclusive, but rather, provides specific information (especially in regards to health) for disabled people who are traveling by airplane or on cruise lines. For example, the site advises people with disabilities to have a pretravel check-up, stating that:

> A travel medicine specialist can help you determine what vaccines and medications you'll need for your trip and give you advice on preventing diseases spread by insects or through food and water. If you have an immune-compromising condition or take certain medicines, you might not be able to get some vaccines, or additional vaccines might be recommended. Your travel medicine specialist can also help you arrange to receive care overseas, if you need it. Check with your insurance company to see if they will cover care received outside the United States. If not, consider buying supplemental travel health insurance.[51]

---

[51] Centers for Disease Control and Prevention. Travelers' health: Traveling with a disability, http://wwwnc.cdc.gov/travel/page/disability; 2016 [accessed 08.10.16].

CHAPTER 8

Athletes at Hotels and Sporting Venues

In this book's previous chapters we looked at sports travel security from the perspective of the individual athlete or the athletic team. In these chapters we examined issues such as health and the athlete's standing in his or her community. We also examined many of the athletes' personal and family travel issues. These issues included issues of perception and community, and the personal and group challenges with which athletes must deal while on the road. In Chapter 6, we turn the page and look at issues of hotel security and the interaction between fans and athletes and what these interactions tell us about security. We can divide these interactions into four groups. They are (1) the interaction between hotel security and athletes, (2) the interaction between fans and athletes (3) the interactions between fans and other fans at sporting events, and (4) the interaction between athletes and other athletes either at the event's venue or off the field.

Many athletes spend a great deal of time on the road, and as such are not only "warriors" on the field but they are true "road warriors." Travel-hardened athletes understand the importance of hotel facilities, hotel privacy, and hotel security. These three pillars of travel interact in the world of sports travel and sports travel security.

Hotel security intertwines with athletic travel security. In reality, there are two parallel security worlds at play. In the first "world" there is the place of lodging's responsibility to take care of all guests, and at the same time, there are "special needs" groups of guests. When the public thinks of special needs groups, the tendency is to think of those who may have a physical or mental challenge. Ironically, one of these groups is often our most physically and mentally fit, the athlete.

In both cases we may argue that hotel security, just as any other form of security, cannot be separated from risk management. Those in charge of any form of security on the macro level, such as a hotel or a stadium, must consider all aspects of risk. In the case of athletics this need to understand risk means that the security professional and/or the individual athlete must understand that a risk level is a function of both the type of risk and issues of vulnerability. The

193

Sports Travel Security. DOI: http://dx.doi.org/10.1016/B978-0-12-805099-6.00008-7

security professional must also take into account special vulnerability factors such as an athlete's (or team's) reputation, and its ability to pay for protection or other services. These additional factors may mean that a less well-known team may have lower levels of risk due to lesser amounts of publicity, but it may also not have the funding to stay in a hotel located in the safest parts of a city or to be able to hire the best trained or most expert security professionals. The security professional then will have to create a ranking of challenges and mitigating factors and determine at what point these two lines meet. Finally, the security professional must never fail to forget that none of these factors is static. What may be a major risk or threat at one point in time may cease to be (or increase being) a risk or threat at another point in time.

When examining these issues it is essential never to forget that the professional athletic industry is first and foremost a business and athletic success means that greater income and greater publicity usually translate into greater exposure to the public. Thus, as success rises so does vulnerability and risk. It goes without saying that in many ways the risk to members of a well-known team (or to a famous athlete) may be greater than to that of a lesser-known team. This statement does not mean that lesser-known athletes or teams do not face risk; it only means that their risks may be different than those of the better-known teams and/or athletes.

The lesser known team, or athlete, may have other factors that increase his or her risk level. These factors include such things as having to be at a hotel that offers less or fewer security devices or security personnel, or having to use less elegant forms of transportation such as vans that may offer lower levels of safety than do buses or air transportation.

Table 8.1, listed below, provides the risk mitigating factors for both well-known teams (or athletes) and for lesser-known teams (or athletes). There is an implied assumption here that in the sports business reputation and income are positively correlated.

Table 8.1 Team Mitigating Factors

	Well-known	Lesser-known
Given best nutrition	Yes	No
Illness prone	Yes	Yes
Magnet for terrorists	Yes	No, unless part of collateral damage
Magnet for publicity seekers/paparazzi	Yes	No
Venue vulnerability	Yes	Yes
Poor hotel security	No	Yes
Poor transportation system	No	Yes

The table above shows that with the change of public perception, risk does not terminate but it rather mutates. For example, in the world of sport, as a person or team's wealth increase, so does the publicity that surrounds that person. In this case, the transformation from a less known and poorer athlete (or team) to a better-known and richer athlete (or team) does not lessen the risk, but merely transforms itself into different or new forms of risk.

To better understand this principle let us create a hypothetical example. Let us assume that a poorly known athlete can only afford to stay at a lower ranked place of lodging. This place of lodging offers fewer security amenities than its more costly competition. This lack of protection may make the athlete more prone to robbery and room invasion, but he or she will be less prone to problems due to high level of publicity. As we shall see later in the chapter, notoriety also increases the passions surrounding the athlete or the athletic team. In this case, few if any of the people interested in a particular sport may even know that this athlete is staying at this particular hotel or that s/he is a competitor in this particular sport. From the perspective of notoriety, the athlete's risk is minimal. However, due to the place of lodging's location or its inability to provide security, our hypothetical athlete may face a greater risk from random acts of violence. Contrasting our poorer athlete with the better-known and (most probably) wealthier athlete we see that the wealthier athlete may have a lower risk of being exposed to random violence, but a greater chance of being the "victim" of publicity seekers, paparazzi, or those seeking to do him or her harm for a specific reason.

HOTELS AND HOTEL SECURITY FOR ATHLETES

The lodging sector plays a vital role within the visitor industry. Contrary to what many people believe this essential component provides the visitor with more than just a place to spend the night. Places of lodging, be they hotels or even motels, are often symbols of the community and fairly, or unfairly, are part of the way that people judge a community. As previously noted, athletes are first and foremost human beings with similar needs, wants, likes, and dislikes as those of other hotel guests. How the place of lodging presents itself to its guest in both appearance and customer service is a good indication of the way that it will also treat its athletic guests.

All lodging establishments, whether they be luxury hotels or simple cottages, have a basic moral duty to provide all their guests with a clean, safe, and secure environment. As customers, athletes, who are away from home, first fall under the category of "guest." As such they, like any other guests, are entitled to the hotel's facilities and customer service, and if available, the hotel's security officer's protection.

It is no secret that hospitality industry executives, like those in other sectors, have traditionally viewed security investments as an unwanted cost and they have held the mistaken belief that security adds nothing to their bottom line. Nonetheless, hotel security has greatly improved over the last few years and hotel management is becoming increasingly aware of the fact that a lack of good security can destroy a hotel's business. Nevertheless, unless there is a "paradigm shift" in the way hotels around the world conceive of and manage this new and rapidly evolving threat, the lives of their guests and employees, their reputations, and indeed their long-term economic viability will be at risk, especially in periods of violence such as that of the 21st-century's early decades.

Surveys indicate that guests rank security as one of their major priorities when choosing a place of lodging. This need for security is especially true in the world of athletics.

The old belief that security will frighten customers has now receded into history and many hotels now understand that security is also a marketing tool. This improvement in hotels' attitude toward security does not mean that all hotel managers understand this principle or live by it. It would be incorrect to state that there are not still some risk management and security department members who report being underappreciated and overworked. Despite the improvements, it is wise for the athlete (or his/her security specialist) to question hotel management about the way that it handles its security and safety issues. Furthermore, in an age of terrorism the better-known hotels may be at a higher risk. Terrorists have come to realize that hotels offer a great potential to inflict not only casualties but also garner publicity. If a terrorist can harm major personalities then the target becomes even more enticing. From this perspective it may pay athletes and athletic teams not to publicize their on-the-road location.

As noted throughout this book, a basic principle of all security is that, despite the public's demand for total security and its belief that it can be obtained, total and complete travel (tourism) security or safety (or any other form of security) does not exist. To live is to live with risk. Sports security specialists can work hard to limit the risk but they cannot eliminate all forms or risk. Despite this reality, there is much that an athlete or sports travel security manager (STSM) can do to determine if a particular hotel's security and safety features are adequate, given budgetary constraints for his or her team or athlete.

The way the hotels treats its athletes, and those either in the athlete's party or who are covering the athlete in the media, can help to build or destroy a city's reputation. Hotels need to satisfy the needs of the socioeconomic group(s) drawn by a locale's attractions and reputation and at the same time provide additional protection to well-known athletes. Visitors will not return to a location if their lodging needs are not satisfied. Both athletes and the media covering the athletic competition may feel vulnerable and/or alone. As the hotel staff may be some of the only locals that these people meet, the staff's actions and attitude may well determine the impression that an athlete has of that locale. Building a good rapport with the visiting athletes and the media is more than good customer service, it is brilliant marketing! Before we look at hotel security for athletes and enter into the narrower confines of sports hotel security, it behooves us to first review some of the basic principles of good lodging security and customer service. Below the reader will find some of the basics of hotel security that apply to all guests, including athletes.

Below is a partial list of some basic questions athletes or their security team may wish to consider. In Appendix 1 the reader will find a full listing of security questions that athletes or athletic security providers may wish to ask hotel management.

It behooves athletes, just as in the case of other travelers, to remember that places with high levels of good customer service tend to be the safest businesses. Hotel service personnel are more than mere employees at a place of lodging, they function as hosts and hostesses and as such many guests ask them for information about their community. Hotel personnel often serve as a front line tourist information resource. Not only do the guests benefit, but the entire local community also benefits when the hotel's staff takes an active role in promoting attractions. On the other hand, hotels and other places of lodging that do not provide good customer service send out a message that they do not care about the well-being of their guests. Furthermore, hotels in which employees tend to care about their guests tend to be safer. Creating a caring environment is the first step toward good guest safety and security procedures.

ISSUE OF PRIVACY

The Sochi Olympics is an example that a person may not enjoy full privacy even in his or her hotel room. For example, a Russian government official commenting on lack of showers at the Sochi 2014 Olympic Games noted that: "We have surveillance video from the hotels that shows people turn on the shower, direct the nozzle at the wall and then leave the room for the whole day," Kozak said, before an aide yanked him away.[1] Of course, such an admission indicates that there were spy cameras inside of the Olympians' showers.

---

[1] http://dailycaller.com/2014/02/06/red-stare-russians-spy-on-media-with-cameras-installed-in-sochi-showers/

Not all hotel privacy issues may have to do with a government of hotel choosing to invade another person's privacy. The Erin Andrews case, in which another person spied on her, is an example that celebrities such as star athlete's (or in this case, a TV personality star covering athletes) are open to privacy invasions even in the sanctity of their hotel (bed)room. The *New York Times* reported that: "A jury awarded the Fox sportscaster Erin Andrews $55 million in her lawsuit against a Nashville hotel and a stalker after she was secretly videotaped naked several times in 2008, according to reports."[2]

The question here is not only one of invasion of privacy but points to the fact that sports and those involved in sports are often the objects of curiosity or of intense emotions (passions) that lead to their dehumanization.

The fact that there are hidden cameras in hotel rooms either for reasons of spying, or for profit, has caused athletic guests to wonder what they can do to protect themselves, especially in the case of high profile people such as well-known athletes. These hidden cameras are often located in such places in other forms of electronic equipment. If trying to determine if there is a hidden camera in an athlete's room (or any guest's room), it is a good idea to examine such apparatuses as: telephones, lamps, alarm or wall clocks, and lamps. Hidden cameras do not need to be placed in electronic equipment and may also be hidden in such places as showers, mirrors, or tissue boxes. The other thing to consider is places where there are small openings such as peepholes, USB ports, or keyholes. It is essential, however, not to become paranoid. Most "paparazzi" type people will not go to the trouble or expense to seek cameras that are so small as to not be visible to the naked eye. The question for the athlete and his or her agent is how much is privacy worth and what amount of expense needs to be spent in order to assure absolute privacy.

Closely related, as to being invasive, is the issue of credit card fraud, and identity theft. Credit card fraud does not compromise a person's personal space or body, but rather it invades a person's financial privacy. Athletes, just as other travelers, may use hotel internet services. Often alongside the hotel's internet service there may be other services that are of an undetermined origin. For example, thieves may steal credit card information by posing as waiters or waitresses (at times these people seek employment for the purpose of credit card theft). It is almost impossible to tell or determine when these thefts have occurred. Below are some ideas that will help:

1. Make sure that the credit card company knows your travel plans prior to travel.

---

[2] http://www.nytimes.com/2016/03/08/business/media/erin-andrews-awarded-55-million-in-lawsuit-over-nude-video-at-hotel.html?_r=0

2. Never give a credit card number to the front desk via the phone. If a person at the front desk asks for this number then go directly to the front desk, ask why they are calling for this information and obtain the person's name that is seeking it.

3. Do not use public Wi-Fi to make purchases via the internet. Public Wi-Fi is great way to read news on line, play games or exchange greetings. Do not use public Wi-Fi if the information you are not prepared to have another unauthorized person read it.

4. Do not take too many multiple credit cards on the road. Having too many credit cards at one time means that most people lose control over which card they have used for particular purchases. It is best to have no more than two credit cards, one for purchases and a back-up card just in case something goes wrong.

A well-trained and caring hotel[3] staff should be able help to coordinate an athlete's hotel experience with the out-of-town visitor experience. Athletes when playing a match or game out of town are both tourists and business people. Just as in the case of other tourists, athletes may have special needs. If the hotel cannot provide basic customer services, this inability or unwillingness may well be an indication that the property will not be able to provide the additional or special services needed by sports teams or traveling athletes. This simple fact means that athletes, just like other guests, need and appreciate lodging information given in a clear and precise manner. Lodging information should not just be about what services the accommodation has to offer but also having information that connects their place of lodging with the community at large. Athletes are also travelers and they too want to know what the community has to offer and which attractions transform a mere work experience into a life experience.

It is essential to coordinate location with the athlete's (or team's) particular needs. Just as in the case of real estate, location means a great deal in the world of security. We cannot separate the security found inside of a property from the environment in which it is located. All visitors need to know if the hotel's management is aware of any crime issues that are found in close proximity to the location in which a particular hotel is situated. For example, if a hotel is located in an area that attracts the homeless, then that fact must be taken into the overall hotel security plan. The first rule of hotel security is that it does not stop at the hotel's doorsteps.

It is essential to remember that at their core, athletes are business travelers, and well-managed hotels cannot only become attractions in and of

---

[3] The word "hotel" throughout this book refers to any place of lodging. It does not only refer only to what tourism industry specialists define as a "hotel."

themselves, but they can also play a role in an athlete's successful work. Hotels with a reputation for good service and fair prices often draw visitors from far and wide. What is true for other visitors is especially true of athletes. These men and women often arrive at (or depart from) the hotel at odd hours. Upon arrival (or departure) they are often tired and hungry and know that the next day will be strenuous. Just as is the case with most other tourists, athletes, especially those who are not part of a team sport that can provide a travel manager, appreciate extras such as a free breakfast, morning newspapers, or a small goodbye souvenir. These extra touches can leave a long lasting positive impression, not only for the hotel, but also for the entire community.

Staff Security

Since staff members may be people who are interested in sports or sports personalities it is essential that a professional attitude be inculcated into each hotel employee. Furthermore, it is important that background checks be conducted on those people who have access to the athlete or his/her personal space and belongings. It is highly unlikely that an athlete, or his/her agent, will know the background of the hotel's employees. Instead, it assumed that a hotel management and its security staff have taken the time to do complete background investigations. Unfortunately, the world of "reality" is different from the world of "should." Too often administrators hire people without even a simple background clearance. This error can cause a great many problems as lodging staff members may have free access to guests' rooms and often know when the guests are in their rooms or not. Security personnel complain that they often have no knowledge as to which employees have access to a guest's room and whether staff members have a previous criminal past. Good tourism security requires that employees be regularly tested for substance abuse. The security staff should also possess a copy of each employee's photo ID and know which keys each employee has in his or her possession.

Despite the fact that hotel security should not be a matter of concern for any guest and especially for guests, such as athletes, who may provoke greater passion, it is incumbent for the athlete or his/her agent to ask questions. For example, a good question to ask is: other than safety fliers or notices, how else does the hotel communicate with its guests about safety and security? Most guests, including traveling athletes, neither read the safety material that has been provided for them nor, in times of emergency, will they remember what it says. Written material exists to make hotel administrators and its lawyers feel better, but rarely do guests read it or remember what is in it. Did the hotel design a hotel safety and security program in such a way as to assume that guests will know what to do during real-life situations when panic often overrides common sense?

Another good question to pose is if the hotel's management staff are trained in tourism security protection. Tourism security is different from standard security. Tourism security emphasizes everything from foreign language communication to heightened anxiety due to a guest's inability to communicate with loved ones during a crisis. Do all staff members receive regular security updates? In the modern world not all athletes on a team are from the same language grouping or have the same nationality. Even if the athlete speaks the local language during an emergency he or she may lose this skill. Is there a plan to handle guests who speak a foreign language? All too often a security plan fails simply because the staff cannot communicate with the people it is serving. Whenever possible, make sure that the hotel staff is certified in its security knowledge by an independent agency.

Athletes and their agents must also ask how well the hotel protects its guests' property. It is the responsibility of the hotel's security specialists to protect not only guests but also their property. There is a close connection between personal protection and property protection. Athletes are travelers and travelers all too often tend to be negligent when it comes to personal property. Phones are often lost, keys are left in doors, and articles of clothing get confused. Does the place of lodging do more than merely run a lost and found? Travelers then are often careless. They may, due to lack of care or as part of anomic behavior, cause all sorts of damage, from fires to permitting unwanted locals to enter onto the hotel's premises. Often, travelers simply forget to care for furniture, appliances, or equipment. A hotel's security must also take into account the needs of the cleaning staff and hotel engineers and seek to assure that site environment is both attractive and as secure/safe as possible.

A traveling athlete of his/her staff need to know if the hotel's security agents are trained in the customs and cultural habits of their guests. For example, some cultures tend to be more trusting than others and different cultures may have distinct patterns for what is acceptable or not for female guests. It is essential that management develop security patterns that meet not only the local environment but also meet the cultural needs of the hotel's guests. Both travel professionals and the athletes should be mindful of the fact that athletes are part of two cultures: their athletic culture and their national or ethnic culture. This duality means that a place of lodging that does not understand cultural diversity may not be able to afford the athlete the protection that s/he is seeking.

Athletes, or their handlers, should know if there is a relationship between the hotel's security staff and the local police department and what type of relationship it is. The local police department should not have to learn where things are in a hotel after an incident has taken place. Regular "walk-throughs" and meetings are essential and these relationships, in the case of athletes, should be both fluid and expandable.

Unfortunately, few athletes or their agents know about the state of a place of lodging's safety and security equipment. Hotel security equipment does not only indicate the level of investment a hotel has made in protecting its guests, but also its level of willingness to provide extra services to its guests. Although not all properties need metal detectors, hotels that have large numbers of VIP athletes may well need these devices. There also are a number of less obvious security modifications to existing buildings that can be made. Among these include the changing of windows to bulletproof glasses in those areas that overlook sensitive or dangerous places, the alarming of exit doors, the upgrading of key systems, and tight controls on who may dispense keys.

Traveling athletes and their travel staff need to ask about a hotel's key return policy, make sure that security cameras create "safe areas" where guests can go in case they feel uncomfortable on an elevator, and do regular reviews of equipment to decide what changes may be necessary. Since we live in an age of terrorism, all places of lodging need to have an overall inspection system. For example, the security staff needs to consider all vulnerabilities such as where trash is disposed and how well-lit are the parking lots.

Athletes, or STS managers, who travel need to ask and to know what types of security upgrades the hotel has and/or is planning to have. For example, does the security staff check the hotel's air ventilation system? Are all fire exits clear of debris? Can the hotel staff evacuate guests from the hotel's roof in case of a terrorist attack or fire? Is there helicopter access? Does the staff have a back-up plan in case there is an electrical blackout and does that plan include an evacuation plan that can be put into action should there be no electricity? Such an evacuation plan means that the hotel can evacuate guests without benefit of lights and communicate with guests even if there is no loudspeaker system. Furthermore, in a world of international tourism, and an age of violence and terrorism, hotels need to have a plan to communicate with their foreign language-speaking guests. Giving orders in a language that is not understood is not useful.

If the athlete(s) is (are) eating at the hotel, then the athletic travel staff should spend the time interviewing the hotel's cooking and wait-staff. Although all means possible should be used in such a background check, nothing is revealing when it comes to security as personal interviews. Personal inspections mean much more than simply asking if the staff refrigerates the mayonnaise. It means making sure that food preparation areas are secure and that there is a close working relationship between a security department and a food preparation service. Food safety in today's world also means that background checks need to be performed on all employees who handle food and that these employees are trained in pertinent aspects of hotel security.

The questions listed above are basic questions that not only should athletes, or their security team ask, but all guests at a place of lodging. Hotels are not only potential targets of attacks but, as has been seen around the world, have had a history of being attacked. For example, in an article published by the New York Fusion Center on threats against hotels, the center notes that:

"Since 2002 there have been 18 major terrorist attacks against hotels world-wide; a major attack is defined as an attack resulting in at least 10 casualties. During this time period there were no attacks against US homeland-based hotels. Groups with a connection to al-Qaeda carried out all but one of these major attacks."[4] The article notes that: "An attack on a hotel within New York State or the US would most likely follow the current predominant worldwide trend and utilize explosives or small arms." Although the New York fusion center notes that: "the likelihood of an al-Qaeda-inspired lone actor successfully attacking a hotel is low. However, lone actors in the US have shown an interest in targeting hotels previously. For example, Farooque Ahmed, arrested in April 2010, conducted pre-operational surveillance at a Washington, D.C. area hotel." The center also notes that: "The most common tactic used against hotels is a vehicle-borne improvised explosive device (VBIED), accounting for 43% of the attacks analyzed in this report".[5]

The above material examines hotels in general and security's role in them. As noted previously, athletes, despite their physical strength, still form a special needs group. As a special needs group athletes must consider, or their security team must consider, a number of issues that do not necessarily impact the general public. For example, professional athletes are often both celebrities and business travelers. Even in the case of university athletes, although technically not business travelers, the sociological profile is often the same and they must be treated as if they were professionals. In fact, there are situations in which a university athlete may be more vulnerable than a professional athlete. Furthermore, athletics tend to create high levels of emotions among their fans. These emotions may be of a love–hate relationship where the athlete is adored by some (his or her fans) and hated by others. Just as in the case of all human beings, athletes make mistakes and these mistakes often provoke a great deal of emotion on the part of some fans. For example, the *Los Angeles Times* (July 3, 1994) reported on the death of Colombian football star Andres Escobar: stating: "Angry at Colombia's elimination from the World Cup soccer tournament, gunmen Saturday shot and killed Andres Escobar, the player who accidentally scored a goal against his own side in a match with the United States and helped seal the team's fate, police said."[6]

---

[4] https://publicintelligence.net/nysic-hotel-attacks/

[5] Ibid.

[6] http://articles.latimes.com/1994-07-03/news/mn-11578_1_world-cup

In this chapter, and until this point, we have discussed basic issues of security. These involve property protection, and freedom from harassment and from criminal acts, be they misdemeanors or felonies. Unfortunately, we live in an age of terrorism and as noted, hotels may be magnets for terrorism attacks. Athletes are not only prone to all sorts of terrorist attacks but due to their high profile may be more vulnerable than the public at large. Below are some of the newer forms of terrorist attacks that can make a hotel's guests vulnerable.

Security In An Age of Asymmetrical Warfare

Chemical, Biological, Radiological, Nuclear, and Explosives attacks are known by the acronym CBRNE. These CBRNE attacks may come in the form of a large explosion that occurs outside of the hotel but impacts the hotel, in the form of a smaller explosion at one of the hotel's sensitive areas such as its air ventilation or air conditioning system, or at a location where people gather such as a hotel lobby or banquet hall. It should be remembered that most hotels are not for the athlete's exclusive use, thus the attack may occur at another location within the hotel and the athlete's death or injury may be nothing more than collateral damage. His or her death may also be intentional as a way of winning publicity or notoriety for a terrorist group's cause. People dealing with athletic security should be aware of the potential for radiological attacks, for bombings and arson, and for other potential chemical or biological attacks. For example, a deadly carbon monoxide attack would be silent, colorless, and odorless. Since many hotels have large amounts of glass surfaces, security personnel must also be aware of secondary damage due to flying or broken glass. The issue, from the perspective of this book, is to understand what counter-measures a hotel may take, and to encourage hotel leadership to continue to have up-to-date[7] equipment and paraphernalia that will permit a smooth and safe evacuation process to occur.

The multiple terrorist attacks that have occurred in diverse places such as Bagdad, Iraq; Brussels, Belgium; London, England; Ankara and Istanbul, Turkey; Munich, Germany; Nice and Paris, France; Orlando, Florida; San Bernardino, California; Sharm El-Sheikh, Egypt, and Tel Aviv, Israel along with ongoing threats throughout the United States, South America, and Europe ought to be a warning to the sports travelers that travelers are entering into a new and dangerous age of travel. People who are concerned with the safety and security of athletes while traveling in an age of terrorism need to consider some of the following principles:

- Athletes and their security staff need to obtain their information from various sources rather than be dependent on single sources.

---

[7] Owing to the constantly changing nature of security threats, no book can provide the most up-to-date information. The material provided here is from 2016 and security experts should use this material as an example for what may lie ahead.

- Athletes and their security staff should learn if there exists a terrorism task force in the location that they are about to visit and connect with such a task force.
- Athletes and their security staff must ask as many questions as possible so as to obtain insights and information.
- Athletes and their security staff law should know members of law enforcement and private security professionals by name and have met with them.
- Athletes and their security staff should realize that acts of terrorism can happen in any community.
- Athletes and their security staff should learn if people in the locale to be visited have brought together industry, civil engineers, architects, and CBRNE experts to find best solutions for future asymmetric-proof hotels.
- Athletes and their security staff can never forget that the best crisis management is good risk management!

VENUE SECURITY

To a great extent, an athlete is only as secure as the venue in which he or she works. The word "work" is used very much on purpose. For both the professional athlete and the university athlete, sports are much more than mere "play," sports are a major form of "entertainment" for millions of people, but are serious work for those participating in the sport. Thus, what the theater or studio is for the actor, the sports venue is for the athlete. The public tends to see these sports venues, be they stadiums, arenas, or playing fields as far from the world of crime and terrorism. Unfortunately, the 20th and 21st centuries have not exempted the world of athletics from the world of violence. Al-Qaeda recognizes sports stadiums as a potential place of violence. Thus, in fact, "Al-Qaeda's Manual of Afghan Jihad proposed football stadiums as a possible terrorist attack site, and the FBI issued an alert in July [2002] warning that people with links to terrorist groups were downloading stadium images" (Estell, 2002, p. 8).

In March 2005, the Department of Homeland Security identified a dozen possible strikes it viewed most devastating, "including detonation of a nuclear device bombing of a sports arena."[8] In 2015, the world witnessed the attempted attack at France's national stadium and on March 26, 2016

---

[8] http://www.thesmartjournal.com/venues.pdf

the United States news network, CNN, reported that at least 25 people were killed at an Iraqi football (soccer) stadium. The CNN report stated that: "A man wearing a suicide belt walked into an Iraqi soccer stadium Friday and blew himself up—killing at least 25 people and wounding 90 more, security officials said. A crowd had gathered for a ceremony to mark a championship for a popular local soccer team when the bomb exploded, the head of the Babil province security committee, Baydhan al Hamdani, told CNN."[9]

Athletes work in multiple types of venue. The venue's risks may depend on anything from building construction quality, to ease of ingress and egress, to fire codes, to weather conditions, to political situations. Additionally, most stadiums were not built for an age of violence. Terrorists are aware that with over 1,000 sports stadiums in the United States it would be cost prohibited to rebuild many of these stadiums. Furthermore, many of these stadiums and arenas are used throughout the year, not only for athletic events but also for other forms of entertainment such as concerts. The US Department of Homeland Security recommends that stadium managers know what it calls the seven signs of terrorism. These seven signs of terrorist activity are: (1) surveillance, (2) elicitation, (3) tests of security, (4) acquiring supplies, (5) suspicious persons, (6) trial run, and (7) deploying assets.[10]

To a great extent an athlete is only as secure as his or her venue. This means that venue security is much broader than mere stadium security; it encompasses everything from a golf course to the open ocean, from a beach to a basketball court, from an Olympic stadium to an ice skating rink or baseball field. The following chart provides some of the world's major sports and where these sports are often played.

UNDERSTANDING RISK AND CRISIS MANAGEMENT

There is no one definition of risk, emergency and crisis management. Often, however, the best way to avoid an emergency and a crisis is through good risk management. The chart below demonstrates some of the differences between risk and crisis management. It is important to emphasize that risk management is always pro-active. Crisis management and emergency management are always reactive. Note following important points concerning tourism risk management.

---

[9] http://www.cnn.com/2016/03/25/middleeast/iraq-violence/index.html

[10] http://www.thesmartjournal.com/venues.pdf

Some Basic Differences between Crisis and Risk Management

	Risk	Crisis
Surety of occurrence	Uses a statistical system	Is a known event
Goal of management	To stop the event prior to occurrence	To minimize the damage one event has taken place
Type of preparation to combat risk that can be used	Probability studies Knowledge of past events Tracking systems Learning from others	Specific information such as medical, psychological, or crime. Developing a "what if" attitude
Training needed	Assume crises and find ways to prevent them	Assume crises and practice reacting to them
Reactive or Proactive	Proactive	Reactive
Types of victim	Anyone, maybe visitor or staff	Can be visitors, staff members, or site
Publicity	The goal is to create nonpublicity by preventing an event from occurring	Goal is to limit the public relations damage that may occur
Some common problems	Poor building maintenance Poor food quality Poor lighting Fear of terrorism Fear of a crime occurring	Rude visitor Sick person Robbery Threat to staff Bomb scare Lack of language skills
Statistical accuracy	Often very low, in many cases the travel and tourism industry does everything possible to hide the information	Often very low, in many cases the travel and tourism industry does everything possible to hide the information
Length of negative effects on the local tourism industry	In most cases, it is short term	Can be long term
Recovery strategies	■ New marketing plans, assumes short-term memory of traveling public ■ Probability ideals: "Odds are it will not happen to you" ■ Hide information as best as one can	■ Showing of compassion ■ Need to admit the situation and demonstrate control ■ Higher levels of observed security ■ Highly trained (in tourism, terrorism, and customer service) personnel

Once a risk has occurred it is no longer a risk but a crisis. This change means that the theoretical has now become the actual and potential action must become real action. Once again the risk manager, now crisis manager, must determine not only the state of the crisis, but also must put a plan of action into place. In the world of risk management, there is time to weigh options and to determine which policy may work best. In the world of crisis management, although flexibility is essential, time becomes of the essence and the worst thing is for over-analysis to set in and thus causing crisis paralysis. Crisis managers must have a system in place that allows them to be notified at all times. In most cases, the crisis manager will be present at the sports venue, but crises can occur either before or after an athletic event, in which case the crisis manager may not be on the scene and a method must be determined how s/he or his or her subordinate can be notified. Since crises do not take vacations or provide us with our optimal times, crisis teams must have a way of being contacted at all times.

Crisis teams must also be aware of different types of potential crisis that may occur at a sporting event. Some of these are:

- An active shooter
- A fire
- An act of terrorism
- A bomb and therefore crowd panic
- An employee who becomes a crisis producer
- An attack on a sports figure by a fellow competitor or fan
- A riot at the event venue or in the host community by fans or by locals.

In a world of chaotic and random violence even smaller venues are open both to safety and security concerns. Safety issues from fire to weather-related panics can occur at any size sporting event. From a security perspective there is always the question of a single terrorist to someone seeking to create havoc for personal or psychological reasons. In all cases during the rescue period the motive is less important than the preparedness to deal with the issue and to save as many lives as possible. That means that all sporting venues must be prepared to save both the athletes and the spectators. Plans must include:

- Evacuation preparation and practice
- Plans for triage
- Lists of back-up personnel
- Awareness of where additional equipment is located
- Regular equipment checks
- Practice so that first responders do not panic
- Training, training and more training
- Listings of who is at charge and what backup plans there are in case those in charge are incapacitated during the emergency.

Some Typical Summer Sports		
Sport	**Venue or location**	**Indoor or outdoor**
Archery	Playing field	
Badminton	Floor/field	Indoor or outdoor
Beach volleyball	Beach	Outdoor
Boxing	Boxing ring	Indoor
Fencing	On matts	Indoor
Equestrian sports	Track	Indoor or Outdoor
Football (US)	Stadium	In Stadium/outdoor
Football (soccer)	Stadium	In Stadium/outdoor
Golf	Outdoor course	
Gymnastics	Matt or arena	Indoor
Hockey	Arena	Indoor or outdoor
Judo	Arena	Indoor
Mountain biking	Trail	Outdoor
Shooting	Range	Indoor or outdoor
Swimming	Natation center	Indoor or outdoor
Tennis	Court	Outdoor
Trampoline	Arena	Indoor
Wrestling	Arena	Indoor

Here are some typical winter sports:

Some Typical Winter Sports		
Sport	**Venue or location**	**Indoor or outdoor**
Alpine skiing	Ski slopes	Outdoor
Bobsleighing	Track	Outdoor
Cross-country skiing	Track	Outdoor
Ice hockey	Arena	Indoor or outdoor
Ice skating (all forms)	Rink	Indoor or outdoor
Snowboarding	Track	Outdoor

The above charts demonstrate large differences between the types of sports and the security issues that are involved. Some of the major spectator sports, such as cricket, both US football and European football (soccer), and base-ball attract large crowds. On the other hand, bobsleighing or archery occurs at venues in which relatively large numbers of people will not be able to gather, and as such their security issues are of a much different nature. We may then say that the person developing security for the venue has to take into account such threat issues as:

- Amount of passion that surrounds a game, match, team, or player
- Amount of publicity that a game, match or player generates
- Expected size of crowd
- Issues of crowd ingress and egress
- Location of event
- Number of spectators who will be in attendance at the event
- Political issues surrounding or connected to the event
- Traffic conditions to/from venue
- Weather conditions (especially if held outdoors).

Additionally, many stadiums have never had a full security assessment. Among the liabilities that can be used as a detriment to both athletes and fans are:

- Lack of emergency and evacuation plans specific to sport venue
- Inadequate searching of venue prior to event
- Inadequate searches of fans and belongings
- Concessions not properly secured
- Dangerous chemicals stored inside the sport venue
- No accountability for vendors and their vehicles
- Inadequate staff training in security awareness and lack of ability to respond to WMD (Weapons of Mass Destruction) attacks.

The list provided above is only a partial list of some of the considerations that must be considered prior to, during, and after an event, and to potential hazards that can be used to cause personal and physical death and destruction. Although all events have major differences as seen in the above list, they all have certain similarities. These similarities coalesce around the issue of risk management. Scholars, management, and security practitioners often spend a great deal of time and effort on crisis management. Needless to say, the best way to manage a crisis is to avoid it with good risk management. No one can assure one hundred percent safety, but the lower the risk the higher the probability that a crisis can be avoided. Risk management is not easy. One of the reasons that risk managers are often frustrated is that when nothing happens, administrators and management tend to question the risk manager's necessity. When a risk does self-actualize and a crisis occurs, then management questions what it received for the time, money, and/or its effort invested.

Although risk is often time-and-place sensitive, there are certain basic principles that touch upon all forms of risk management including sports and athlete risk management. Since risk management is both essential and difficult to demonstrate, risk managers have developed a number of these assumptions, which they then adapt to a specific circumstance, person, time, or location. It should be noted that when we are speaking about personal risk management rather than place or group risk management, we often call this personalized form, "personal protection." In reality, it is risk management on the micro rather than on the macro level. Below are many of the working assumptions that risk managers use in dealing with both sports and athlete risk management.

CRITICAL RISK MANAGEMENT STEPS

Even before considering what form of protection (risk management or mitigation) may be needed the risk management professional needs to consider:

- How many people will be at the sporting event?
- Is there one or are there multiple venues for this athletic event?
- What are the event's demographics and its demographic make-up?
- Is the sporting event's location a normal event-staging place or used only from time to time?
- How well publicized is this sporting event?
- What groups might attempt to politicize this event?
- The circumstances under which the event will occur: from outside to stadium politics, from changeable weather conditions to traffic flows, and potential road failures.

Once the risk manager or risk management team has ascertained these basic "facts" they need to begin to address the following issues:

- There is no event that is 100% free of risk. No matter how good the risk manager or his/her team may be the issue of risk is still ubiquitous. Perhaps the biggest error that risk manager can commit is to believe that s/he has considered all possible risks. Thus, risk management is statistical in nature. The good risk manager must create a stochastic model and realize that s/he is playing a probability game.
- Travel involves risk. Although there is risk at being at home, to be away from home is to accept as normative the fact that as we enter un- or less familiar surroundings risk grows.
- Sporting events are attended by choice. In the case of the public, a sporting event is a volunteeristic activity. Thus, the lack of security is not only a physical risk but also an economic and psychological risk. No sports fan ever has to attend a sporting event. Attendance is purely by choice.
- Most athletes and fans assume that management has taken the necessary precautions to assure their safety and security.

- As world tension mounts, the demand for risk management increases. Sporting events are no longer worlds that are immune to acts of terrorism or to other forms of criminal or violent political activity.
- In sports risk management, as in tourism, there is no distinction between security and safety; the two are intertwined. In both cases the person has a negative experience that may well impact future attendance. Many fans will be highly unsophisticated when it comes to issues of a locale's geography or of a stadium's evacuation routes.
- Different types of athletes and fans require different forms of risk management.
- Often as efficiency increases so does the risk. Efficiency does not mean enhanced security. It may streamline the process so much that simple risks may be overlooked. Technology does not necessarily mean less insecurity but rather a change in the form of insecurities and risk. A simple rule of thumb is that if the risk generator understands high tech, then low tech may trump high tech, but if the risk generator does not understand high tech then high tech may mitigate low tech. In a like manner, as we script our security and try to rationalize it, we discover that irrationalities often become part of the event.

It is also essential that a risk manager or his/her team understand that just as fans and athletes are human beings with both strengths and weaknesses, so are risk managers. Thus the risk manager has to take into account his (her) personal strengths and weaknesses, the politics and expectations of the tasks, and the mix of personalities involved.

TYPES OF STADIUM PROTECTION

In reality there are multiple issues of stadium, arena, and venue protection. These "protections" can be viewed as:

- Physical protection via stadium lighting. Good lighting is an essential part of any security and safety plan. Most cameras require lighting and lighting is essential not only as a means to hold down crime but to protect the public from undue falls. Lighting should be used in all aspects of the sporting venue. Fields and courts need to be well lit. Other areas include the need for lighting, but not limited to, are: the outside parameters and parking areas, stairwells and back accesses, hallways and rest room areas. A general rule of thumb is that if the area needs to be protected or patrolled, or if there is danger due to slips or falls, then the area needs lighting. It is essential in any lighting plan to have back-up power sources. This back-up lighting plan, or redundancy in a more technical language, is essential not only due to outages caused by weather, but also due to manmade violence such as a terrorist attack.

- Issues of fire protection. There is a wide range of fire potential due to the fact that sporting venues range from a stadium with wooden benches to large concrete stadiums. All sporting venues must meet fire codes and sports venue security teams should work with local fire marshals on a regular basis. Fire safety plans should be coordinated with any structural changes and even the most open area should have, in an age of terrorism, a constant updated evacuation plan.
- Outside of stadium protection—weather protection. Often we do not think of weather protection in the same way as protection from violence. However, the weather can be an ever-present safety issue. Protection from the weather includes everything from a spectator or athlete getting wet due to rainfall to a person being struck by lightning, or suffering from severe heat or cold. There is no 100% sure ways to protect a person against a freak weather occurrence. Game managers should be responsible to know the weather forecast and put life and limb ahead of financial loss. In the case of lightning, the FAA (Federal Aviation Authority), NASA (National Aeronautics and Space Administration), and the US Department of Defense have developed lightning protocols that can be adapted to a sporting event. Joel Gratz and Erik Noble writing for the American Meteorological Society recommend in an article entitled: "Lightning Safety and Large Stadiums" note the following:
- Stadiums should designate a responsible person(s) to monitor the weather and initiate action when appropriate. Monitoring should begin hours and even days ahead of an event. Computer-based lightning monitoring is suggested for large venues because crowd noise and lighting make visual and audible lightning observation difficult.
- A protocol needs to be in place to notify all persons at risk from the lightning threat.
- Safer sites must be identified beforehand, along with a means to route the people to those locations. The all-clear signal must be identified and should be considerably different from the warning signal. The signal should be sounded 30 minutes after the last sound of thunder. Clearing skies and an end to the rain do not guarantee that the lightning threat is over.
- Lightning safety tips and/or the action plan should be placed on game programs, flyers, the large television screen at stadiums, and on placards around the area. Lightning warning signs are an effective means of communicating the lightning threat to the general public and raising awareness (Bennett et al. 1997).[11]

---

[11] http://journals.ametsoc.org/doi/abs/10.1175/BAMS-87-9-1187

DETERMINING WHICH TYPE OF RISK IS GREATEST

As noted, different sporting events have different types of risk. When determining risk it is important to remember that no event is ever 100% risk free. No matter how large a staff or budget, neither the staff nor the budget will ever be adequate. Thus, the only alternative is to prioritize risk and to determine which risks have the greatest potential to harm an athletic event or athlete. Here is a list of types of risks that have occurred at athletic events in the past. They are given without prioritization either regarding frequency or consequences. It is the task of the risk management team to determine which of these has the highest potential of occurrence and what the consequences of such an occurrence might be. Here, then, is a listing of negative events that have occurred at sporting events:

- A car being stolen
- A murder
- A riot
- Gang violence
- Crime of distraction
- Sexual assault
- Vandalism
- "Con" game
- Prostitution or public nudity
- Purchases of illegal drugs
- Natural event, storm, tornado, sun poisoning
- Food poisoning

To help determine which of these and other risks may be most critical for a particular event consider the following recipe:

1. List all potential risks. Do not rank these risks merely list them as above.
2. Next to each risk label it as highly likely to occur, likely to occur, or not likely to occur. Grade each risk with a number from 1 to 10 with 10 being the most likely to occur and 1 being the least likely to occur.
3. Return to your list and assign a second set of numbers indicating if the consequences of such a risk from 10 to 1, with 10 being the worst consequences (multiple deaths) to least consequential (someone spills their drink).
4. Average the two sets of numbers. Then re-rank the risks: with the risks receiving the higher averages on top, and those with a lower score on the bottom.
5. Take the top half and assign them a number according to the amount of media coverage this event might receive. Once again grade each of these risks with the most amount of potential negative media coverage receiving a 10 to the least amount of potential media coverage receiving a 1.

6. Repeat the process this time assigning a number from 1 to 10 based on the event's expect news cycle life. For example, will the event be covered for only a day or two or might this negative event be in the news for a month or even a year.

7. Average these two numbers. The total averages should provide the risk manager with a good idea as to where he or she will want to spend mitigation resources. It should be emphasized that this exercise should be redone prior to each event as security is never stable and what may not be a risk factor on one day may become a risk factor on another day.

Once the events' risks priorities are determined, the risk manager can then begin to develop lists that will allow him (her) to mitigate these risks. The risk manager will want to determine such things as the following:

- Best evacuation routes
- Need for additional entrances and exits
- Natural or nature threats such as snakes at outdoor locations
- Locations and number of first aid stations and personnel
- Number and locations of rest room facilities
- If lighted routes to parking areas are necessary
- Location and need for emergency access phones.

Risk managers will also want to ask themselves if they have worked with first responders on such issues as:

- Traffic flow
- Divisions of labor
- Times when staff is not on duty
- Dealing with out-of-towners
- Language crises
- Package and delivery of packages and parcels review systems
- Crime prevention.

A high level of cooperation and collegiality is essential for good risk management. Risk managers do not have to like everyone with whom they work in their own agency or in another agency, but they do need to form a professional working and respectful relationship with them. Areas where stadium managers, risk managers, and first responders need not only to collaborate but also to develop joint plans are in such areas as:

- Fire prevention. Even in concrete stadiums the potential for fire is always present. It is essential that risk managers along with fire department not only do a regular review of fire safety procedures, but also interact on a regular basis. Fires can spread very quickly and for this reason it is important for all employees to know about what to do in case of a fire. Even before a fire department arrives, the risk management team should have sports venue employees trained as to what to do regarding:

- Smoke. Many employees know that not all smoke means a major fire. Their prime objective should be to evacuate the site or isolate the fire at the first sign of smoke. Smoke accumulates at the ceiling. If exit signs are placed only at higher levels then they may be not seen during a fire. Do employees know that fresh air for breathing is near the floor?
    - Panic. How to handle panic and how not to panic. People who panic rarely save themselves or others. The more information that a guest and an employee have the less likely they are to panic.
    - Exits. Make sure guests and employees know where the exits are located. This is especially important in enclosed visitor or information centers areas. We can almost be sure that the evacuations will be needed when guests and fans are least prepared. It is important that multilingual signage provide evacuation instructions.

Furthermore, it is essential that risk managers be sure that they have:

- Visible guards. Contrary to what some visitor/information centers professionals may believe, professional security guards are greatly appreciated and make guests feel secure. This sense of security is especially true for female guests and visitors from foreign lands. Professional security guards, if trained properly, not only do not hurt profits, but also can add to a bottom line. Since this work is often tedious, it is the risk manager's responsibility to know that his personnel are at work and alert.
- Done good background check as to the criminal history of all employees. Find out, for example, does the person have an arrest record?
- Gotten to know the people who work at local police departments and hospitals. Often police and medical officers can point out errors and easy ways to correct problems. It is a lot cheaper to avoid a crisis than to have to deal with the crisis after it has occurred.
- A clear policy as to the type of keys used throughout their facility and who controls these keys. It is also the risk manager's responsibility to have a missing or lost key policy.

ALCOHOL

Many people believe that alcoholic consumption is part of the sports spectator experience. In many places in the United States alcoholic consumption is considered a potential liability and therefore banned during games. This banning may lead to three new problems:

1. It does not prevent alcoholic consumption prior to the event. In many cases, tailgating parties have become part of the "spectator experience."
2. The banning does not prevent someone from trying to bring alcohol into the stadium as a form of hidden contraband.
3. The banning policy may encourage alcohol displacement. In other words, during the postgame experience alcohol may be consumed at off-venue sites and although it has displaced the problem at the sports venue it may have created new problems at off-site locations resulting in the loss of reputation and even lives.

There is now a counter theory that argues that the controlled permitting of alcoholic consumption at athletic events may actually be preferable. Those in favor of this policy argue that stadiums that serve alcohol during games can attempt to assure that the drinker:

- Guests should have some food along with the alcohol as a way to mitigate its negative effects.
- Foods served can be low salt and high protein, another way to lower the alcohol's impact.
- Amounts of liquor consumed may be controlled by the venue staff and by both public and private security teams.
- Stadium personnel can watch for "fighting/angry" drunks, and thus monitor events.
- They also argue that liquor served at a stadium will assure that these alcoholic beverages will be distributed by trained and licensed bartenders and will be able to document with witnesses all alcoholic incidents.

    It should be noted that a person who chooses not to abide by these rules may be just as likely to break these policies both inside and outside of the stadium setting.

CHAPTER 9

Athletes as Idols

Being a sports enthusiast means that a person is either a spectator or someone who cares about sports. To be an athlete, on the other hand, a person needs to participate in sports. Being an athlete, however, is often a lot more than being simply a paid professional or even unpaid "amateur,"[1] whether simply a person who practices a sport, or a person who is a highly trained, with special talents or skills.

Often, athletes are also media personalities. A successful athlete might become a news figure and as such, she or he is often idolized. Fairly or unfairly, the media might turn the athlete into a role model. Since all too often, athletes' personal privacy is both ephemeral and questionable, they have special needs. These needs exist both at home and most especially, when away from home. If privacy is hard to obtain at home, it is even a harder "commodity" to find when traveling. Also, despite the belief of many of the members of the public that athletes, especially well-paid professional athletes, live a "charmed" life with few responsibilities or cares, in most cases, quite the opposite is true. Despite the athlete's desires or wishes, the public often views these role-model athletes as heroes, or figures to be studied and/or emulated. This often-contradictory public perception means that well-known athletes are objects of admiration and also jealousy, adored by the public and yet, when their human foibles come to light, there may be a stated (or even unstated) sentiment that the athlete "got what she or he deserved."

Although some athletes seek the limelight, many neither seek nor relish this public posture or position. Those who fall into this latter group tend to see themselves as merely men (or women) who are doing a job. No matter into which group the athlete may fall, these imposed public perceptions create special issues and problems for the traveling athlete. He or she is not merely a traveler or business traveler, but must live with the knowledge that whatever she or he does, there is someone watching and critiquing his or her actions.

---

[1] The term *amateur* here does not mean "less able," but merely refers to the person's paid or unpaid status vis-à-vis that sport.

Sports Travel Security. DOI: http://dx.doi.org/10.1016/B978-0-12-805099-6.00009-9

In an age of social media, to be known is to surrender much of one's privacy. Travel, for the athlete on whom unrealistic expectations are placed, is often more of a challenge than a pleasure. It is against this background that we examine the athlete as bigger than life and beyond being a mere mortal. The athlete then becomes a "person" who has been transformed willingly (or not) into a superhuman hero or symbol.

THE ATHLETE AS HERO

Around the world, nations and societies have developed some form of hero or role model. Sociologists and social observers have noted, and classified, different types of heroes. For example, J.S. Morin[2] spoke of the "perfect hero." This type of hero is the near-perfect person, the demigod or almost demigod, who is kind, decisive, uncompromising and, at the same time, selfless. The exact opposite of the perfect hero is found in Spanish literature and called the *pícaro* or loosely translated as a "lovable rogue." The *pícaro* is the anti-hero hero, someone whom we admire for not fitting into a mold, and for breaking the rules and getting away with it. Often, the person is greedy or selfish, yet packaged in a way that we feel sympathy for him (it is usually, but not always, a *him*). In American literature, we read (or watch programs) about *pícaros* such as Bonnie and Clyde. We know what these people are doing is wrong, but on some level, we still root for them.

Not far removed from the anti-hero is the "un-hero." This is the person who does everything wrong, but despite being the wrong person at the wrong time at the wrong place, falls into a heroic act or receives credit for something that she or he simply does not deserve. The un-hero is the eternal, yet lovable, social klutz. The list of un-hero types is long. For example, we have the misfit or outsider who, despite being an outsider, commits a heroic act, and the "old timer" hero, the person who is now past his or her physical or mental prime, but whose knowledge saves the day. She or he is often the person who is ignored by those who are younger. Despite being discounted, she or he uses past experience and saves the day. There is also the "everyman" hero, who never thought of himself or herself as heroic, but just happens to be at the right spot at the right time to perform an act of heroism. Being the "everyman," we relate to this type of hero. The everyman hero is the person who has no special powers, abilities, or charms, but whom fate has placed into a hero's position.

---

[2] Morin, J.S. 7 types of heroes, http://www.jsmorin.com/2013/02/7-types-of-heroes/; 2013 [accessed 08.15.16].

Some heroes are prodigies. The "prodigy hero" is the person who is meant or destined to be a hero and whose life's course is nothing more than a series of lessons that help the prodigy develop into the hero that he or she was destined to be.

We only need to look at the athletes who appear in advertisements to understand that Western societies often assign the hero role to many of its sports figures. The athlete who appears in an ad is indicating that the person who purchases said product or service not only has the athlete's "approval" but also shares in the hero's qualities.

Often, athletes fall into one of the categories mentioned above. They not only are looked up to or despised, but become the fodder for multiple publications and news reports. The cynic might well believe that this status has more to do with off-game marketing than with on-game activities.

As such, these well-publicized athletes are often subjects of controversy or gossip, and have name recognition far beyond what many of them seek, or perhaps deserve. This love–hate sense of being a hero is perhaps what makes sports "hero worship" unique. Many athletes neither see themselves, nor desire to be seen, as heroes, yet they are given the role of hero despite their desires. For example, in his article published in *Esquire* magazine, Kareem Abdul-Jabbar noted that:

> Heroes provide models of exemplary behavior to emulate. Heroes inspire kids to achieve more than they thought they were capable of, to find strength when they thought they didn't have any more, to follow a code of moral conduct when it would be easier and maybe more popular not to. But when it comes to sports figures, Americans seem a little confused about what defines a hero.[3]

Abdul-Jabbar noted that in most cases, athletes have not done anything "heroic." From his perspective, (professional) athletes receive a salary for a job, nothing more and nothing less. His sports capabilities are a business deal in which his purpose is to win games. Of course, the other side of the coin is that businesses must make money, and if a team does not attract fans, it will lose money (either directly or indirectly) and eventually become unsustainable. Thus, ironically, even the salaried athlete, who claims not to be an entertainer, must become, to some degree, just that. Abdul-Jabbar correctly noted that although athletes work hard, and are often proud of their accomplishments, they have chosen to sacrifice some parts of their lives in order to excel in other parts of their lives. What is said of athletes could also be said of

---

[3] Abdul-Jabbar, K. Esquire. Are professional athletes heroes? http://www.esquire.com/lifestyle/health/news/a23707/kareem-are-professional-athletes-heroes/; 2013 [accessed 08.15.16].

millions of other professionals, including teachers, doctors, lawyers, and factory workers. Abdul-Jabbar went on to state that

> To be a hero means to risk something considerable in order to accomplish a goal that serves a greater good than the individual. It's not even important that you are successful, merely that you sacrificed something to try to make things better for someone other than yourself.[4]

Abdul-Jabbar raises important points about the athlete in our collective psyche. Since many of these people come from the poorer ranks of society and rose principally due to hard work by taking advantage of a God-given talent, they fit the mold of the American Dream. Also, because many of these people have obtained fame and fortune, this "rags to riches" epic is the modern American version of the Horatio Alger myth, in which the poor boy through hard work and perseverance becomes a success. Not only are athletes considered by many to be "heroes," but they also are often placed in the position of being "role models." As we have seen above, not all heroes are role models, but most sports heroes are assigned the additional role of being a role model and the person whom others seek to emulate. As a role model, the athlete is expected to be able to inspire others. In the United States, we often expect our role models to embody our national dreams, to show no prejudice, and to be accepting of the other person. Role models do not cheat or act in an unbecoming manner; they not only have a clear set of values, but also live these values. As such, to a greater or lesser extent, they lose their "personhood," and when they act in human ways, the media often castigate them. Perhaps sports figures fit into the role-model category because many of them have overcome obstacles in their lives. Dr. Marilyn Price-Mitchell wrote that:

> Research studies have long shown a correlation between role models and higher levels of civic engagement in young people. Positive role models are also linked to self-efficacy, the ability to believe in ourselves. In fact, the young people in my study admitted that had they not learned to believe in themselves, they would not have been capable of believing they could make a difference in the world![5]

Is it fair to impose the title of role model on our athletes? Are they heroes simply because they know how to throw or kick a ball? Dr. Philip Zimbardo, professor emeritus of psychology at Stanford University, has sought to create a paradigm of heroes. His research supports Abdul-Jabbar's statements. Zimbrado's hero paradigm includes the following items that are summarized

---

[4] Ibid.

[5] Price-Mitchell, M. Roots of Action. What is a role model? Five qualities that matter to teens, http://www.rootsofaction.com/what-is-a-role-model-five-qualities-that-matter-for-role-models/; 2011 [accessed 08.15.16].

below, along with potential alternative reasons for the acts of potential role-model heroism:

1. Heroes surround us. Zimbrado argued that there are many more people who are heroes than we realize. Most of these people help others and get little or no recognition. They simply help because there is someone who needs their help.

2. Opportunity to be a hero matters. Most acts of heroism occur in urban areas, where there are more people and more people in need! Thus, the greater the number of hero-type opportunities, the greater the number of heroes.

3. Zimbardo also argued that education seems to matter. He assumes that the more educated a person is, the more the person is aware of his or her surroundings. In reality, people in poorer neighborhoods might also be very much aware of their surroundings as a survival technique. However, for a poorer person, being aware of one's surroundings might be an indicator that it is wise not to get involved.

4. Volunteering matters. One-third of all the people whom Zimbardo sampled, who also were heroes, had volunteered significantly, up to 59 hours a week.

5. Gender matters. Males reported performing acts of heroism more often than females. Zimbardo believed that this lack of female heroism might be because women tend not to regard a lot of their heroic actions as heroic, but just what they think they are supposed to do for their family or a friend. Another possible interpretation is that men tend to use heroism as a form of machismo; they are supposed to be the saviors. For example, it is worth noting that despite the fact that we are now many years after the feminist revolution, the media report that an attack was "also against women and children," assuming that males are supposed to self-sacrifice, and perhaps that their lives matter less. It is also worth noting that only in 2016 did the United States Congress consider the question of the female draft.

6. Race matters. Blacks were eight times more likely than Whites to qualify as heroes. Zimbardo hypothesized that this difference might be due in part to the rate of opportunity. He connected the rate of heroism to location, and inner cities provide greater hero opportunities than do suburbs or wealthier areas. Yet, he noted that although location mattered, so, too, did educational levels.

7. Personal history matters. Having survived a disaster or personal trauma made a person three times more likely to be a hero and a volunteer.[6]

---

[6] Zimbardo, P. Greater Good. What makes a hero? http://greatergood.berkeley.edu/article/item/what_makes_a_hero; 2011 [accessed 08.15.16].

According to Zimbardo, athletic abilities have nothing to do with heroism. In fact, he did not even mention strength as a hero-factor. Despite this fact, the media often classify athletes as heroes or judge them as role models. This fact might be because the American athlete often seems to be a modern-day combination of the Horatio Alger story with the need for some form of hero-worship. Psychologists have questioned if hero-worship, especially the athletic form, is a healthy phenomenon. Writing in *Psychology Today* and citing the research of Dr. Michael Hyman and Dr. Jeremy J. Sierra, Matt Beardmore noted that: "Hero worship (among adolescents) seems like an innocuous act, but there is definitely a dark side, he told me [the interviewer], adding that he wouldn't be surprised if '2 percent of the U.S. population had a serious problem with some type of hero worship.'"[7]

William C. Rhoden, writing in a *New York Times* article of October 21, 2012, in reference to Charles Barkley of the Phoenix Suns basketball team, noted that:

> We (the public) crave illusion, and athletes have historically been vessels of our self-deception. In light of the dramatic falls of Michael Vick, Marion Jones, Barry Bonds, Roger Clemens, Tiger Woods and now Lance Armstrong, we need to either recalibrate our definition of the sports hero or scrap it altogether. The concept is based largely on ignorance: the less we know about an athlete, the easier it becomes to invest him with lofty ideals. The ideals have little to do with the athlete's character and everything to do with creating an artificial construct that serves a need.[8]

Barkley argued that the line between the sports hero and the sports role model is very thin. In reality, both categories demand supermen (or superwomen). He went on to note that these individuals ceased to be judged on facts, but rather on emotions. Emotions not only are difficult to control, but also often lead to bouts of fantasy, whether negative or positive.

Athletes as heroes are people about whom myths develop. Since human beings not only identify with heroes, but often project themselves onto the persona of the hero, these people must live public lives that are often removed from reality. When traveling, they are placed in the position of a double flight from reality. If to travel is to leave reality behind, the athlete must experience both the fantasy of the hero-role model combined with the fantasy of travel. These flights of fantasy also create a great deal of

---

[7] Beardmore, M. Psychology Today. Is it safe to workshop athletes? https://www.psychologytoday.com/blog/time-out/201310/is-it-safe-worship-athletes; 2013 [accessed 08.15.16].

[8] Rhoden, W. *The New York Times*. Seeing through the illusion of the sports hero, http://www.nytimes.com/2012/10/22/sports/seeing-through-the-illusions-of-the-sports-hero.html?_r=0; 2012 [accessed 08.15.16].

disappointments and anger at unfulfilled expectations. As will be seen later in this chapter, fallen heroes often are assigned to a special world of purgatory. For example, when Nike abandoned Lance Armstrong, it stated that:

> ... it was betrayed and misled, though certainly no more than the world was deceived by Woods, who implied—or allowed marketers to infer—that his great character was at the root of his athletic success. Armstrong was simply an illusionist: he told us he was riding up the sides of mountains without chemical help.[9]

Was the reason that Nike dropped Armstrong one of morality, or was it the case that once an athlete is finished being a hero, he or she can be discarded like an article of used clothing? Sports heroes have a fine line in which to walk. The public expects athletes to be disciplined and full of passion; athletes are expected to help others and be models of perfection. Since they are not gods but humans, athletes, like other people, will at times fail, and unfortunately, as the media all too often thrive on negative news, there are those in the media who seek to destroy their reputation or turn a minor or private incident into a major, public incident.

Psychologists have argued that these myths or assumptive behaviors create what Jungian psychologists call "archetypes." In Jungian psychology, the hero archetype is the person who overcomes adversity, challenges, and demonstrates honor, strength, and victory. Heroes provide a narrative for what some psychologists call "sensemaking," which refers to an ongoing interpretative process that allows a person to rationalize and understand a series of events and experiences (Weick, 1995).

To take these ideas and apply them to sports, we see that from this theoretical perspective, the hero's journey often seeks to bring order to disorder or make right situations that have gone wrong. The athlete ceases to be a businessperson, but now moves to an almost angelic or saintly state. We expect our athletic heroes to have a supernatural talent, to achieve set out goals and bend reality to their will. It is not a stretch to argue that many desire to emulate such mythic accomplishments and to possess such power. It is also understandable to why athletes fail at this superhuman task.[10]

Since we learn about archetypes through the media and through marketing, we turn celebrities into semigods or heroes. Our daily language tends to reflect this semigod quality through the use of such terms as sports idol, hero-worship, and through a "cult of personalities."

---

[9] Ibid.
[10] Shadraconis, S. Lux. Leaders and heroes: Modern-day archetypes, http://scholarship.claremont.edu/cgi/viewcontent.cgi?article=1048&context=lux; 2013 [accessed 08.15.16].

The sports hero soon becomes the figure upon whom we project our own desires, or use his (or her) skills as ways to cover over our own inadequacies. Sophon Shadraconis wrote about some of the reasons we emulate heroes. It is interesting that although people of color are often underrepresented in much of the media, they are well represented in the world of sports and athletics. Thus, they become symbols for those in the inner cities. Shadraconis stated that:

> The emulation and idealization of leaders does not end with physical features. Individuals may also project heroic qualities and idealized images on leaders such as strength, courage, and a strong moral compass.
> The development of para-social relationships with idealized leaders, or heroes, may address of the loss in meaning in work and allow individuals to connect with their true selves. Idealization is the process by which some object is removed of any negative features and comes to be overvalued and emotionally aggrandized. (Laughlin, 1970, p. 123)[11]

Brown and Starkey (2000) argued that it "implies the exercise of an unrealistic judgment, and it results in the creation of a 'fantastic' and 'impossible' person, standard, or other entity" (p. 106). When we idealize leaders, these idealized leaders may result in being modern-day heroes to be worshiped. When leaders do not live up to our expectations, no matter how unrealistic, this may elicit a disgusted response."[12] In other words, these figures take on a larger-than-life persona, and when they return to being merely human, disappointment sets in.

It is not easy to be a sports hero at home, and it is even more difficult to be one on the road. At home, there are moments of privacy; on the road, there is, as has been seen in other chapters, little or no privacy. At home, many athletes have the support of family and friends; on the road, there is a great deal more loneliness, frustration, and the requirement to almost always be "on display." Travel adds a great deal of stress to a person who is already under stress. The athlete travels for two reasons: either as part of his or her business (sports) or passion, or for vacation or relaxation. At home, athletes are able to escape, to be more themselves. On the road, the situation changes radically. The athlete will not only be "on view," but might have to share a room with a colleague. Personal quirks might come to the forefront, and locations where an athlete might "enjoy" privacy or alone time could be minimal. Constantly being on public notice means that the athlete becomes objectified rather than humanized.

---

[11] Ibid.
[12] Ibid.

We might expect that being a "hero" would create a protective aura around the person. Many athletes, however, are placed in the role of disappointer and thus, his or her security is diminished, rather than augmented. Since many athletes do not seek the status of role model, their failure may be seen as a form of betrayal. This often misplaced admiration causes the admirer to feel betrayed, which can lead to both anger and the potential for violence. Citing a study by Marongui and Newman, Dr. Sandra L. Bloom wrote that:

> ...[T]he abuse of power on the part of the perpetrator and the helplessness experienced by the victim are hallmark characteristics of interpersonal violence and, therefore, we can expect that a victim will be highly motivated to seek revenge. The desire for vengeance/justice becomes a part of the trauma response and may be directed at the original perpetrator or may be displaced onto others, often those entirely innocent of the initial injury. Placed in the role of the hero, the athlete is bound to disappoint his or her fans, and his or her inability to live up to this assigned status places the athlete in double jeopardy.[13]

THE MEDIA, NEGATIVE PUBLICITY, AND THE FALLEN ATHLETIC HERO

Many marketers believe that on some level, all publicity is good publicity, no matter how bad the publicity might be. The 19th-century Irish playwright and humorist Oscar Wilde made this assumption when he stated that "the only thing worse than being talked about is not being talked about."[14] Certainly, in a world of social media and 24/7 news cycles, there is no dearth of opportunities for people in the public eye to receive publicity. In today's world, almost anyone can have what Andy Warhol is misquoted as calling "their 15 minutes of fame."(The actual quote is, "In the future everybody will be world famous for 15 minutes.")[15] Not everyone agrees, however, that all publicity is good, and in an age of paparazzi and social media, there are a great many celebrities who would argue that even if they are public figures, they are still individuals who should enjoy the right to personal privacy.

---

[13] Bloom, S. L. Center for Nonviolence and Social Justice. Reflections on the desire for revenge, http://www.nonviolenceandsocialjustice.org/Research-Literature/Sanctuary-Model-literature-and-works-by-Sandra-Bloom/Reflections-on-the-Desire-for-Revenge/75/; 2001 [accessed 08.15.16].

[14] Wilde, O. Goodreads. Quotes by Oscar Wilde, http://www.goodreads.com/quotes/5560-there-is-only-one-thing-in-the-world-worse-than; 2016 [accessed 08.15.16].

[15] The Phrase Finder, http://www.phrases.org.uk/meanings/fifteen-minutes-of-fame.html; 2016 [accessed 08.15.16].

Perhaps the best example of this "privacy versus publicity debate" takes place in the world of sports. A landmark case involved Terry G. Bollea, better known by his wrestling name of Hulk Hogan, who was awarded some $115 million in damages due to his being photographed in a compromising situation without his knowledge or consent. The March 18, 2016, edition of *The New York Times* reported that "Mr. Bollea's (legal) team said the verdict represented 'a statement as to the public's disgust with the invasion of privacy disguised as journalism'," adding, "The verdict says, 'No more'."[16] The article then went on to state that:

> The meaning of the verdict will not be clear for some time. But the perception that a Manhattan media company, noted for its wry tone and its insistence that nearly any topic is fair game, was brought low by a celebrity fighting for privacy is most likely to resonate widely across the industry.[17]

This loss of privacy is not only restricted to professional athletes. University athletes also can become the center of attention. This attention (so-called fame) could be destructive both to their careers and personal lives. Heisman Trophy winner Johnny Manziel is an example of a university star athlete who became a media attraction, and for whom we could say, the media became a major distraction, or perhaps, detriment. In 2012, Manziel became the first freshman to win the Heisman Trophy. Perhaps because Texas A&M University is a football school located in Texas, a football state, or perhaps because his freshman status was unique, Manziel became a media celebrity. Not only was his private life turned into a real-life soap opera, but the impact of that much publicity coming so early in his life might have had a part to play in his personal problems once he became a professional football player.

Not everyone sees publicity as a good thing. There are those who view the entire football mystique as contributing to the downfall of young athletes. For example, in writing about Johnny Manziel, Darren K. Roberts of the *Dallas Morning News* (April 27, 2016) noted that:

> We have created the toxic environment that strips premier athletes of perspective and accountability. We want our touchdowns, and we want them now. We crave wins and despise losses. We have demoted the ability to cope with adversity, empathize and lead with integrity to backup on our depth chart for life. Consider this: Of the 10 largest stadiums in *the world*, eight are American college football stadiums. The combined capacity of those stadiums stands at roughly 830,000. Rest assured, that will top 1 million

---

[16] Madigan, N., Somaiya, R. Hulk Hogan awarded $115 million in privacy suit against Gawker, http://www.nytimes.com/2016/03/19/business/media/gawker-hulk-hogan-verdict.html?_r=0; 2016 [accessed 08.15.16].

[17] Ibid.

as rival schools double down in the infinite game of "construction dare." And schools have the money to do it—the 128 teams of the Football Bowl Subdivision (FBS) have a combined value of $20 billion.[18]

Roberts focused on the spectacle and the fact that these young men (and perhaps young women, too) have become pawns in the business of university sports when he wrote:

> We should not be surprised the first freshman Heisman Trophy winner falls from grace. In a society that pays more attention to falling 40-yard dash times than rising SAT scores, it is time for us to encourage athletes to create an identity outside of their sport. The truth of the matter is that at some point, the ball will go flat for every player. And when it does, he will be left to pick up the pieces.[19]

There are numerous other exceptions to the rule that all publicity is good publicity. When the person about whom the public is hearing or reading is considered a hero or a role model, negative publicity cannot only destroy a reputation and career, but also the person's private life, or his or her relationship with a spouse and children. For example, highly derogatory actions such as those by music star Chris Brown in his treatment of his "significant other," Rhiannon, might have well cost Brown more than merely a good number of fans; it might also have added to his psychological problems. *Time* magazine wrote the following about the Chris Brown incident:

> The violent episode between Chris Brown and Rihanna in 2009 instantly became one of the most notorious domestic abuse incidents of the 21st century after photos of her battered face were leaked to the press. The assault had ramifications for both of their careers and in a new trailer for a documentary about his life, Chris Brown says he contemplated suicide in the aftermath. "I went from being on top of the world, No. 1 songs, being kind of like America's sweetheart to being Public Enemy No. 1," Brown said in the trailer for *Welcome to My Life: The Official Chris Brown Documentary*. "I felt like a f—ing monster ... I was thinking about suicide, I wasn't sleeping, I barely ate."[20]

Since Chris Brown was not a sports role model and admitted to his "indiscretions" (assault), he might have been able to somewhat recover at least a part of his reputation. The expectations placed on him as a professional and an

---

[18] Roberts, D. Dallas Morning News. Blame yourself for Johnny Football's fall from grace, http://www.dallasnews.com/opinion/columnists/dmn-contributors-network/20160427-blame-yourself-for-johnny-footballs-fall-from-grace.ece; 2016 [accessed 08.15.16].

[19] Ibid.

[20] Begley, S. Time. Chris Brown says he felt like a "monster" after Rihanna assault, http://time.com/4298397/chris-brown-rihanna-assault-trailer/; 2016 [accessed 08.15.16].

adult, then, were less than those placed on the (at the time) underage university player, Johnny Manziel.

When we turn from professional singer to a professional sports hero, note that the media often treat the sports hero in a very different way. For example the Chris Brown case to a great extent paralleled the case of Baltimore Raven (US football team player) Ray Rice. In Rice's case, we also see an abused woman, but the forgiveness factor decreased as the hero expectations increased. In the Ray Rice case, the denial level at first took precedence. CNN reported that:

> The Baltimore Ravens released Ray Rice on Monday after a video surfaced showing him punching his then-fiancée and dragging her limp body out of an Atlantic City casino elevator. He was originally suspended for two games over the February fight, a punishment that many considered too lenient.
> Rice was just weeks away from returning to the gridiron when the new video surfaced, spurring swift responses from the Ravens and the NFL that sent his professional football career grinding to halt.[21]

At first, due to the fact that Rice was known as a nice guy, fans and even members of the media began to make excuses for him. The media portrayed him as a role model. Thus, when the incident became known, people at first entered a state of denial, which then went from disappointment to anger. It took professional football some time to come to terms with the case's new reality. For example, Steve Bisciotti, owner of the Ravens football team, had, at first, come to Rice's defense and stated the following:

> He's just been lauded as the nicest, hardest working, greatest guy on the team and in the community. So we have to support him. I think we'll be rewarded by him maturing and never putting himself in a situation like that again.... I've been on record of saying my definition of character is repeating offenses. If we're all one strike and you're out, then we're all in trouble. It's how you respond to adversity.[22]

During the initial stage of this "fall from grace," Rice's wife, as is often the case following assaults, came to his defense. It also became clear that there were two emotions occurring at the same time. On one hand, we see that there was a sense of denial. Simply put, although the incident was videotaped, people did not choose to believe that a role model might fail. On the other hand, there is a human tendency to go after those who have succeeded,

---

[21] Fantz, A., Levs, J., Shoichet, C. CNN. Ray Rice's wife slams his punishment for violence against her, http://www.cnn.com/2014/09/09/us/ray-rice-nfl-janay-rice/; 2014 [accessed 08.15.16].

[22] Bien, L. SB Nation. A complete timeline of the Ray Rice assault case, http://www.sbnation.com/nfl/2014/5/23/5744964/ray-rice-arrest-assault-statement-apology-ravens; 2014 [accessed 08.15.16].

to bring down the mighty. Thus, within a relatively short time after the incident, and with the release of a new video, the National Football League had to change directions due to heavy criticism, not only by groups that fight domestic violence, but also by the public at large. The new video meant that:

> According to ESPN's Chris Mortensen, the NFL requested the tape from law enforcement during its investigation, but was denied. The Ravens also reportedly hadn't seen the video until TMZ released it. According to Mortensen, the Ravens are preparing for the running back to miss more time.[23]

In the world of publicity, the quality or meaning of actions is often determined by who the person is and what expectations are placed on that person. Unfortunately, all too often, actions are judged not by what the person did, but by who the person is (or is not), and the public's pre-perception of that particular person. For example, if we create a hypothetical case, we can easily see the difference. Let us assume that a porn star releases (makes) a sex tape. The sex tape will barely cause a ruffle in the media. Now, let us assume that the same sex tape is produced not by a porn star, but by an academic or political leader. The tape is the same as that made by the porn star, but the consequences are very different. The same hypothetical sex tape, and the person who made it, are now judged differently and the tape's production becomes a scandal. We can then define negative publicity by three major factors: what the action is, what the preconceived assumptions are about the actor, and who comprises that portion of the public that views and has an interest in that particular action. From the set of factors above, we can determine that Hollywood stars who are not seen as role models are less likely to suffer from a negative action than are sports heroes. The reasons for this differentiation are the following:

1. Sports and athletes often assume the position of role models even if they do not seek that role.
2. Sporting events are usually considered a form of "family entertainment." Thus, when a sports hero falls from grace, the fall is a tragedy that produces both disappointment and anger.
3. The media often place higher standards on sports heroes than they do on other public personalities. Sports heroes are expected to be "on" even during their free time. When traveling, the sportsman (or sportswoman) has less time and fewer places in which to escape public view.
4. Sports heroes are subject to high levels of media attention. Thus, when they commit a personal error, or are involved in a scandal, these

---

[23] Ibid.

"banner yellow journalism" type headlines are seen as a means by which a newspaper, magazine, or television station might be able to increase ratings or readership. A scandal involving an athlete might be bad for the athlete, but at the same time, could be excellent or good for media ratings.

Scandals are not limited to any one type of athlete. Below, the reader will find summaries of some of the major, negative publicity scandals involving athletes in the United States. These scandals touched men and women, people from different races and ethnic backgrounds, and involved single-player athletes and also whole teams:

- Lance Armstrong. The Lance Armstrong scandal might be the "mother of all (sports) scandals," the perfect storm. Being a cancer survivor and a world-class athlete, Armstrong was everyone's definition of the clean-cut athlete. Good looking, intelligent, and with a desire to help others, he was the perfect role model. Armstrong was living proof that despite great adversity, the human spirit could conquer illness. Viewing Armstrong's successes, many in the world saw him as an inspiration that humans could do more than merely survive; they could flourish in the face of diversity. There were some who questioned Armstrong's success in the bicycle racing world, and Armstrong took numerous drug tests to prove them wrong. Unfortunately, despite years of denial, it finally became clear that he had used performance-enhancing drugs. The revelations shattered his image and created a sense of betrayal among his many, now-former fans, and as we have seen above, it cost him his contract with Nike.
- O. J. Simpson is another example of reputational self-destruction. Simpson was one of the greatest (American) football players, and his acting roles and television ads made him famous. These ads, along with a brilliant football playing style, made him a household name. The police charged Simpson with murdering his former wife and her friend. His trial was one of the most publicized trials in American history. Although the jury acquitted him of murder, he was found guilty in civil court and later ended up going to jail following a felony arrest in Las Vegas. There are those who defend Simpson and believe him to be the victim of racial prejudice. Others believe that the original acquittal might have been due to preexisting emotions, either based on his notoriety or skin color. The scandal not only destroyed his personal stature, but might also have hurt, for at least a few years after the trial, the sport of (US) football in general.
- Pete Rose. Pete Rose was one of America's great baseball players. In the United States, baseball often is seen as more than a mere sport, but the US national pastime, and as such, its players hold a special place

in the US pantheon of sports heroes. Since there are more baseball games in a season than in many other sports, baseball players travel more and have more contact with their fans. In the case of Peter Rose, his downfall was not due to a felony or the use of illegal drugs, but rather to being accused of illegal betting (on his game of baseball). Rose did not go to jail, but baseball, afraid of the potential stain on its reputation, banished him, and he has never been able to enter baseball's Hall of Fame.

- Tiger Woods was more than a great golfer. He seemed to be the perfect gentleman and a potential national "hero." Being part African-American, he was the perfect role model for young Black men in a game and world principally inhabited by upper-class White men. Tiger Woods fit the perfect stereotype of the sports hero/role model. By 2009, however, he seemed to be on the path of self-destruction. His many mistresses came to light, his wife divorced him, and he went from being a media "idol" to an almost "devil." It should be noted that Tiger Woods has worked hard at recovering his former reputation, and for that reason the public has judged him much less harshly than other fallen heroes.

- Tonya Harding. Almost every child knows, or thinks that he or she knows, that the Olympic Games are about great sportsmanship. Olympic players are not supposed to be professionals, and are supposed to compete for the love of sport rather than profit. Children are taught that it is not who wins, but how one plays the game, that is important. Thus, the fact that Tonya Harding and her husband were accused of assaulting Tonya's fellow ice skater, Nancy Kerrigan, by hitting her on the leg with a club in order to disqualify Kerrigan from competing in the 1994 Winter Olympics, came as a total shock not only to the sporting world, but also to all those who tended to see the Olympics as a symbol of what good sportsmanship was about.

It is not only professional sports that sometimes find themselves in the negative limelight. Unfortunately, teams also can become part of a negative story.

- Penn State University sex scandal. The child sex scandal at Penn State might have centered on one or two people, but the scandal often is also associated with Penn State's entire football team. The Penn State sex abuse scandal not only hurt the university's team, but might have also harmed the university's overall reputation.

- Soygate and Deflategate. As an example of a team touched by scandal, we may consider the Boston Patriots (football team) and their quarterback, Tom Brady. At the time of this writing, it was unclear what the NFL and the courts' final verdict would be. What is important from the perspective of this book is that the scandal, now known as "deflategate," impacts not only the team's quarterback, but also imputes the entire team's reputation. Jim Rapoza noted the importance of reputation when he stated that:

> But the other side of the coin here is that the Patriots shouldn't be surprised by this treatment, given their negative reputation. Of course there's Spygate, which had a huge negative impact on the team's reputation. And by pretty much any measure the Patriots are probably the least media friendly team in pro sports, so they shouldn't be surprised when the media piles on. In fact, one could say that the most damaging and long lasting penalty for Spygate is this negative reputation. Because of that reputation, the Patriots get no leeway and are punished for transgressions that would be ignored by others.[24]

Sports scandals might not only be about an individual athlete, or even a team. International soccer (called football in Europe) in the years 2015–16 was subjected to one of the great scandals of all time, involving members of its governing commission, known by its French name, The Fédération Internationale de Football Association, or FIFA. Top FIFA officials were indicted for an alleged scheme involving more than 150 million (US) dollars in kickbacks and bribes. The scandal erupted in May 2015 with seven top FIFA executives being arrested in Zurich, Switzerland. The scandal became worse when the United States indicted some 14 FIFA officials, both current and former. Eventually, another 16 officials also were charged. The British Broadcasting Corporation (BBC) reported that "former Brazil football federation chief Ricardo Teixeira was among those accused of being involved in criminal schemes involving well over $200 m (£132 m) in bribes and kickbacks."[25]

The BBC also noted that many of these scandals touched on the FIFA head, Charles "Chuck" Blazer, and noted that

> between 2004 and 2010: he [Blazer] and others on the FIFA executive committee agreed to accept bribes in connection with the selection of South Africa as the host of the 2010 World Cup. The scandal was highly complex. Here are a few of its many parts:

1. One of Blazer's co-conspirators received a bribe in Morocco for its bid to host the 1998 tournament, which was eventually awarded to France.
2. Blazer and others also accepted bribes in connection with broadcast and other rights to the *Concacaf* Gold Cup tournament in 1996, 1998, 2000, 2002, and 2003.

---

[24] Rapoza, J. WIRED Innovation Insights. Deflategate and the impact of a bad reputation, http://insights.wired.com/profiles/blogs/deflategate-and-the-impact-of-a-bad-reputation#axzz47EliIYss; 2015 [accessed 08.15.16].

[25] BBC. Fifa corruption crisis: Key questions answered, http://www.bbc.com/news/world-europe-32897066; 2015 [accessed 08.15.16].

3. Much attention has been focused on a $10 m deal that US prosecutors say was a bribe to secure the 2010 World Cup for South Africa.[26]

The materials above provide us with a number of lessons regarding how some athletes are perceived, and some might argue, unfairly judged. It should be emphasized that only a small portion of athletes, and managers or athletic officials, bring scandal to themselves, their teammates and communities. However, as is all too often the case, the public and media tend to focus on the negative rather than the positive. Simply put, an athlete's fall from grace is much more interesting to many people than the personal history of a hardworking athlete who lives his or her life in a community-minded and ethical fashion. From the examples above we see that in all cases, there was a "disconnect" between the expected behavior and the demonstrated behavior, and this disconnect produced not only disappointment, but anger and scandal.

In some, but not all, cases, the public has unrealistic expectations, and these (perhaps unfair) expectations result in a communal sense of betrayal or "hurt." As noted, "the athlete" is not seen as a mere mortal, but rather as a demigod who has no right to disappoint his or her fans. Since the public and sports fans have certain preconceived notions regarding the expected behavior of their heroes, any human failing by athletes is judged more harshly than those of politicians or entertainers. In the case of the latter two groups, the public expects moral failure, a sense of moral impropriety and scandal. Many people simply expect politicians to be dishonest, and entertainers to push or ignore society's bounds. The same cannot be said of athletes. When these expectations are not met, more than disappointment sets in; instead, there is psychological hurt and anger. Since athletes are people and not demigods, the more that they are exposed to the public, the more likely their character flaws might be noticed. At home, these character flaws can be hidden from the public's view, but in public or on the road, flaws are not as easy to hide.

Thus, we see that on the road, what might not be noticed has a higher probability of being noticed. A clue to understanding this stress comes from studies of family vacations. The travel magazine *HomeAway*, reported that "researchers noted that 55% of Americans found certain components of travel to be stressful."[27] According to the magazine, there are two primary sources of irritation for traveling families: the lack of privacy from friends and family members, and/or other travelers not in their group. In the case of athletes, these people are traveling with "business" colleagues and not family members.

---

[26] Ibid.

[27] HomeAway. HomeAway survey reveals stress keeps nearly half of families from enjoying vacations, https://www.homeaway.com/info/media-center/press-releases/2013/VRM-summer-2013; 2013 [accessed 08.15.16].

More successful or better-known athletes are constantly in the public's eye, and in a world of image manipulation and social media, where every telephone is also a camera, the athlete never knows what will be posted about him or her. With almost anyone having the ability to doctor a photo, seeing is no longer believing; rather, seeing is a constant threat to one's well-being, and as seen in an NFL interview from October 18, privacy might be a thing of the past as videos of naked athletes preparing to shower were (unbeknownst to them) broadcast on national television.[28]

ISSUES OF INSURANCE

The word insurance covers a great many categories. It appears that the insurance industry has created a form of insurance for almost everyone. From health insurance to disability insurance, from loss of reputation insurance to change of airline insurance, the offerings might seem to many to be unlimited. Athletes and sports enthusiasts need to consider what, if any, insurance they need, and what types of insurance they already have. Athletes and sports enthusiasts who travel as part of a team might not have to worry about travel insurance. The team might have already purchased it, or the athletes might travel by private motor coach or airplane. What could be true of the top tier of athletes might not be true for athletes in lower categories, however. To a great extent, their business trips might be subject to sudden changes resulting from an event being canceled, weather issues, or changes of schedule. In playoff games, teams must be prepared to travel if they win, but might have to cancel a trip if they lose.

Trip cancellation insurance is not the only form of athletic insurance that an athlete might need. All sports have a certain amount of risk involved, and many sports also incorporate controlled violence, or what is called in the sporting world, "competition." Whether at home or on the road, sports figures, especially those desiring to become major players in their sport, most focus on the physical. This physical focus means that many athletes tend to worry more about their speed and skill than about their safety. In the world of athletics, good health is a tool to succeed, but not a goal in and of itself. Sports insurance is not merely about team sports. Often, it is relevant in personal sports, from swimming to horseback riding, and from sailing to mountain climbing. For this reason, the sportsman or sportswoman needs to have not only a rescue plan, but also a way to pay for medical care. In some ways, the individual athlete might be at greater personal risk than the team athlete.

---

[28] Love, B. Scott. Oh my! NFL network accidentally broadcasts a locker room full of naked Bengals players, http://www.lovebscott.com/news/oh-my-nfl-network-accidentally-broadcasts-a-locker-room-full-of-naked-bengals-players-video; 2015 [accessed 08.15.16].

Individual athletes might travel alone, their support staff may be minimal or nonexistent, and they might not have anyone to hold them back when it would be wise for them to reconsider the adventure.

On the team side of the athletic equation, many team members believe that insurance is a way to protect themselves against economic loss should they be injured. Marc Tracy, writing in the May 8, 2015 issue of *The New York Times*, disagrees. He cited the case of Cedric Ogbuehi, who chose to finish his college career, but unfortunately, tore a ligament at the Liberty Bowl, which lowered his value and potential earning power in the professional football draft. Ogbuehi had purchased loss-of-value insurance. The *Times* noted that:

> To the extent that loss-of-value insurance helps persuade elite athletes to return, it is a boon to their teams, which get to use their talents for another season. But Ogbuehi's story highlights the perils of top athletes who extend their college tenure, during which they may be compensated only by a scholarship. In many cases, they cannot enter professional leagues because of age restrictions. N.C.A.A. rules barring agents and requiring players to declare for drafts soon after their seasons end make a tough decision even more difficult, some observers say.[29]

Yet the *Times* also reported that:

> Ogbuehi does not stand to collect on his insurance, his agent, Ryan Williams, said. Because most income is taxable but the insurance's benefits are not, a player typically must fall precipitously in the draft for the policy to take effect. "Although we believe he would have been drafted higher in 2014, he's pleased with the outcome this year," Williams said.[30]

What is seen in these examples is that there are numerous forms of athletic insurance, and the wise athlete needs to know which form works for him or her. To determine insurance needs, once again, the athlete has to understand risk and should review the risks that he or she faces with a qualified risk manager and a trusted insurance agent before considering types of insurance to purchase.

The athlete also needs to understand who he or she is within the world of sports, and how the purchased insurance might or might not be of benefit. To accomplish this goal, the athlete or sports enthusiast should begin by asking many of the basic questions found throughout this book.

---

[29] Tracy, M. *The New York Times*. Insurance doesn't eliminate risk for top college athletes who forgo draft, http://www.nytimes.com/2015/05/09/sports/ncaafootball/insurance-doesnt-eliminate-risk-for-top-college-athletes-who-forgo-draft.html; 2015 [accessed 08.15.16].
[30] Ibid.

PARADES, SPORTS FIGURES, AND SECURITY

Parades are celebrations in motion. We hold parades to laud winners and to declare victories. Parades are a celebration of our heroes and a way to say "well done." As such, it should not come as a surprise that there is a close connection between parades and athletic competitions. Parades draw large crowds. They are a way to show gratitude or veneration, congratulations, or victory. We give parades for winning. Occupation armies might use parades as a way of indicating to the vanquished that it is they who now hold the reins of power. In this case, the parade serves as an open symbol not only of victory, but also of control. In peacetime, military parades indicate a nation's strength. The peacetime military parade is a way of telling the world that if another threatens or attacks, then the attacker will be destroyed. Since military parades provide a sense of superiority and of victory, it likewise is not hard to understand why parades are important in sports. The psychological relationship between competition in sports and the parades that often occur after a team wins a major tournament may be similar to a military parade after a victory. Sports teams on a subconscious level resemble armies. In many ways, competitive sports are a socially acceptable manner to channel aggression. Jeff Deitz, writing in *The New York Times* on November 21, 2009, noted that:

> Aggression is a basic component of human instinct. Without it, no athlete can succeed. But if it runs amok or is misguided, it can undermine the most-talented competitor. When athletes lose it—that is, lose control of their aggressive impulses—fans are right to wonder, what was he thinking? Or even, was she thinking at all?[31]

Many sports psychologists seem to agree. Thus, in Gordon W. Russell's book, titled *Aggression in Sports: A Social Psychological Perspective*, Lise Joern, in analyzing Russell's work, noted that:

> The sporting community, however, draws a distinction between aggression and aggressiveness, and the (brutal) body contact that is seen as integral to some sports such as rugby, boxing or the martial arts. This kind of contact conforms to the rules of the sport and is completely legitimate even when the same sort of behaviour (sic) outside the sports context is defined as criminal. Also, participants in these sports, by the very act of taking part, have implicitly accepted the inevitability of rough contact. They have implicitly consented to the probability of minor injury and the possibility of serious injury.[32]

---

[31] Believe Perform. Aggression in sport, http://believeperform.com/education/aggression-in-sport-2/; 2013 [accessed 08.15.16].

[32] Arvid. Idiots Forum. Aggression in sport—ugly, or just part of the game? http://idrottsforum.org/joelis_russell081001/; 2008 [accessed 08.15.16].

Other psychologists connect sports and war. For example, J. A. Mangan noted that:

> The sports field and battlefield are linked as locations for the demonstration of legitimate patriotic aggression. The one location sustains the other, and both sustain the image of the powerful nation. Furthermore, the sports field throughout history has prepared the young for the battlefield. Throughout history sport and militarism have been inseparable. More than this, heroes of sports field and battlefield have much in common. They are both viewed as symbols of national prowess, quality and virtue. The warrior and the athlete are crucial to the perceived success of the state. Less often, sport has been an attempted antidote to war—bloodless competition with the purpose of assuaging bitterness, seeking reconciliation, attempting conciliation, pursuing comity.[33]

The same theme is noted in the work of Dr. Steve Taylor. Writing in *Psychology Today*, Taylor stated that:

> Sport satisfies most of the same psychological needs as warfare, and has similar psychological and social effects. It certainly provides a sense of belonging and unity. Fans of soccer, baseball or basketball teams feel a strong sense of allegiance to them. Once they have formed an attachment to a team (usually during childhood) they "support" it loyally through thick and thin. The team forms part of their identity; they feel bonded to it, and a strong sense of allegiance to the other supporters, a tribal sense of unity. Sport also enables the expression of "higher" human qualities which (sic) often lie dormant in ordinary life. It provides a context for heroism, a sense of urgency and drama where team members can display courage, daring, loyalty, and skill. It creates an artificial "life and death" situation which is invested with meaning and importance far beyond its surface reality.[34]

It is not hard to see the relationship between sports and war, and sports and victory. Just as in most wars, in a sporting event there is the victor and the vanquished, the person or team that celebrates and the person or team that leaves the playing field as the defeated. Since major sport teams often are closely related to the community, state, or nation with which they are associated, or the locale that they represent, victories go far beyond the team or mere sporting event. Sports victories become community (or national) moments of pride that transform into celebrations. To beat a rival's team is a form of play-war; it permits aggression without long-term destruction. In

---

[33] Mangan, J.A. SGI Quarterly. Sports and war: Combative societies and combative sports, http://www.sgiquarterly.org/feature2006Jly-2.html; 2006 [accessed 08.15.16].

[34] Taylor, S. Psychology Today. Sport and the decline of war, https://www.psychologytoday.com/blog/out-the-darkness/201403/sport-and-the-decline-war; 2014 [accessed 08.15.16].

some ways, nations have used sports as a political metaphor and have tried to apply the rules of sport to "game" war. For example, if we read the various Geneva Conventions on war, promulgated after World War II and including numerous treaties attempting to regulate the rules of war promulgated after World War I, we see that they are an attempt to create "rules of war" that are not terribly dissimilar to the rules of a sporting event. In *American Umpire*, Elizabeth Cobbs Hoffman's book on United States diplomatic history, Cobbs Hoffman noted that: "Umpire is an imperfect metaphor, but it fits more closely than 'empire'. It reasonably approximates the ways in which the United States brought action to a halt, exacted a penalty, and then tried to get out of the way to allow competition to resume."[35] In other words, Cobbs Hoffman connected the rules of the sporting event to the rules of war.

We find another similarity between the violence of war and sporting events in the fact that both sporting and military victories often are celebrated with some form of parade. In many locations around the world, both professional and university sporting events encompass more than the mere game. They are spectacles that occur both on and off the field. For example, Pasadena (California) holds a yearly Rose Bowl parade. Once, protection at these parades was merely an issue of crowd control or parking control. In an age of terrorism, however, what was simple is no longer simple. Thus, Steve Gorman, writing for *Reuters*, in reporting on the preparations for the 2016 New Year's Day Rose Bowl Parade wrote that:

> More than two dozen federal agencies are joining forces with police to bring an unprecedented level of security to the annual Rose Parade in Pasadena, California, in the aftermath of the deadly mass shooting this month in nearby San Bernardino Extraordinary security measures planned for the New Year's Day event include more than a dozen armed tactical "rapid-response" teams to be posted along the parade route, along with dozens of surveillance cameras, bomb-sniffing dogs and radiation-detection devices, law enforcement officials said. Some 700,000 spectators are expected to turn out in Old Town Pasadena, north of the Los Angeles, for the 127th Tournament of Roses Parade, a 5½-mile procession of flower-adorned floats, marching bands and equestrian teams.[36]

Among the additional precautions that the police used included undercover officers, surveillance cameras, and license-plate reading devices. Although there is no exact figure as to how much these precautions cost the city, it is reported that the parade's protection costs exceed $1 million. This situation

---

[35] Cobbs, E.H. American umpire. Boston: Harvard University Press; 2013, p. 17.

[36] Gorman, S. Reuters. Unprecedented security set for California's Rose Parade, Rose Bowl, http://www.reuters.com/article/us-roseparade-security-idUSKBN0UC04Q20151229; 2015 [accessed 08.15.16].

is not unique to California. For example, New York City provides extraordinary protection for its Thanksgiving Day Parade, using everything from plainclothes police officers to bomb-sniffing K-9 (dog) units.[37]

Professional athletes draw people to parades. Not only is there the hope of seeing the athlete, but bystanders also become part of the spectacle. As such, protection must be provided not only for those attending a parade, but also for those in the parade. Those participating in the parade are the center of attention, yet are almost bereft of protection. In most cases, the person participating in the parade not only has little physical protection, but his or her distance from the crowds, filled with anonymous spectators, is often minimal.

No matter what the size of a parade, there are certain principles that all parades organizers must consider. Even before planning a parade route, it is essential to know what regulations, laws, or local ordinances govern the parade. At first, these regulations might seem to be a major inconvenience or worse, but in reality, they provide a structure for the parade and permit the organizer to begin to develop an overall risk management plan. These risk management plans must address at least four special groupings: (1) protection against risks to the parade participants, (2) protection against risks to the parade's spectators, (3) protection against risks to the objects, floats, or equipment used in the parade, and (4) protection against damage to the parade's locale. Furthermore, parade organizers need to have both an evacuation plan for those participating in and those observing the parade. Unfortunately, in today's world, evacuation plans must be subdivided to address an evacuation due to a natural risk and one due to an act of violence. Parade organizers must know where their ambulances are at all times, and should a pedestrian or participant be hurt, how long it will take to get this person to a hospital. Parade organizers also need to have not only lists of essential contact people, but also a way to find these people. It is important not only to have contact information for key people (email addresses, telephone numbers, etc.), but also to know how to reach this person, should the necessary person be unavailable. Once these basics are completed, parade organizers need to understand the parade route and preferably to have walked the route or followed it in a mock motorcade. This real-time exercise allows the parade providers to identify potential problems from the same perspective as that of the parade participants. By actually conducting a pre-parade exercise, the organizers are able to see problems that could occur from the same perspective as that of the participant.

---

[37] Thomas, T., McShane, L. New York Daily News. NYPD rolling out extra security ahead of Macy's Thanksgiving Parade after Paris terror attacks, http://www.nydailynews.com/new-york/nypd-increases-security-thanksgiving-parade-article-1.2445756; 2015 [accessed 08.15.16].

Once this initial planning is completed, the organizers can create a written plan for the parade's safety, security, and hazard protection. Within this plan, the organizers need to account for everything from challenging weather conditions to potential terrorist attacks. They will need to know what type of vehicles will be used, and who is conducting these vehicles' inspection. Likewise, simply having a driver's license may not be sufficient. Questions need to be asked regarding the driver's experience with large flatbed vehicles, or if the driver has anything in his or her personal history that should raise a red flag. In a world in which there is both violence and terrorism, a vehicle at a parade can become a deadly weapon. Parade organizers also should have some knowledge of who will be in the crowd. Since crowds tend not only to be free flowing, but also offer the protection of anonymity, crowd control is especially important when personalities such a major sports figures are participants in a parade and therefore placed in what might be an insecure situation. It should also not be forgotten that some spectators might choose to bring an assortment of animals with them, which might cause additional problems, not only from the perspective of security, but as related to crowd control and health.

Where people watch the parade is also of great importance. Will there be public viewing stands, and in the case of authorities or VIPs, special viewing stands? Will these stands be used to block or reroute both pedestrian and automobile traffic patterns? Will vendors be allowed to enter the stands, and if so, is there a plan to know who these vendors are, and if they pose any potential risk? In other words, how do we do background checks on both vendors and spectators who are in the stands? Are permits required, and if so, what type of permits are required?

Although we might not expect that sports figures would be concerned regarding the assembly and disassembly of a parade, the opposite might well be true. For example, when assembling, the mere presence of these athletes (especially in a team) encourages people to approach them. This potential public–athlete interaction brings up numerous issues regarding personal protection. Since athletes are dependent on their body, a slip or fall while getting on or off a float could have dire consequences, not only from the standpoint of a physical injury, but also economic consequences.

PROTECTION OF VIPS AT PARADES

Parades offer a special set of challenges to security personnel. Although the parade permits an interaction between VIP(s) and parade watchers, it also means that the VIP often has less protection. For example, on May 13, 1981, Pope John Paul II was attacked while riding in an open car. Although the

Pope survived the assassination attack, the incident forced Vatican officials to create a special, bulletproof vehicle called the "Popemobile." The 1981 incident serves as a relatively recent reminder that parade protection is not an easy matter. Although there is no one, single formula for protecting both parade viewers and participants, some of the risks that must be considered include the following:

1. Friendliness of the crowd, its reason for being at the parade, its expected density, and knowing whom the crowd might anger.
2. Location of the parade and places from which a gunman might attack.
3. The potential for the parade to become a target of a terrorist attack.
4. Specialists will also need to know how they might handle unexpected forms of attack, such as a biochemical or radiological attack.
5. Major attacks are not the only threat to a parade. Thus, due to crowd density and the fact that parades take place in open spaces, parade specialists will need to know how to handle lost children, people who need medical attention, and the available evacuation routes.
6. In the case of sports parades, there are two types. There is the controlled parade, such as at an Olympic Stadium. These assume that the protection procedures at the stadium also will apply to the opening parade and closing ceremonies. There is also the open air, tickertape-type parade. These assume goodwill, but in reality, they are extremely hard to protect. It should be emphasized that the fact that an athlete or team has a great deal of goodwill does not necessarily mean that the athlete(s) will not be attacked by someone seeking publicity or trying to create terror. The sheer size of the crowd is enough to become a magnet for those seeking to do harm. Once again, the basic rule, especially in an age of terrorism, is that the more popular the team or the athlete, the higher the potential for random violence.

CHAPTER 10

Interview

In the past nine chapters, we have looked at many forms of sports tourism security. We have also examined many of the issues surrounding sports and athletic travel. We have viewed these issues from both academic and business perspectives, and we have examined issues of safety and security and the ways in which they intertwine.

This chapter is different. Rather than writing about the athletes, the chapter gives voice to the athletes, allowing them to speak for themselves. It is fair to say that most famous athletes have the luxury of additional security. For this reason, this chapter focuses on athletes who are not famous (or are no longer are famous), because they represent the vast majority of athletes and are the norm, rather than the exception to the rule. The athletes chosen for this chapter represent a broad spectrum representing how athletics touch many people's lives. They, like most athletes, are ordinary people who are not household names, but rather, individuals who love sports and live lives similar to most people.

Some of the athletes interviewed are still active in their sport; others are now retired. Taken together, they weave a representative tapestry of the average athlete. Their story is not about the athletic elite, but rather reflects the "athlete" found deep within each of us.

METHODOLOGY

Since this chapter is different from the other chapters, it begins with a methodological section. In reality, developing a methodology is a challenge, as there is no single definition of who is or is not an athlete. In the end, an athlete is a person who proclaims that she or he is an athlete. Furthermore, the number of people who participate in athletic activities is so large, and the types of sports practiced by athletes so broad, that no one image of an athlete comes to mind when we use the word. These variations, both within the term and within the types of sports practiced by athletes, created multiple methodological issues. On the one hand, a statistical quantitative methodology

245

Sports Travel Security. DOI: http://dx.doi.org/10.1016/B978-0-12-805099-6.00010-5

would require the distribution of a large sample size of questionnaires. The questionnaires would then have to be broken down into so many sub-categories (e.g., team sports vs individual sports, by gender, and by professional vs amateur status) that statistical analysis would become meaningless. Additionally, unless thousands of questionnaires were distributed, it would be almost impossible to conduct a scientific (assigning of a p-value) survey, especially as there is no one, universally accepted definition of the statistical universe. Even if thousands of questionnaires were distributed, the survey would still have been nothing more than a convenience sample rather than a systematic sample. In order to allow athletes to express themselves freely, the quantitative approach was replaced with the qualitative. The qualitative approach, although not scientific, allows for a broad spectrum of reported activities and demonstrates the wide variety within the world of athletics.

What follows in this chapter is a series of vignettes representing different sports and athletes at different stages of their lives. To capture these vignettes, open-ended questionnaires/interview guides were distributed, and then follow-up calls were made, or face-to-face meetings were held.

The interview guides were developed in both English and Spanish. The guide was first written in English and then pretested to be sure that the Spanish version reflected not only the question, but also the spirit of the question, and culturally made sense. The cultural part of any translation is almost always the hardest part. For example, the simple question: "How many people are in your family?" in English, usually refers to a person's nuclear family, while the same question in Spanish tends to refer to the extended family. To avoid confusion, the interview guide (questionnaire) was distributed about one week prior to the follow-up conversation. The book's author translated the answers of those athletes who answered in a language other than English. The English translation was then returned to the athlete so that she or he could verify that the translation expressed his or her views accurately. Athletes were also asked to sign a release form so that no athlete's name appears without expressed, written permission.

Since sports tend to be universal, and both university and professional athletes, like the population at large, are not homogeneous, it was also important to take into account the following factors:

- Age of athlete.
- Amount of time spent on the road.
- Athlete's civil status.
- Athlete's financial situation.
- Athlete's gender.
- Athlete's level of religiosity.
- Athlete's religion.

- Athlete travels as part of team.
- Athlete's travel patterns.
- Cultural factors.
- Legal factors.

This list is not meant to be extensive or complete, but rather, it provides us with an entrance into the complexity of the situation. Thus, although some patterns may be recognized across cohorts, reality dictates that we view each athlete as a single and unique individual.

Found below are the stories of several athletes. They are representative of all athletes, and yet, no two are the same. Each athlete has a unique story, and yet each has similarities with his or her colleagues. As we read the tale that each sportsman or woman tells us, we learn how each one provides us with insights into the world of travel for the professional or university athlete. All athletes received the same questions, yet each answered in his or her own way. Every athlete was encouraged to tell his or her personal story in a way that reflected him or herself. Often, the questions asked sparked additional comments or recollections, and these, too, were recorded. Each person is unique, but all of us will recognize something of ourselves in the other.

The following questions, however, were posed to each athlete, either in English or Spanish. Some soccer players were more comfortable in Portuguese than in English or Spanish, and they were permitted to answer in their native tongue. The author translated the Portuguese commentaries into English.

THE INTERVIEW GUIDE

The interview guide consisted of the following questions. The Spanish guide, found at the end of this chapter, is not an exact word-for-word translation, but rather reflects cultural differences and assumptions. Verbiage was changed to elicit the same cultural response as in the English language guide.

- Please tell me your name and current age.
- What professional or university sport(s) did you/do you play?
- In what years did you play this (these) sport(s)?
- Did you play only university sports?
- Did you play only pro sports?
- Did you play on both university and professional team?
- When playing sports, did you travel?

Only answer these questions if you played (or are playing) university sports:

- Would you describe your travel experiences as a university athlete as positive or as a hassle?

- What three things did you like about travel as a university athlete?
- What three things did you dislike about travel as a university athlete?
- Were your professors supportive of your absences while on the road?
- Did your travel negatively impact your formal education?
- Did travel help you bond with your teammates?
- Did you share a room when on travel or have your own room?
- Did you go into the locale when visiting?
- Did you see yourself more on short vacation experience or on a business trip?
- Did you have fun while on travel?
- Were you under a guardian's supervision?
- Did you ever have any safety concerns while away?
- Did you ever have any security concerns while away?
- If you could have changed two things about your sports travel experience, what would they have been?
- What three things would you recommend to a freshman athlete about being on the road while at school?
- What else should I have asked you that I failed to ask?

If you played or are playing in a professional sport, then answer these questions:

- For the most part, would you describe your travel experiences as a professional athlete as positive or as a hassle?
- How is professional athletic travel different from university athletic travel?
- What three things did you like about travel as a professional athlete?
- What three things did you dislike about travel as a professional athlete?
- Was your family supportive of your absences?
- If not married, was travel a positive or negative factor in your social life?
- If married or a single parent, did your travel negatively impact your home situation?
- Did travel help you bond with your teammates?
- Did you share a room when on travel or have your own room?
- When not playing ball, when on the road did you go into the locale when visiting or did you or just stay at the hotel?
- Did you see away games as more of a short vacation experience or more as being on a business trip?
- Did you have fun while on out-of-town travel?
- Were you under a security guard's supervision?
- Did you ever have any safety concerns while on sports travel?
- Did you ever have any security concerns on sports travel?
- What three things would you recommend to a new professional athlete about being on the road?

- If you could have changed two things about your sports travel experience, what would they have been?
- What else should I have asked you that I failed to ask or would you like to tell me?

THE NARRATIVES

Below, the reader will find a number of narratives. They are presented in alphabetical order. After all the athletes tell their stories, a general analysis of the collective whole is provided.

HECTOR ENRIQUE AMADOR RUIZ:[1] PROFESSIONAL SOCCER PLAYER

Hector Enrique Amador Ruiz, age 18,[2] is a Honduran soccer player who currently plays for the Houston Dynamos as a midfielder.[3] Amador has been playing professional soccer, or youth soccer, since the age of 14. His soccer career has taken him from his native Honduras to numerous countries including Brazil, Guatemala, Mexico, and Portugal. As a young man from a poor part of a poor nation, Amador was fascinated by the chance to travel to foreign lands. Travel also gave Amador the gift of bonding with his teammates and having the opportunity to make new friends. As a young professional athlete, he was thrilled to be able to wear a team uniform, see distant lands, and visit new places. His only bad (travel) experience was in Brazil, where the hotel provided the team no essential services (including food) on Christmas Day. As Amador traveled more, he also learned the frustrations of travel. He discovered that often, travel meant long waits at the airport, flight delays, and missed connections. Amador used these delays to his advantage by deepening his relationships with his teammates and finding creative games and conversation by which to pass the time. Once at the site of play, Amador reported that the team distributed rooms in such a way to prevent cliques from forming, and as a way to assure that all of the teammates had the opportunity to know each other. The hotel experience, then, became another way for team members not simply to bond, but to learn to work together and form a single social unit.

---

[1] Please note that Spanish last names are composed of the father's last name and the mother's last name. The second last name adds precision to the first last name. For legal purposes, it is the father's last name that dominates.

[2] All athletes' ages are given at the time of writing of this book. Their given age reflects their age in 2016 and not at the time when they were engaged in their sport.

[3] Interview given in Spanish and translated into English by the author.

Since Amador was basically on his own from the age of 14 years onward, he had no real family support. On the other hand, many of his teammates did have the support of a loving family. Amador noted the importance of having a supportive family not only to alleviate times of loneliness, but also to have a trusted older person as both a mentor and guide.

Amador viewed his soccer trips as business trips rather than social trips. Despite the fact that he was in another city for reasons of business, he also reported that whenever he visited another location, he spent as much of his free time as possible getting to know the host city. These excursions afford the players the opportunity to learn something about the local culture and cuisine. He noted that players are not permitted to consume alcoholic beverages while on travel. Although he does not specifically know of any player who bent the rules, he does admit that there are rumors, or gossip, about players who found ways to do so. He emphasized that from his perspective, these are only rumors, and that he does not know personally, nor is acquainted with, anyone who has not followed the rules. Similarly, there were rumors that some players found ways to seek out prostitutes. Once again, Amador emphasized that he personally did not know anyone who hired a prostitute and that not only did most players abide by the rules, but the players with whom he came in contact were careful not to do anything that might even remotely be considered illegal or immoral.

He also noted that the team almost always had professional protection. The soccer club provided this protection, and due to these protective services Amador never felt fearful, with one exception that took place in Colombia. When asked to explain this fear, Amador indicated that although nothing happened to any of his teammates or himself, Colombia's reputation at the time of his visit provoked fear. This was compounded when in Colombia, some people confused his team for a Nicaraguan team and several of the fans verbally attacked the team. It should be stated there was no physical abuse, only verbal abuse.

Although Amador plays in a post September 11th world, terrorism issues so far have not been a problem. However, he is slated to become part of Honduras' national team (*La selección nacional de Honduras*), and this higher profile on the world stage may mean that there will be a need for greater caution and security.

When asked what advice he would give a new player, starting as he did at 14 years of age, he immediately answered that a young soccer player must be physically, mentally, and emotionally strong. He notes that there are a great many disappointments along the way, and there are always people prepared to take advantage of a young soccer player. This is especially true for a young man first starting out in any professional sport. The player, especially if he comes from an underprivileged background, at first sees himself as living a charmed life. Everything is taken care of for him. It is only later that the player comes to realize that professional sports are like any other business, and to be successful, one must produce. Thus, to be a success, a player must enter the game prepared to work hard and sacrifice for the future.

JOVANA DIMOVIC: PROFESSIONAL AND UNIVERSITY TENNIS PLAYER

Jovana Dimovic, age 33, tells an unusual story, in that she played professional tennis before she played university tennis. Dimovic came to the United States from Serbia at the age of 18. Prior to receiving a full tennis scholarship, she played European tennis at the professional level. Since her professional career occurred during her years as a minor, she traveled under the guardianship of her father or coach. She noted that when traveling with her coach, and not a parent, a colleague's parent was also present.

From Dimovic's perspective, professional tennis travel afforded her the opportunity to experience local cultures and sample local cuisines. Her tennis experience was both athletic and educational, and helped shape who she is today. Travel occurred on weekends and permitted Dimovic to participate in her sport, attend school, and develop a special bond with her father, as well as special friendships with fellow athletes. On the road, especially as a young girl, she shared a room with her father. When traveling with a coach, accommodations were always made so that she was appropriately watched over.

For Dimovic, the travel experience was intertwined with her professional sports experience. These experiences not only paid off in monetary value, but also in cultural and educational value. Her professional career gave her more than mere prize money. It also provided a sense of personal pride and feeling of accomplishment. Since she was less than 18 years of age when she played professional tennis, she had to give up some of the activities typical of young people. Dimovic today realizes that she missed spending time with other members of her family and sacrificed much of her (high) school social life for her commitment to tennis. In retrospect, she sees these sacrifices as trade-offs. Dimovic learned that everything in life comes with a price, and part of the price for being a professional athlete at an early age is that she often did not have the same experiences that other young women had. On the other hand, she gained in many other ways. For example, since same people tended to compete in tournaments, when not on the court, there was a great deal of bonding and these young ladies established deep friendships. The basic modus operandi was similar to that of many trial lawyers and in her adult life, these experiences have served her well; for example, with her tennis competitors, she learned to separate friendship from work. She was a friend with her tennis colleagues off the court and fierce competitors with these same people on the court.

Since professional travel was for Dimovic as much a learning and bonding experience as a competitive sports experience, she tended to see these short journeys as more weekend excursions rather than business travel. Security was not a problem for her because she traveled with her father. Playing professional tennis as a minor meant that there was no need for additional security. Although she admits that sexual harassment was always a potential problem, due to the fact that her father or guardian was with her, she had no concerns. She noted that tennis does not arouse the same passions that may result in violence that are associated with some other sports.

When asked what she would advise others who seek to be underage (minor) athletes, Dimovic spoke about the need for a parent to have good communication with a child, and make sure that the athlete knows how much hard work and sacrifice are involved. Dimovic noted that the hours are long and tedious, and the work is hard, but the reward is great.

Since Dimovic's university sports experience occurred after her professional experiences, she came to the university with a different perspective than people who entered university life without such life experiences.

Owing to her athletic skills, perfect English, and quick mind, Dimovic was able to win a full scholarship to an American university. She found the university travel world to be quite different from the world of professional sports that she knew in Serbia. If her professional travel was a mixture of cultural learning and playing tennis, her university world was very much more businesslike. University women's tennis travel was often composed merely of going from Point A to Point B. Her travel tended to consist of arrival and check-in at a hotel, eating as a team at a restaurant, returning to hotel to sleep, playing her match, and departing for home. These trips were not meant to be learning or cultural experiences, but rather, were all about winning tennis matches.

Travel was not, however, a total hassle and the joy of bonding and making friends with her teammates or fellow players added much to her travel experience.

When asked if her professors were supportive, Dimovic answered that this was a mixed bag. There were definitely professors who went out of their way to be supportive, and there were those who noted that athletics were an extra-curricular activity, and felt no compulsion to go out of their way to accommodate her needs. From these professors' perspectives, it was her responsibility to create a life balance and blend her athletics with her academic work. She noted that the team traveled every weekend, leaving on Thursday or Friday and, at times, getting back late on Sunday. Dimovic argued that her sports travel had a negative impact on her academic career in that there was not sufficient time to study and she often suffered from sleep deprivation. At times, she realized that due to travel stress and time restrictions, she would have to accept a grade of C or B instead of seeking an A, because there simply was not sufficient time to travel, do school work, and play tennis.

These academic tennis travel experiences were definitely more business-oriented than educational, and the university was interested in going to the destination, winning, and returning. For example, although she traveled with coaches and trainers who were there principally to handle someone being injured, there was little or no concern shown about food intake or types of food provided. Often, meals consisted of fast food or all-you-can-eat buffets, and there was no real supervision when it came to hours of sleep or intake of vitamins.

Owing to the need to overschedule, players often suffered from undue amounts of stress. Furthermore, the team often traveled via 15-seater vans, the most dangerous form of transportation. The vans were often uncomfortable, and although the athletes did not perceive the danger, they were in significant danger. In a study by Tarlow and Island, the authors noted that:

> The National Health and Transportation Safety Administration (NHTSA) has demonstrated that these vans are excessively risky; yet, despite the fact that this mode of transportation has resulted in many injuries and deaths among collegiate athletes, their use continues.[4]

Despite the travel challenges, these were good experience and Dimovic stated that during her years of travel, she was never subjected to issues of sexual harassment, and never had anything stolen. Her advice to a future student athlete was to manage your time well and understand that, in life, there are always trade-offs.

ERIN LECHLER: VOLLEYBALL

Erin Lechler, age 36, played volleyball during her Texas A&M University years of 1997–2001. Lechler stated that her sports experience was very positive, and she still has fond memories of her time spent playing intercollegiate volleyball.

Lechler grew up in a family that did not travel much. In fact, prior to entering college, she had never been outside the state of Texas. It was only through her university athletic travels that she was able to see much of the United States.

---

[4] Tarlow, P. Island J. *Sports Team Travel Security*. CRISP Report, ASIS, 2016, p. 12.

Lechler traveled as far away as Hawaii, and was fascinated by the variety of scenery and cultures that she found across the nation. For someone not used to traveling, university travel had the additional advantage that she did not have to worry about travel details. She merely had to show up on time and the university made all the travel arrangements for her. Lechler stated that she found her travel experiences a wonderful way to make new friends or deepen already existing friendships.

Lechler noted that she played volleyball during the precellphone era. This fact meant that the women on the team spent a good deal of their free time chatting, going shopping, or simply getting to know each other rather, than being on their phones. She also complimented the coaches in their room assignments. The coaches did a good job of mixing roommates so that team members got to know everyone on the team, and these interactions helped develop a team spirit and camaraderie.

The pleasures of travel did not mean that Lechler did not have travel challenges. She discovered that studying on a plane can be a challenge, and mixing sporting activities with study and class scheduling was especially difficult as volleyball games were played on Wednesdays and Saturdays. This schedule meant that she had to travel on Tuesdays, play volleyball and return home on Wednesdays, and then travel again on Fridays so that she could play on Saturdays. On the other hand, there were many weeks when she had plenty of time for class and she did not remember missing many class sessions.

Lechler made a point of speaking to professors at the beginning of each semester, and then periodically reminding them when she needed to travel. Lechler stated that using this methodology, she rarely had problems, and that most of her professors were supportive. The method worked so well, and her careful planning paid off to such a degree, that Lechler believed that her sports travel had a positive impact on her education and did not permit her to slough off or become lazy.

Lechler divided her volleyball games into two separate sections: conference trips, which were all business, and tournaments, which were more relaxed and permitted more flexibility.

Travel safety was not a problem. She never faced any form of sexual harassment or physical threat, and stated that the university did a good job of protecting the women. Lechler also remembers that they did not travel in the 15-seat vans that have caused so many problems. In most cases, the team used either the smaller, private (university) airplanes or large university buses. When vans were used, they were of the smaller and safer variety. Travel on private planes had some challenges, such as lack of adequate restroom facilities, and in more turbulent weather, travel on a small plane could be a challenge to the stomach. On the other hand, small, private planes were convenient and got the team back in time to attend classes. When asked what advice she would give to a new student who wanted to be a student athlete, she immediately responded to take an early initiative with professors and let them know that you appreciate their class.

SOLOMÓN LIBMAN: PROFESSIONAL SOCCER PLAYER

Solomón Libman, age 32, is a professional soccer player and part of Peru's national soccer team. Libman has played professional soccer for the last 14 years. He began his soccer career at the age of 5 and by age 15 he had been on his country's national junior teams: on the team for those under 15, on the team for those under 17, and on the team for those under 20. He now plays both for a professional local Peruvian team (called "clubs" in soccer) and as part of the national team (selección nacional). He began his adult professional career in 2002 and continues to play professional ball, currently as a member of Club Deportivo: Universidad César Vallejo (UCV).

Libman's sports career has taken him to a wide variety of nations, including Austria, Denmark, France, Japan, (South) Korea, Russia, and the United States. He has traveled throughout Latin America. He not only enjoys these international matches but also reports that playing in international competition is a major career boost.

Since soccer has been a part of his life since childhood, he always has enjoyed the support of his family. He grew up with soccer and it has become a part of his daily routine. He reports, however, that his frequent trips and his consistent having to be on the road meant that he not only missed his family but at times missed important family occasions. On the other hand, Libman states that these frequent trips meant that he was able to bond with his teammates, and in some ways they became his "other family." In fact, he says that the bonding experiences is one of the best parts of team travel.

Although Libman never played on a university team, he attended university while playing professional sports. His university-plus-professional soccer play was a mixed experience. As a professional soccer player he had to balance his work (soccer) with his academic studies. During his time at college, Libman had some professors who were understanding of his need to balance practices and games with studies. He stated that these professors were more than willing to help him receive an education and understood his need to work. Unfortunately, he also had other professors who were not helpful. He speaks of professors who had the attitude that he needed to dedicate himself either to sports or to his academics. These professors held the position that the two simply do not mix and they were not going to bend their courses around his needs. When traveling professionally he also had to find ways to do his class work. This work–study routine was a consistent balancing act throughout his university career.

The need to travel professionally while studying also presented other personal challenges. As a professional, he had to travel to a wide variety of locations and at the same time he had to share a room with colleagues. The room-sharing experience was positive, but of course it also meant a decrease in personal privacy. Libman reports that it was important for him to learn, whenever possible, something about the city or locale in which he was traveling. These cultural excursions, however, were not always easy and it was clear to him that travel was not about fun but rather that being on the road to play an away-game was strictly business.

On the rare occasions when it is possible, he will leave a hotel to get to know the locale in which he is playing, but in most cases he only has time for practices, scouting out the stadium, and rest before a game. When he travels with Peru's national team these trips are purely business trips. If there is any non-business activity or cultural activity it is after the game has finished but these outings are rare.

Libman was never worried about his safety or security. He reports that a player who follows the rules and does what he is asked to do is not in danger. The key is to follow the coach's (director técnico) guidelines and schedule. When traveling with the Peruvian national team there is always security. Security may come in three ways: security provided by the hotel, security provided by the team, and security provided by the locale.

When asked about advice for other players or future players, Libman emphasizes the importance of acting in a way that enhances rather than diminishes one's reputation and the importance of following team guidelines. He reminds up-and-coming athletes to enjoy what they do, but take their work seriously. He stresses the importance of learning how to live with others, bonding with others and respecting their boundaries. Finally, for those who play at the level of a national team, to never forget that they are not merely athletes but also representatives of their nation and what they do reflects not only on their reputation but the reputation of their team and country.

CORY MALTZ: UNIVERSITY BASEBALL PLAYER; UNIVERSITY OF NEW MEXICO, USA

Although Cory Maltz, age 26, was drafted into professional baseball, he chose not to pursue this career. His story, then, is typical of thousands of university athletes who enjoyed their sports experience, and after finishing university, went on to other careers.

Maltz played baseball beginning in 2008 at Weatherford Junior College; he then played at the University of New Mexico for a season, after which time his father passed away. Upon the death of his father, he returned to Stephen F. Austin State University in Texas, playing there through the 2013 season and graduating. His athletic experience in theory was different from that of older players in that his entire college career occurred during what security analysts often now call "an age of terrorism." From this perspective, his story demonstrates the "disconnect" between the news we consume and most people's daily lives. Although Cory did not play baseball for a salary, he attended college on a scholarship, and as in all of these cases, the line between scholarships and "play for pay" (professional salary) can be somewhat blurry. University students do not receive a salary per se, but universities often treat athletes on scholarship as if they were "employees." Although students do not receive a salary, they do receive "services in kind" (education for their time on the field).

Maltz reported that his baseball travel experiences were a mixture of fun, and at times, stress. In contrast to football players, those who participate in baseball have many more games in their season and spend a great deal more time on the road. This fact means that university student baseball players, unlike student football players, may have to spend a great deal of time away from the classroom, and that class participation might be either challenging or downright impossible. Finding ways to balance time for school work and baseball could often be a major challenge.

When speaking with Maltz, it became clear that he divided the actual travel experience, being on a bus or plane, from the "being there" and the post-travel experience. He found the travel experience to be fun, and the buses to be both adequate and safe, although he expressed the need for more legroom. Baseball players, and particularly student baseball players, however, have hectic schedules, and there were times when after an eight-hour bus ride, Maltz would return home only to have to depart for another road trip on the next day. Maltz also reported that at times, he would come back to campus entirely exhausted and then have to be in class the next day or spend time preparing a class project that had to be presented the following day.

When asked if his professors understood his situation, Maltz stated that some of his professors were supportive and allowed him to adapt his academic schedule to his travel needs. Others were less flexible, and some clearly resented his absences and insisted that he take exams in the presence of a proctor while riding on the team bus to the next game. Despite the challenges of constantly being on the road, Maltz saw these challenges not as a negative, but rather as lessons in balancing various sides of his life. His need to juggle time forced him to find ways to transform school athletic trips into life learning experiences. Maltz stated that he benefited from these trips, as they provided team members the opportunity for bonding experiences and learning to work together as a single unit.

Maltz comments about his fellow students' attitudes reflect the research in the academic literature. He remembered that some students might have resented his absences or shunned him, and that most of the athletes tended to socialize among themselves. He reported that few of his fellow students sought out athletes as friends, and thus, he was unaware of most people's feelings. Personally, he did not face any overt hostility but could understand why resentments might occur.

At away games, Maltz's experiences were typical of those of many other athletes. Soon after arrival for an away game, team members usually went straight to practice, followed by a team dinner and free time. During free time, athletes were able to go into town as long as they were in the hotel by the set curfew. Curfew was normally 10 pm, but if the team had an extra day before the game, the coach would extend curfew to 11:00 or 11:30 pm. When team members visited the local entertainment district, they did so without chaperones.

Game days were almost a relief, and from Maltz's perspective, the practices were often a lot harder than the actual games. As university football players also noted, Maltz indicated that once having arrived in the destination city, the mindset changed and the athletes saw their presence as "work." Departures were as soon as possible after the game ended.

University baseball players have a very strenuous travel schedule. To keep the players in top physical condition, the team has a number of strength trainers who coached the team members on everything from proper food intake and nutrition, to types of exercise and physical activity. Maltz indicated that these people were essential to his physical and mental well-being.

Despite the fact that Maltz played in the post September 11 period, he stated that he never thought about, or was concerned about, issues of safety or security. Trainers watched over the athletes and perhaps because college baseball does not create the passion of sports such as football or soccer, the players did not worry about acts of terror or crazed fans. It should also be noted that although many people attend baseball games, because there are many more games in the baseball season than in football or soccer, attendance at each individual game tends to be much lower than at these other sports. This lower attendance may mean that baseball is a less attractive target.

When Cory was asked what he would change about his baseball travel experience he stated a desire for more comfortable travel, the need to have tutors during travel due to the fact that baseball players miss a great deal of classroom time, and consistency of hotel quality. He would remind new players to stay on top of their schoolwork and to remember that these trips are not vacations. Finally, he recommends incoming students to eat right and sleep when they can!

SETH MCKINNEY: UNIVERSITY AND PROFESSIONAL FOOTBALL

Seth McKinney, age 37, played university football for Texas A&M from 1998 to 2001. Beginning in 2002, he played professional (NFL) football for the Miami Dolphins, Cleveland Browns, and Buffalo Bills from 2002 until 2010.

When speaking about his university travel experiences, McKinney described these trips as "not unpleasant." Although he was well treated he noted that it is hard for a football lineman to be comfortable on a small (chartered) plane. He also remembered that chartered airplane food was not always enticing. Despite the smallness of some of the aircraft, accommodations to the players' size and comfort level were made. For example, there were never three players in a row, and the empty middle seat between the players provided some extra room.

McKinney noted that because the football season is relatively short in comparison to many other sports, and 50% of games were played at home, he never really had to adjust to travel in the same way that, for example, baseball players did. On the other hand, players spent the night before all games, including home games, at a hotel, and thus during the football season, he had an ongoing hotel experience.

McKinney played at Texas A&M, a major, college-football school. Most students there are enamored with their school's football program and are extremely loyal to it. Perhaps this might be one of the reasons that McKinney did not come across any of his fellow students who might have had disparaging remarks. Most professors were supportive, and even those who were not were, for the most part, "noncombative." He also had high praise for the university's athletic academic advisors. These men and women tried to steer athletes away from professors who, when it came to student athletes needing to travel, have uncooperative attitudes. When asked about conflicts between practices, travel time, and academic schedules, McKinney explained that these conflicts were kept to a minimum or resolved either by taking a particular course, with a schedule that would not conflict with practice, in the postseason semester, or by assuring that courses were finished prior to practice and travel time. McKinney observed that as football players travel only on Fridays, they have less of a time conflict than those in sports that have longer seasons and where travel is more frequent.

When asked how he saw his sports travel from the human or social side, McKinney stated that these trips were a good relationship-building (bonding) experience. Players shared a room, ate together, and watched movies together. This bonding experience occurred both when the team was on the road and at home, as nights before all games were spent at a hotel.

On the evening before a game, the players were expected to be in their room by curfew time (10:30 or 11:00 pm) and were checked on by monitors (coaches or security officers). When asked if he viewed these trips as "fun/ mini-vacations or more as business trips" McKinney used the phrase *non-stressful business travel*. He noted that players were well cared for. For example, after team meetings, there was pizza in their rooms, and they had access to pay-for-view movies. Part of their being cared for extended to what they were not allowed to do. They were not free to roam around a city as they pleased, and for the most part, they merely stayed at a hotel, went the next day to the stadium, played their game, and left. Most of McKinney's university football experiences took place prior to the attacks of September 11, 2001. McKinney expressed the fact that he had no safety or security concerns while on travel.

He understood that although he might have fun on a trip, the purpose of the trip was not to have fun, but to do a job. When asked what advice he would give an incoming player, he immediately answered: "Be on time and follow the rules!"

McKinney's professional experiences have points of similarities with his university experiences, but also a number of contrasts. His professional time occurred post-9/11. He described this professional travel as "real" business trips, and that professional sports are not play, but work. For the professional player, football is a job, and players are expected to perform. In some ways, travel is easier for the professional. There is a certain amount of freedom and comfort that is unknown in the world of university football. Players can go out to eat prior to a game. They travel out of town on larger planes, for example a 757 or a 747, and during the outbound portion of the trip, key players, such as the quarterback, are provided with first-class tickets. After team meetings, players are provided with an array of snacks, they stay at trusted hotels, and there are security guards posted on the players' floor(s). Once the player becomes a "veteran" (having played for about 4 years) he no longer has to share a room with a teammate. Although the players' wives might come to a major game, such as a Super Bowl, in most cases, travel consisted of a one-day event and players traveled without family. Since professional players are only on the road for eight games, their travel experiences are somewhat limited. Once the game is over, players return home as soon as possible. This shortness of stay reinforces the idea that these are pure business trips rather than cultural journeys or short vacations. Although McKinney played in the post-9/11 period, when stadium security became an issue, he was aware of what we might call minimal security challenges. Players were now expected to go through some form of megatometer or metal detector. There were times when some fans may have thrown an egg at a team's bus, but he called these actions "controlled anger." He also remembered that there were stories about late night "hassle" telephone calls but he never experienced any of these calls. In a like manner, he never saw any of the violent fan actions (or reactions) that might be typical of a European soccer match. McKinney's advice to a young player was the same as to a new player at a university: "Follow the rules and be on time!"

ANTHONY (TONY) PAIGE: UNIVERSITY AND PROFESSIONAL FOOTBALL

Tony Paige, age 52, is the Executive Vice President of Football at Perennial Sports and Entertainment. Prior to his retirement, Paige spent 9 years playing on three different professional football teams.

Paige's sports career is extensive. He played for both university and professional (US) football teams. His university career was at Virginia Tech, where he played football during the early 1980s. In 1984, he made the transition from university football to professional football and joined the New York Jets professional football team. His professional football career lasted 9 years: 3 years with the Jets, three with the Detroit Lions, and finally, 3 years with the Miami Dolphins. He retired from professional football at the age of 30.

Paige did not describe his university athletic travel experience in either positive or negative terms. He emphasized that his university football travel experience was limited. His trips were of short duration, and because football is played only once a week, his football trips were limited in number. As is true of many who play football, Paige would leave for the host city on a Friday, then have dinner, and see a movie at the hotel with teammates. On Saturdays, he played football and soon after the game ended, returned home.

From his perspective, these journeys were pleasant, but not necessarily cultural or educational experiences. Paige emphasized that football players travel less than many other athletes who have more games or competitions within their schedule.

Paige noted that his schoolwork came first. When he traveled, if he had schoolwork that needed to be finished while he was on the road, he brought it with him. He found his professors to be understanding of his situation, and they treated his absences as they might have treated any other university-excused absence. He did not speak of any conflicts either with faculty members or fellow students.

When asked if these travel experiences were also team-bonding experiences, Paige stated that as a university team, the members ate together. When on travel he shared a room with a teammate and the team members and staff shared a Friday evening movie together. As a university football player, he was under the supervision of the coaches, who controlled the players' travel time, which included pregame curfews. From Paige's perspective, even his university trips were a sort of "business trip" in that he traveled to another location to do a job (play football), did his job, and then returned home. During his university years, Paige did not have any travel security or safety issues. What was important was learning team discipline, which perhaps was best exemplified by being on time! It should be noted that he played in an age that was less complicated, and few Americans were aware of any threats from terrorists or other acts of violence.

Paige's professional period was in many ways different from the university period of his life. Paige noted that his professional athletic travel was both more and less regimented than university travel. While he had greater flexibility in going out to dinner on the night before a game, time management was a major factor. For example, if he arrived late to the football team's complex, where the team met to depart for the airport, then in the professional world, fines were levied. As a professional player, he clearly understood that travel was part of the job, and that 50% of his games would be played away from home. According to Paige, his wife understood the necessity of travel. He noted that if they wanted to eat and pay the bills then "travel was a part of the package." Although rookies and younger players shared a room, once one became a "veteran" (more established members of the team with perhaps 4 years of experience) players were given their own rooms.

Travel was strictly travel and not tourism. Once the game was over, players went almost directly to the airport. Thus, Paige saw these trips as business trips. During Paige's time playing football, he was never afraid and security was never an issue. When asked what advice he would give to a new NFL player, his answer was almost immediate: "Be on time!"

DINIS RESENDE:[5] EUROPEAN FOOTBALL (SOCCER) (PORTUGAL)

Dinis Resende, age 49, is a former Portuguese soccer (known as *futebol* in Portuguese) star. He played soccer for his university club and upon completion of his university studies, he played professional soccer. His professional soccer career lasted from 1981 until his "retirement" in 2005. From that point until the time of this book's writing, Resende coached (técnico) soccer.

Resende sees his travel experience as a positive one. He stated that he enjoyed seeing new cities, meeting new people, and experiencing different cuisines. Being in Europe, Resende had ample opportunity to experience various

---

[5] Interview given in Portuguese and translated by the author.

cultures, especially as the cultural and cuisine differences might be more marked than in the United States and the distances between cultures are shorter. Resende's positive experience was based not only on his personality and positive outlook on life, but also on the fact that his university professors were highly supportive of his sporting activities. His teammates were also supportive, and he found travel to be a bonding experience both on and off the field. When on travel, Resende shared a room with other teammates. It is interesting to note that Resende's travel experiences included a tourism component. The team not only encouraged this curiosity about other cultures, but also facilitated daytime (nighttime) excursions. These visitations, however, were not, random. They were almost predetermined by the (soccer) sporting association.

There were also travel challenges. For example, during his university days, the frequent changing of hotels, and the need to take non point-to-point flights, made travel often longer and more arduous than he would have liked, and travel fatigue was always a possibility.

As a student, Resende did not see these travel experiences as work, but rather as additional cultural learning experiences. The same was not true once Resende entered the world of professional soccer. During his professional career, these journeys were much more serious, and for the most part were business trips in which his athletic capabilities and results determined, at least in part, his professional reputation and potential earning capacity.

Resende indicated that as a university student, he felt well protected. His team had the support of local authorities, such as police departments, along with private, contracted security companies.

Despite these security precautions, Resende noted that security was a major concern even on the university level. When facing rival teams, personal security was a concern, stemming from the fact that European soccer fans are highly passionate, at times so passionate that violence is an ever-present threat.

When asked what he would recommend to a student athlete who was just beginning his or her career, Resende noted first, the importance of listening to coaches and trainers; second, meeting and being mentored by upper classman; and third, developing a sense of sportsmanship where personal ambitions are set aside. Perhaps the key question for Resende was the following:

> *How do you understand your motivation and do these motivations match your personal goals?*
> *How does working with a team fit into these goals? What motivates you?*

Resende's professional experiences were different from his university experiences. Perhaps the reason is that once he entered the world of professional sports, his "playing" became his "work." He noted that as a professional athlete, he felt emotional pressure to win, and the fact that these matches were now pay-to-play rather than merely play, transformed the experience. Travel as a professional meant that he had to be precise in his planning. As a professional soccer player, Resende had a much greater amount of technical support. The team also had staff members dedicated to making travel as hassle-free as possible. When his team traveled, staff dealt with everything from psychologists to physicians. While Resende reported a relatively open or unregulated travel experience on the university level, he could not say the same for the professional level, where food choices were limited or nonexistent, and access to the media and telecommunications was restricted during travel.

There were also difficulties in being both father/husband and traveling athlete. He missed family events, and family schedules had to deal with an absentee father. Despite these "home front" challenges, Resende reported that he enjoyed the full support of his family.

As noted, visitations to local sites were much more controlled during Resende's time as a professional player than during his time as a university player. Part of the reason might be due to the fact that the players had professional security. A second reason might be that emotions run extremely high in professional soccer, and confrontations with opposing teams had to be avoided at all costs.

His advice to up-and-coming professional athletes did not differ greatly from his advice to young university athletes, but he would ask young professionals to think about why they chose a collective, rather than individual, professional lifestyle, and what soccer philosophically or emotionally means to them.

JAKE ROTHER: UNIVERSITY AND PROFESSIONAL TENNIS

Jake Rother is a 23-year-old tennis player who has played both competitive university tennis and professional tennis. Like many tennis players, Jake's competitive career began at an early age; in this case, in 1998, at the age of five. Rother played tennis, either singles or doubles, for the University of Indiana. He reports that his university travel experience was mostly positive, although having four players assigned to a room was challenging both from a personal perspective and from a competitive perspective. He noted that this many roommates did not encourage sleep, and that not sleeping well the night before a competition could be a real challenge. Despite the cramped quarters Jake enjoyed his university travel experiences, especially the bonding that occurred with other team members, although the tightness of quarters and the lack of personal space did produce some difficult situations.

Rother had some professors who were supportive of his athletics, but others were unbending when it came to rescheduling exams or deadlines for handing in assignments. Tennis required a great deal of time on the road and this meant that he often missed classes. Although he was able to make up much of his work, he missed out on lectures and class discussions. There was a clear trade-off between his sport and his academic career. Rother saw his university tennis trips more as business travel than as pleasure travel. However, because he loves competitive tennis, these trips were still enjoyable. Rother reported that he had a good amount of freedom when on university tennis trips and that often his "guardian" was himself.

On the other hand, and perhaps because the world today is a more dangerous place than even 20 years ago, the students were warned to use extreme caution in certain locations. For example, when traveling along the Mexican border, Rother and his teammates were warned by their coach not to open their (hotel) door to anyone. When asked what he would recommend to a new student-athlete, Rother answered that he would tell the student to pack as lightly as possible, heighten flexibility, lower expectations, and have fun.

Rother took a different view when it came to his professional tennis experiences. He noted that tennis on the professional level is both a gamble and a job. The professional player must cover his own expenses in the hopes of recovering the "investment" in winnings. Additionally, travel arrangements must be made by the player, rather than having a university department where someone else handles these arrangements. Since Rother did not play in the top tier of professional tennis, he noted that he often lacked resources and was not given "royal" treatment. Despite that, as a young professional, he enjoyed the opportunity to take responsibility for his life and to share time with fellow athletes. He also enjoyed the support of his family. Most of Jake's professional career occurred when he was under the age of 18. He traveled with friends who lived in Europe, and was under the supervision of a friend's parent or coach.

Rother expressed travel concerns, especially when traveling outside the United States. During this period of travel, he was either with older friends who had family living in Mexico, or with friends living in Europe.

Rother noted that travel at the lower end of the professional scale is an investment or a gamble based on the hope of winning. He pointed out the fact that wealthier players, or players who had greater economic backing, were able to absorb some of the hassles of travel, (e.g., staying in nicer hotels) than those whose resources were more limited. When asked what Rother would advise a young, up-and-coming professional, his number-one answer was: "Bring lots of money!"

TIMOTHY SPEAKMAN: UNIVERSITY AND MINOR LEAGUE PROFESSIONAL BASEBALL

Timothy Speakman, age 51, played both college and professional baseball. He played at Fullerton College in Fullerton, California, in 1984–85, and from 1985 until 1989, he played professional, minor league baseball for the Boston Red Sox organization. In 1986, Speakman was injured, and although under contract, he did not actively play baseball for his last two-plus seasons.

Speakman described his college travel experiences as pleasant. He was able to see new places and meet new people. Baseball travel afforded him a break from his normal, daily activities, and permitted him the opportunity to bond with fellow teammates. On the other hand, the travel part of the trip (versus the social part) was not always easy, even in the 1980s. There were logistic problems and few, if any. Extracurricular (other than game) social or cultural activities were provided. Other hassles were lack of access to clothes washing machines and dryers. He noted often it was easier to wash his uniform at home.

As a student athlete, most of his professors understood his need for class absences, although he reported that other professors made it clear that they did not believe that sports had a legitimate part in a college curriculum. Despite some pushback, Speakman did not see his baseball activities as interfering with his college education. As in most cases in academic sports, Speakman was expected to share a room on travel, and on those occasions when time allowed and transportation was available, visited the locales in which he was playing.

Speakman described his collegiate baseball travel as "business trips with pleasurable intervals." Speakman played ball in the 1980s, and this period in the United States was a time of relative safety and security. During his years in baseball, he noted that he considered both the buses used to transport the team and the hotels in which the team stayed to be safe, and he had no concerns regarding his travel safety. When asked what he would tell a new student athlete who plans on playing collegiate baseball, Speakman recommended that the young athlete find a mentor, an upper classman with whom to room and from whom to learn. Also, he would advise this sportsman to remember that he is not playing for himself, but his actions represent his school and his school's image.

Speakman saw his time in professional, minor league baseball as similar to his college athletic career, but with a great deal more travel. Once he began to receive a salary, it was clear that these were business trips. Not only was he paid to play, but also, the minor leagues are showcases for the major leagues.

Thus, players are always aware of the fact that their goal is to move from the minor to major leagues, and therefore, they are always under observation.

Just as in collegiate baseball, minor league travel afforded bonding time with teammates and greater possibilities to see new places. Since baseball was the player's primary job, the conflict between sports and academics ceased to be an issue. Although Speakman reported that during his minor league career, his family was supportive, he had to face the reality of hostile fans and of meal quality that was inconsistent at best.

As a professional baseball player, Speakman reported having much more freedom of movement than when he was a collegiate athlete. When public transportation or taxis were available, he was able to use his free time to visit the cities in which he was playing. Possibly because minor league games draw less attention than major leagues, and passions are often less, security was not provided to the players. When asked what changes he would have made or what advice he would give a rookie, his answers had an academic bent. He suggested that new players use their free time to improve their knowledge base and learn more about the cities visited during this time on the road. In that sense, Speakman became a symbol of the scholar athlete!

T. J. MARCUM: KYLE FIELD AND BRIGHT FOOTBALL COMPLEX AT TEXAS A&M UNIVERSITY

This chapter has presented the reader with a number of interviews of athletes who represent not necessarily the elite or big names of the athletic world, but rather the average athlete, the man or woman whom we may not know by name, but through whose efforts the world of athletics exists. Throughout the interview process, the issue of stadiums constantly arose. To round out these interviews, T. J. Marcum of Texas A&M's Kyle Field and Bright Football Complex was kind enough to sit down for a long interview. Marcum is unique in that he has been both a basketball coach and intimately involved in the workings of one of America's largest sports stadiums. He sees the world of athletics from the perspective of a player, coach, and one who must worry about the venue's safety and security.

There is no doubt that Texas A&M's football stadium, Kyle Field, is large. It holds just under 103,000 fans and sits between the university campus and city streets. It is a stadium that has grown with its school and reflects the passion for sports, and football in particular, of Texas A&M.

The interview with T. J. Marcum revealed how complex and intertwined are questions of safety and security, building security, fan security, and player/

coach security. It should be noted that his interview reflects not just the world at Texas A&M, but also to a great measure, any athletic venue throughout the country. For example, Marcum's greatest day-to-day fear is of a broken pipe or pipes that could cause water damage to the entire facility. In terms of events and/or competitions, he noted that in a post-9/11 world, we no longer live in a make-believe world, but rather one of harsh realities. The stadium authorities are well aware of the fact that it would take just one deranged, crazy, or evil person to create havoc. The havoc would not only result in actual tragedy, but would also harm the school's reputation.

Marcum also is well aware of the fact that this person (or persons) with harmful intent need to use a gun. For example, a person on an upper deck who throws an empty bottle or other object(s) from a higher deck can cause great harm to guests below. Thus, security personnel and stadium authorities have to worry about everything from an unintentional flying object to a bomb. Furthermore, in an age of terrorism coupled with fear and crowd paranoia, there is always the potential for panic. In many ways, a panic could be as deadly, or even more deadly, than an intentional act of violence. In discussions about the stadium with Marcum, the old adage that "there is no person, object, or reputation that cannot be stolen, harmed or destroyed" became evident. For example, despite numerous security precautions, no one can guarantee 100% absolute security. To attend an athletic event is to understand that there is always an element of risk. For this reason, stadium managements across the country are continuously measuring the balance between risk and reward.

One of the points that Marcum made about large, university athletic programs is that often, the coaches are of a higher profile, and better known, than the athletes. In the world of large university sports, it is the coaches who might need extra protection. Speaking about the university world, Marcum noted that the documented instances in college athletics cases of when/where an athlete being in danger are relatively few, and furthermore, because coaches tend to be better known, they might be, at times, in greater potential danger.

Marcum spoke about the fact that athletes often are sequestered (watched over and kept away from the public) when they travel and wondered if some of their greater dangers were not when on the road and protected, but rather when they were at home. From the team's perspective, a college athlete is probably more likely to encounter a safety/security issue while at home than on the road. At home, there is less "team" supervision. He also noted that many less-than-desirable people have opportunities to seek out athletes. When athletes are not in a protected situation, such as at their home, these people could cause problems.

In the case of football players, they are sequestered before a game even if it is a home game and, of course, when they are on travel. This policy is also enforced in professional soccer, and for some basketball teams. The practice, however, is not necessarily true for other sports.

Concerning the stadium, safety and security must be viewed from at last six different perspectives:

- Public ingress into the stadium.
- Public attendance at the game or sporting event.
- Public egress from the stadium and use of public roads.
- The pregame athlete experience.
- The game period.
- The postgame athlete experience and egress.

Focusing on the athletes' experience, we can divide the athletes' experience into three subsections. These are the athlete's protection prior to the time of play, his or her protection during play, and the after-game experience. As noted in the case of football and professional soccer, and in some schools for basketball, players are sequestered prior to the game. In other sports, they are more on their own. Marcum stated that we hope that our student-athletes during play are safe; we take every precaution possible to ensure their safety and security while participating. From Marcum's perspective, the focus on safety and security has been on our guests/fans rather than the athletes/participants. The problem might be that in large stadiums, no matter how well prepared a first responder team might be, streets can carry only a specific amount of traffic and there is a limited quantity of first responders, doctors, and ambulance units. Stadiums are well aware of this problem and are prepared to use the most sophisticated systems of triage.

Players are well protected while getting ready for a game or in the postgame period. For example, locker rooms are sealed off and there is a vetting process in place for all those who have entry into the locker or other private areas. Special attention is given to the day when a sporting event takes place. Thus, athletic event days have a different set of rules than do other days.

In summation, Marcum noted that all athletic venues do their best to protect the public, but there is simply no way to protect the public completely from diseases, mishaps, and acts of treachery. To be alive is to balance risks with benefits.

SUMMARY AND ANALYSIS

It should be noted that these interview do not represent a scientific statistical analysis, but merely a cross-section of different athletes in different sports and at different stages of their lives. The following chart provides a comparative summary of these interviews.

Name	Type of Sport, and University or Professional or Both	Protected While on Travel	Used Travel to Bond	Visited Host Location While on Travel?	Saw Travel as Business or Pleasure Travel
Amador	Soccer, professional	Yes, team provided professional security	Yes	Yes	Business
Dimovic	Tennis, professional and university[a]	Yes (by parent of guardian)	Yes	Yes	Midway, both business and also educational
Lechler	Volleyball, university	Minimally	Yes	Yes	Business
Maltz	Baseball, university	No	Yes	Yes	Business and pleasure
McKinney	Football, university and professional	Yes	Yes	No	Business
Paige	Football, university and professional	Yes	Yes	No	Business
Resende	Soccer, university and professional	Yes	Yes	Yes	Cultural as student and Business as professional
Rother	Tennis, university and some professional	No	Yes	Yes	More business than cultural
Speakman	Baseball, college and professional	No	Yes	Yes	Cultural at college and business as professional

[a]Dimovic played professional tennis in Europe prior to attending university in the United States

Everyone interviewed expressed the fact that their sports travel was both a competitive experience and a bonding experience. Perhaps the number-one complaint, especially among student athletes, was regarding exhaustion and lack of sleep. All the athletes learned the life lesson that they could be competitors on the field and friends once away from the game. On the other hand, the soccer players noted the highest degree of potential interteam and interfan problems. Those playing nonteam-oriented sports expressed the opposite viewpoint. There was some division of opinion concerning security between the younger and older athletes. This dividing line may have three causes: location where the athlete found himself or herself, the passions that a particular sport aroused, and the fact that younger athletes live in a more violent age than the other athletes interviewed.

Those participating in football and soccer produced a limited, direct economic impact for the local community. It should be noted, however, that this situation reverses itself when we speak of indirect economic impact, such that the impact on places of lodging or of fans coming to see the game and filling not only the stadiums, but also renting cars, going to restaurants, purchasing food and liquor for parties before and after a game, and hotel occupancy. The team sports tended to leave the host location as quickly as possible after the event's conclusion. This rapid departure was especially true of those playing professional sports.

The student athletes universally expressed the challenge of combining athletics with academics. Most, but not all, of the student athletes found that their athletic career had a negative impact on their academic achievements. Some people expressed the fact that lack of sleep was a problem and that time management was a skill that they had to learn to succeed in both their academic and athletic careers. For some athletes, their professors were understanding, and for others, university professors could be a challenge that required interpersonal skills.

Finally, no athlete expressed regret. All were pleased to have practiced their sport and all were thankful for the chance to play. No athlete interviewed was so fearful of the challenges of travel or issues of security that he or she would have done things differently. All would agree with the American football player and coach Vince Lombardi, when he stated: "The spirit, the will to win, and the will to excel are the things that endure. These qualities are so much more important than the events that occur."[6]

SPANISH-LANGUAGE INTERVIEW QUESTIONS

- Por favor dime tu nombre y edad actual
  Salomon Libman Pastor
- ¿En cual deporte profesional participaste o participas?
  Futbol soccer (futbolista profesional)
- ¿Para cuantos años participas en este deporte/desde cuando?a nivel profesional 14 años. Pero comencé desde muy pequeño 5 años,

---

[6] ThinkExist. Vince Lombardi quotes, http://thinkexist.com/quotation/the_spirit_the_will_to_win_and_the_will_to_excel/12311.html; 2013 [accessed 08.15.2016].

estuve en las selecciones nacionales sub 15, sub 17, sub 20 y mayores actualmente de la selección peruana,

- ¿Jugaste su deporte en la universidad?

  No, pero estudie administración de empresas en la universidad Ricardo palma.

- ¿Jugaste su deporte en un equipo profesional?

  Si, sport boys (2002 a julio 2008).

  Alianza Lima (julio del 2008 al 2012).

  UCV (2013 a la actualidad).

  Cuando participaste en este juego ¿viajaste a otras ciudades?

Si, la mayoría de ciudades las conozco por el futbol, viaje desde muy pequeño, conozco algunos países como España, Austria, Suecia, Dinamarca, noruega, Francia, Rusia, estados unidos, japon, corea, y todo latino america.

Si participaste (o participas) en un deporte universitario:

viajes como un estudiante universitario

No, me dedico al futbol profesional

- ¿Cómo fue su experiencia de viajar como atleta universitario, te fue algo positivo o negativo?

  Nunca lo hice, porque estudiaba mientras jugaba y siempre mi prioridad fue jugar en las ligas del futbol profesional.

- Como atleta ¿cuáles son tres cosas que te gustaron?

  Hacer lo que me gusta y que me paguen por eso, siendo mi profesión.

  Conocer países y diferentes culturas.

  Jugar por la selección peruana.

  Que la amistad vaya más allá del futbol, el poder conocer amigos.

- ¿Te apoyaron tus profesores/catedráticos cuando tenías que viajar durante el año académico?

  Muchas veces me apoyaron y otras no, recuerdo una aneecdota estando en la universidad, tenia que sacarme 6 en un final y no pude ir al final, porque tenía que jugar un partido de futbol profesional, le pedi al profesor que me postergue el examen y me dijo o te dedicas a una cose o a otra, al final me tomo el examen sustitutorio cambiándome todo, no pude aprobar el curso, hice una cosa que nunca había hecho, le dije a mi padre que vaya hablar y al final mi padre fue pero no hubo solución, mi padre entro a la sala de profesores explicándole mi situación y le dijeron lo mismo, fue allí donde mi padre reacciono y le dijo que es por eso que el peru esta donde esta…en el tercer mundo.

- ¿En tu vida como estudiante universitario, ¿Te impactó en forma negativa tus viajes al participar en actividades deportivas?

No, con la universidad nunca viaje.

- ¿Cuándo viajaste había una relación especial con los otros deportistas de tu equipo?

    Si, siempre hay afinidades con algunos deportistas, por lo general, en el futbol hay muchas concentraciones (vivir en hoteles, dormir allí antes de los partidos para descansar)

- ¿Compartiste una habitación o cuarto de hotel cuando viajaste para jugar o tenías su propio cuarto?

    En el futbol profesional, lo hago una vez a la semana, por motivos de concentración antes de un partido d efutbol

- Al estar visitando otro lugar para motivos deportivos, podías entrar en la ciudad para disfrutar de su vida o te quedaste en el hotel?

    A. veces es posible conocer la ciudad, en mi caso casi siempre que puedo lo hago, pero a veces por los tiempos solo es hotel entrenamiento, conocer el estadio y descansar, sobre todo cuando viajas con la selección Peruana.

- Al viajar para jugar en un deporte universitario ¿Te viste como si estuvieras de un viaje de placer o de un viaje de negocios? nunca

- ¿Cuándo viajabas para practicar tu deporte te divertiste?

    Si, ha habido momentos de diversión, obviamente con responsabilidad, después de los partidos. Hay viajes que han coincidido con visitas de mi familia.

- ¿Qué clase de supervisión o vigilancia tenías cuando estabas en otra ciudad?

    Siempre la seguridad en el hotel y a veces la seguridad del equipo. Y horarios que se tenían que respetar.

- ¿Tenías preocupaciones por tu seguridad personal?

    No, siempre hemos estado bien resguardados, aunque a veces se han perdido cosas dentro del hotel. Lo bueno es que casi siempre sin sonar soberbió siempre vamos a buenos hoteles.

- Si pudieras cambiar dos cosas acerca de tus viajes deportivos cuales serían?

    Por el futbol he perdido muchas cosas, y a la vez he ganado, el hecho de estar en viajes o concentrado me pierdo matrimonios, reuniones familiares, hasta entierros, me sucedió con mi padre.

- ¿Cuáles son tres cosas que recomendarías a un nuevo estudiante (un estudiante del primer año universitario) para mejorar su experiencia viajera como atleta?

    Ser perseverante.

    Mantener sus convicciones y confiar en su capacidad-

- ¿Qué otras cosas debería yo haberte preguntado?

Preferiría que la entrevista sea personalmente, de hecho que hay muchas anécdotas, ya que el futbol que es el deporte que practico, es un mundo aparte.

Si participas o participaste en un deporte profesional:

Viajes como deportista profesional

Si. Siempre lo hago

- ¿Cómo fue su experiencia de viajar, incluyendo el tiempo en otra ciudad, como atleta profesional, te fue algo positivo o negativo?
  Siempre es positivo, a pesar de que se presenten temas como el cambio de hora y comida etc.
- Si viajaste como atleta universitario y profesional, ¿hay diferencias entre las dos experiencias y cuáles son?
  Nunca he sido atleta universitario, siempre me dedique al futbol profesional, lo que si hay diferencia es cuando viajas con la selección peruana y el equipo para el cual trabajas, en muchas oportunidades el nivel de seguridad se da con el equipo de la selección peruana.
- Como atleta profesional ¿cuáles son tres cosas que te gustaron cuando estabas de viaje?
  La competencia internacional.
  El conocer la ciudad.
  Salir de compras.
- Como atleta profesional ¿cuáles son tres cosas que NO te gustaron cuando estabas de viaje?
  El estar lejos de mi familia y perderme ocasiones y eventos importantes.
- ¿Te apoyó tu familia cuando tenías que viajar?
  Siempre me apoyo, no solo al momento de viaja, si no para ser futbolista profesional, sobre todo mis padres.
- ¿Te impactaron tu vida de casa/tu vida de familia los viajes profesionales? ¿Cómo te impactaron?
  Como me inicie desde muy pequeño, aprendí a convivir con ello, y todo se volvió muy natural, parte de mi vida cotidiana
- ¿Te ayudaron tus viajes a tener una relación más fuerte con tus colegas de equipo?
  Si, sobre todo generar grupos, eso es el resultado de la convivencia con otros deportistas, además de ser el capitán del equipo y referente en todos los equipos que jugué he sido el capitán y líder.
- ¿Cuándo viajabas tenías una habitación solamente para ti o tenías que compartir tu habitación con otra(s) persona(s)?
  Siempre comparto habitaciones ya sea con mi equipo profesional o con la selección peruana.
- ¿Cuándo no jugabas visitaste la ciudad anfitriona para divertirte?

No, ya que estaba concentrado he iba a competir, porque es el futbol profesional, después de los partidos de futbol, a veces se puede salir, no siempre.

- ¿Para ti fueron estos viajes unas breves vacaciones o más bien un viaje de negocio?

  Casi siempre resultan siendo viajes de trabajo.

- Cuando viajabas ¿te divertiste? Siempre con responsabilidad, ya que es mi profesión, lo mejor para un futbolista, son las competencias internacionales.

- ¿Tenías protección profesional y/o seguridad cunado viajabas? Con la selección peruana hay mucha seguridad policial y personal y con el equipo profesional donde trabajo una seguridad mas leve. Todo esto es dependiendo a que ciudad viajas y contra quien juegas.

- ¿Tenías preocupaciones por tu seguridad?

  No, siempre me he mantenido dentro de las reglas del director técnico, cuidando mi imagen e integridad profesional.

- ¿Cuáles son tres cosas que recomendarías a un nuevo atleta profesional acerca de sus viajes?

  Disfrutar lo que hace, normalmente uno va a competir.

  Saber y aprender a convivir con los demás.

  Saber respetar y comportarse a la altura de la situación este en el evento que este, ya que pertenece a una delegación o representa a un país.

- Si pudieras cambiar dos cosas con referencia de tu experiencia de viajes deportivos ¿cuáles serían?

  La vestimenta en algunas ocasiones, ya que a veces es en ropa deportiva, a veces en terno o ropa de gala.

  A. veces viajar con más tiempo de anticipación.

- ¿Qué otras cosas deberías haberte preguntado y te pregunté?

  Prefiero una entrevista personal.

Index